HAVING BEEN EDITED BY THE CAPABLE HANDS OF

LYTA GOLD & NATHAN J. ROBINSON

AND PUBLISHED WITH TIRELESS CRAFTSMANSHIP BY

CURRENT AFFAIRS

NEW ORLEANS LONDON DELHI RIO TOKYO STOCKHOLM LAWRENCE

Current Affairs Publishing, Incorporated
631 Saint Charles Avenue
New Orleans, LA 70130

First U.S. Edition

LIBRARY OF CONGRESS
CATALOGING-IN-PUBLICATION DATA
Gold, Lyta and Nathan J. Robinson (eds.)
The Current Affairs Big Book of Amusements / Lyta Gold and Nathan J. Robinson
ISBN 9780997844733

COVER DESIGN BY
Jon White
jonwhitestudio.com

Table of Contents

"YOU'RE GETTING YOUR MONEY'S WORTH"

THE CURRENT AFFAIRS™
"BIG BOOK OF AMUSEMENTS"

Amazing Activities

CAN YOU SPOT WHAT'S WRONG WITH THE
GREAT BARRIER REEF?
Things are not quite right in the Great Barrier Reef. There are five things wrong in this picture. Can you spot what they are?
ANSWERS ON PAGE 182

JEREMY

You are the Labour Party's chief media strategist. You have a problem. Nobody can agree what sort of clothes Jeremy Corbyn ought to wear to optimize his electability. Should he be himself and wear the old beige jumper his mum knitted him in 1985? Should he make some kind of modest attempt to look like the leader of a major political party, with, like, a suit or something? Or should he appeal to millennials with a branded T-shirt and a pair of designer jeans? It's your job to find the outfit that will reverse the party's electoral fortunes! Good luck.

CORBYN

DRESS HIM FOR SUCCESS

Create your own...

FAKE STUDENT ID

EVERYONE LOVES A GRADUATE STUDENT!

Miss those occasional minor discounts? Trying to impress a girl by convincing her you're doing a Master's in Social Work? Or perhaps you just want to sneak into the library to catch a quick nap or place flyers for your yoga studio inside the books. Use our handy kit and you can live the dream of being a student forever.

FABULOUS UNIVERSITY

YOUR VISAGE HERE

Card #60760000212458

EXPIRES 05/19

STUDENT

INSTRUCTIONS

1. Cut out the letters that will spell your name when combined in the correct order.
2. Carefully place these letters, in the order that spells your name, above the Card #.
3. Place a flattering photograph of your head and shoulders in the Visage Box.
4. Cut out, photocopy, and laminate. Now you're ready for those discounted admissions!

The fun kind of fraud...

A	A	A	A	B	B	B	C	C	C	D	D	D	D
E	E	E	E	F	F	F	G	G	G	H	H	H	I
I	I	J	J	K	K	K	L	L	L	L	M	M	M
N	N	N	N	O	O	O	P	P	Q	R	R	R	S
S	S	S	T	T	T	U	U	V	W	W	X	Y	Z

DISCLAIMER:

It is almost certainly some sort of misdemeanor to use a fake student ID to get into a campus rave-up or get a dollar off a taco. We strongly discourage any and all persons from using our service.

a courtesy of: LEGITIMATE IDENTIFICATIONS INCORPORATED, 5800 S. PALO VERDE BLVD. SUITE 400, LAKE HAVASU CITY, AZ, 86403

COLOR the FLINT

WATER SUPPLY

Thanks to the gross negligence of state officials, the city of Flint, Michigan discovered to its horror in 2014 that its water was flowing in a toxic range of colors. Use your crayons to show Gov. Rick Snyder and various municipal bureaucrats some of what their pitiless indifference has wrought.

SOME PUZZLES FOR LIBERTARIANS

CANNIBALS, COERCION, AND THE INFINITELY WEALTHY MAN. ANSWERS ON P. 182

1

Deep in the forest, thousands of miles from civilization, there is an isolated village. It has not seen contact with any other humans for a long time. It is, however, a pleasant and flourishing community, which strongly values freedom and entrepreneurship. There is, however, one tiny quirk. In this village, there is a ritual. Every year, a boy who reaches 18 is cannibalized. It brings the rains, or something. But despite its taste for cannibalism, this village wishes to live in accordance with libertarian principles. Thus, they will only cannibalize the boy if he consents. In order to encourage this to happen, they will put tremendous social pressure on the boy. All through his youth, they will tell him they believe the future of the village depends on his consenting. His parents tell him that he would bring great shame on the household if he refused, which is true. The choice nevertheless rests with the boy, and whatever he chooses will be respected. The parents and villagers attempt to persuade him, but never lie to him, and make clear that they would never force his choice. However: if the boy refuses to be cannibalized, the village has a backup plan. The boy will be blacklisted. No shopkeeper will sell him food, no hotel will give him a room, no hospital will treat him, no employer will hire him. After all, under libertarian principles, nobody can be told how to use their property. The boy's parents, ashamed of him, will turn him out of the house with no money. He may leave the village, but it is certain death, for thousands of miles of desolate wolf-infested wilderness stand between him and other humans and he has no food. (The wilderness is also privately-owned, and he cannot pay the admission fee.) He is shunned and despised, left to wander the streets in a futile search for shelter and sustenance. However, no force is exercised against him. He is never touched or arrested. He is treated as nonexistent, as the villagers await his demise. So the boy starves to death. The villagers then cannibalize his emaciated corpse, reasoning that they cannot be compelled to give him a dignified burial (plus he died on private property, collapsing in a flowerbed).

QUESTION: IS EATING THE BOY'S CORPSE AFTER HE DIES THE ONLY POTENTIAL VIOLATION OF LIBERTARIAN PRINCIPLES IN THE VILLAGE? IS EVERY SINGLE OTHER ASPECT OF THIS COMPLETELY PERMISSIBLE?

2

IS THERE A DIFFERENCE BETWEEN STATE AND PRIVATE COERCION?

3

CAN YOU CONSTRUCT A THEORY OF PROPERTY RIGHTS THAT DOES NOT SUFFER FROM INTERNAL INCOHERENCE OR DEPEND ON SPECIOUS NATURAL LAW ASSUMPTIONS?

4

The Infinitely Rich Man is not infinitely rich. He is just very, very rich. Nobody knows quite how rich. One day, you happened to meet the Infinitely Rich Man in a bar. At first he was friendly, but soon you found yourselves in an argument about horses. You were for them, and he was against them. Or perhaps you were against them, and he was for them. You don't actually remember how it went. As you parted ways, you expected never to see the Infinitely Rich Man again. Little do you know: the Infinitely Rich Man now despises you. His sole desire on earth is to see you unhappy. This should hardly trouble you, though. After all, you have a good job at a castanet factory. You own your own home, which has a picturesque lake view. You have a wife, whom you love and who loves you. You also have a prized possession, your 1972 Pontiac LeMans. You don't have much spare cash, but this never bothers you because of your stable job. The Infinitely Rich Man is also a strict Libertarian. He believes it is illegitimate for anyone to initiate force against another. And because you are fortunate enough to live in a Libertarian world, you are free to enjoy those things you treasure most in the world without being bothered by the state or the Infinitely Rich Man. The Infinitely Rich Man is not discouraged, however. He still believes he can ruin you. He will be a Count of Monte Cristo, but an extremely law-abiding one. The first thing the Infinitely Rich Man does is buy the castanet factory where you work. He immediately fires you. He also makes sure that if any other employers inquire about you, the castanet factory will refuse to serve as a reference. Not that this matters, for he intends to bribe any other castanet company who hires you into firing you. (There are four castanet companies.) You therefore find yourself unemployed. Fortunately, you have a skill. You know how to make castanets! (Castanets are very popular.) So you scrape together what money you have, and you open a little drive-thru castanet stand out on Route 9. But the Infinitely Rich Man has a plan. He opens a stand next to yours. At his stand, castanets are free. He gives them away by the truckload. He sets the whole world clacking. You cannot compete. You are ruined. At least you still have your wife, your friends, your lakeview home, your 1972 Pontiac LeMans. But the Infinitely Rich Man has a plan. First, he buys the lake. He fills it with concrete. No more lake view, and your property value diminishes by $100,000. Then, he buys every house around yours, flattens them, and turns the neighborhood into a landfill. The smell doesn't reach your home, but it turns the neighborhood unsightly and desolate. Your house becomes worthless. The Infinitely Rich Man buys the heating company and refuses to provide gas to your home at any price. (You try to talk other gas companies into competing, but they refuse; laying a new main for a single home would be absurd, they say.) But you have a wife! And friends! And you get to drive a 1972 Pontiac LeMans! The Infinitely Rich Man offers a bribe. Any of your friends who refuse to speak with you ever again will receive a salary of one million dollars per year. At first, many decline to take the bribe. But sooner or later, most of them have one or another sticky financial situation, and they give in. Goodbye, vast majority of your friends! At least your wife loves you. But one day, she becomes ill. She finds out that she will die, unless she goes on a treatment regimen for the rest of her life. The regimen costs $100,000 a month. The Infinitely Rich man pops up, and offers to pay. The one condition is that she divorce you, cut contact, and never speak with you again. As soon as she breaks the agreement, he will cease to pay for the treatment. You love your wife, but you do not want her to die. You both agree that it is better that she should accept. At least you can drive your 1972 Pontiac LeMans. Oh, but wait. The Infinitely Rich Man invests heavily in electric energy. Slowly, he makes gasoline-powered transit obsolete. He buys the oil companies, burns the gasoline, and converts every gas pump to a charging station. You can only drive your LeMans short distances, using some of the last gallons of available petrol, which you ordered from the internet. (That is, if the Infinitely Rich Man didn't outbid you!) They don't make the Pontiac LeMans anymore. Parts therefore exist only in small quantities. The Infinitely Rich Man buys up all existing LeMans parts. The moment it breaks, you are out of luck. As you sit alone, broke, and starving in the garage of your unheated home, caressing your disabled LeMans, thinking about your long-gone wife, your lake view, and your job, you are thankful that you live in a world of freedom, where nobody can encroach upon the liberty of another.

QUESTIONS FOR LIBERTARIANS: HAS THE NON-AGGRESSION PRINCIPLE BEEN VIOLATED? SHOULD THE INFINITELY RICH MAN SUFFER ANY CIVIL OR CRIMINAL PENALTIES FOR HIS ACTIONS?

CLANDESTINE
FUN, FUN, FUN PAGE

SPONSORED BY THE UNITED STATES DEFENSE INTELLIGENCE AGENCY

ANSWERS ON PAGE 182

ACROSS

2. Civil Rights Leader ____ was surveilled, harassed, and blackmailed by J. Edgar Hoover and the FBI.

3. Operation Midnight _______ was a subproject of MKULTRA where CIA agents did all sorts of bizarre things like dose one another with LSD as a prank. One famous plot involved luring johns into a CIA safe house with a prostitute, giving them a large dose of LSD without telling them, and watching them from behind a two-way mirror.

8. The Church Committee found that COINTELPRO was designed to deny citizens the right to free association and free speech, and the FBI had violated ________ rights of Americans.

10. George ____ was responsible for some of the most bizarre and illegal LSD subprojects of MKULTRA. His resignation letter to the CIA read: "I was a very minor missionary, actually a heretic, but I toiled wholeheartedly in the vineyards because it was fun, fun, fun."

11. ________ police dropped a bomb provided to them by the FBI on a city block. The MOVE bombing happened in 1985.

12. U.S. President Gerald Ford signed an executive order forbidding US-backed political assassination on _________ 18, 1976.

13. J. Edgar Hoover's illegal COINTELPRO ordered that agents expose, disrupt, misdirect, discredit, neutralize, or otherwise eliminate leaders and movements that were deemed ________.

14. In December of 1981, Ronald Reagan signed an executive order allowing the government to retain, modify, and distribute "________ collected information" that contains evidence of crimes. It is considered a key authorization of NSA mass data collection. In this same executive order, he also echoed Jimmy Carter's EO against direct or indirect support of assassination.

15. U.S. President Harry S. ______ said of J. Edgar Hoover: "[The FBI is] dabbling in sex-life scandals and plain blackmail. All congressmen and senators are afraid of [J. Edgar Hoover.]"

17. It was revealed in the 1970s that the CIA was responsible for failed and illegal assassination plots on Fidel ______, Congolese leader Patrice Lumumba, the Dominican Republic's President Rafael Trujillo, and René Schneider, commander-in-chief of the Chilean Army.

18. In _______ of 2014 the CIA Torture Report found that the CIA had routinely used ineffective and brutal torture techniques without oversight during the "War on Terror." Prisoners were kept awake for periods of over 180 hours, subjected to psychological humiliation, physical abuse, and sexual abuse. CIA officials lied to Congress and the White House about these abuses "to try to protect their budget."

19. Booz Allen IT contractor Edward Snowden blew the whistle on the NSA in 2013, including PRISM, which is a program that 'incidentally collects' information on American ______.

20. Former CIA agent Victor Marchetti wrote a book called "The ____ of Intelligence" in 1974 which alleged the CIA had fallen into a foolish obsession with clandestine operations. Marchetti was placed under CIA surveillance for this.

DOWN

1. Fred ______ was shot to death in his bed by Chicago police as part of a COINTELPRO operation to suppress the Black Panthers on December 4th, 1969

4. Jimmy Carter signed an executive order forbidding anyone in the US government from directly or ______ being involved in any type of assassination on January 24th 1978.

5. The CIA illegally opened domestic mail going to and from the Soviet Union and ____ in a program called HTLINGUAL.

6. Although 3 executive orders have forbidden state-sponsored assassination, these rules have been reinterpreted to not be applicable during wartime. Needless to say, we have been at war for the last 16 years and will probably continue to be at war for the foreseeable ______.

7. The FBI was created in 1908 under the name Bureau of ______ (BOI.) It didn't become the FBI until 1935.

9. In 1973 the CIA Director James R. _________ commissioned an internal report on 'current or past CIA actions that 'may have fallen outside of the CIA's charter.' That report was nicknamed "The Family Jewels" and was 693 pages of CIA-backed illegal activity.

16. The reason that we know COINTELPRO existed: a group of left-wing activists broke into an FBI field office and ______ a bunch of paperwork.

HOROSCOPES

ARIES
You've got an opportunity to knock a bad habit today. Your legal right to a fair trial has been suspended under the jurisdiction of laws, which are not made public. You will be detained indefinitely.

TAURUS
Someone from your past will contact you, possibly seeking a recommendation or renewed partnership. You will be held indefinitely by the U.S. government without a trial.

GEMINI
You might not like it at first, but the change in weather will also bring changes in the way you relate to your career. During the night your house will be raided and you will be taken to a black site. You will not get a trial.

CANCER
The universe is giving you the chance to break out of your rut and learn something new. Take advantage of it. You will be indefinitely detained without trial.

LEO
Being in charge will come easily to you, and you'll gain new admirers and lots of new friends who can't believe you're not too good to be true. You will spend an extended period of time in solitary confinement before you receive a trial.

VIRGO
The stars are on your side if you're planning a hot date with a new flame or a weekend getaway with your love. This will be a bad month for fair and legal trials. Expect indefinite detention.

LIBRA
Your job might feel just a touch too demanding. Cultivate efficiency and you'll have plenty of time for other pursuits. You will have your rights suspended without oversight.

SCORPIO
Get a groove, find your rhythm, and beautify your space! You will be taken to a detention facility without trial.

SAGITTARIUS
If you've got your heart set on a trial remember to keep your chin up if you get disappointing news. You'll be detained.

CAPRICORN
Your natural talent for charming chitchat will be even more useful this week than normal. You may even be able to have a positive impact on a tough family situation. You will be held indefinitely without a trial.

AQUARIUS
I know you've been feeling locked down. Now is the time to be spontaneous. Throw off your inhibitions and live without plans for once. You're going to jail without trial.

PISCES
If there is something you feel guilty about nagging at your conscience, now is the time to own up to it. The stars tell us that you will have your rights suspended and you will be detained without trial indefinitely.

PLUCKY APARTMENTS
LOW COST LOW SPACE LOW PRESSURE
POLICERA
Contract your own cops! No liability! No problem! Even more volatile and under-trained than regular cops!
"DOWNLOAD PORT-A- GO! ONLY $99.99 A MONTH!"
COFFEE PLAN
GOLD MEMBERSHIP
MELTINGLY RICH COFFEE MADE FROM THE FINEST KONA BEANS TENDED BYTHE FINEST WHITE-COLLAR PRISONERS.
SILVER MEMBERSHIP
HIGHLY CAFFEINATED: PERFECT FOR-ON- THE-GO GIG MANIACS! WILL ONLY VERY SLOWLY ROT YOUR INSIDES.
BRONZE MEMBERSHIP
QUICK, AFFORDABLE COFFEE WITH ONLY A 10% CHANCE OF LISTERIA POISONING!
JEFF WATANABE, CREDIT SCORE 610, BIFOCALS, SOCIAL ANXIETY FIFTEEN MINUTES TO YOUR NEXT GIG! YOUR CAR WOULD GO FASTER IF YOUR CREDIT SCORE WAS HIGHER!
Google
amazon

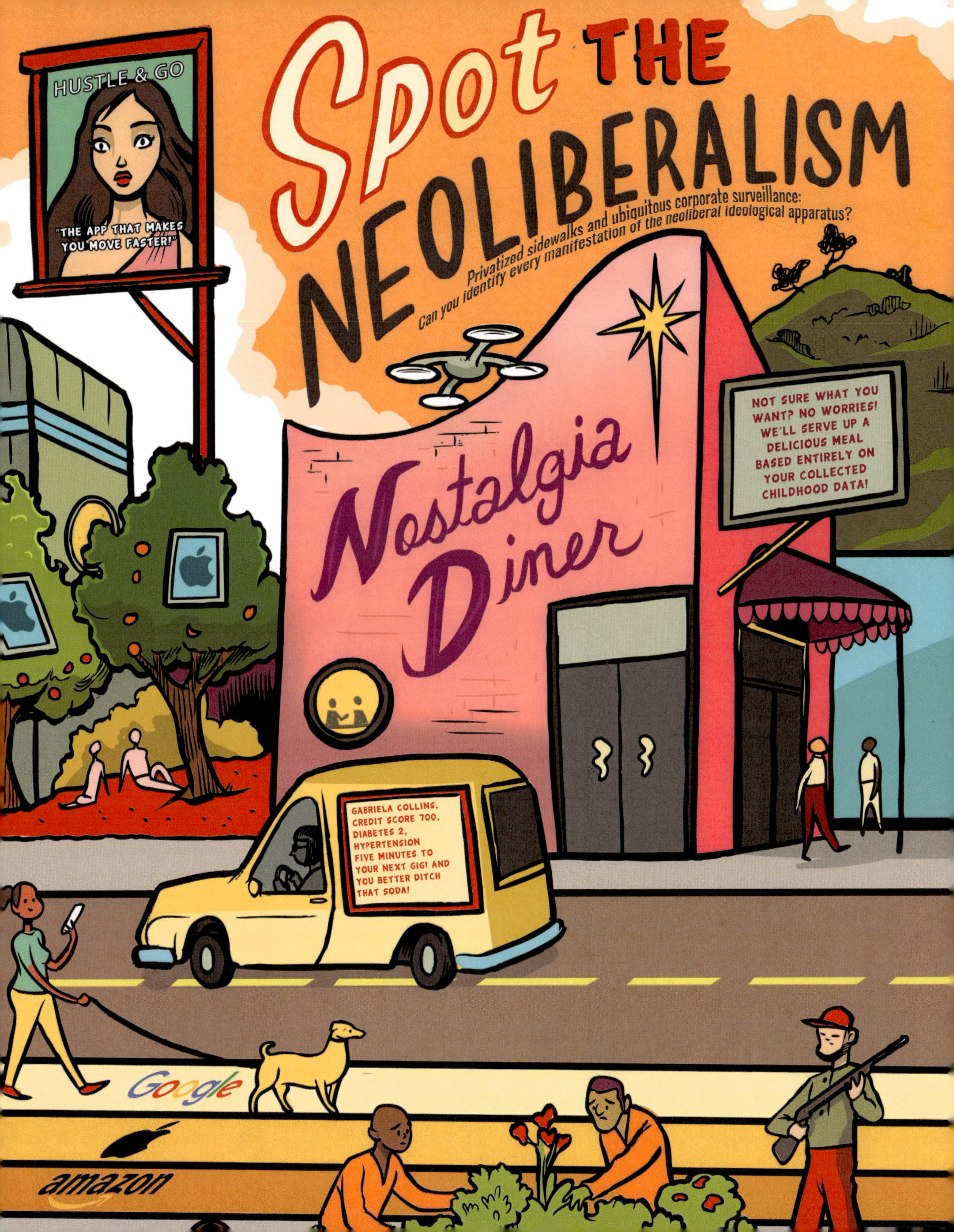
Spot THE NEOLIBERALISM
Privatized sidewalks and ubiquitous corporate surveillance:
Can you identify every manifestation of the neoliberal ideological apparatus?
HUSTLE & GO
"THE APP THAT MAKES YOU MOVE FASTER!"
Nostalgia Diner
NOT SURE WHAT YOU WANT? NO WORRIES! WE'LL SERVE UP A DELICIOUS MEAL BASED ENTIRELY ON YOUR COLLECTED CHILDHOOD DATA!
GABRIELA COLLINS, CREDIT SCORE 700, DIABETES 2, HYPERTENSION
FIVE MINUTES TO YOUR NEXT GIG! AND YOU BETTER DITCH THAT SODA!
Google
amazon

BLOCKS

to spell the acronyms of the horrible U.S. government agencies?

1.

2.

3.

4.

5.

PIN THE MIDDLE FINGER ON
MAYOR
RAHM EMANUEL
Hey kids! Do YOU want to flip the bird to the labor movement, teachers, and the whole city of Chicago in general? Sure ya do! Just have an adult cut along the dotted lines (careful not to cut off your OWN finger), close your eyes, and try to pin the middle finger on Mayor Rahm!
TEACHERS ON STRIKE
FAIR CONTRACT NOW!

The results are IN: American teenagers are totally done with capitalism. "The system doesn't work," says Tara McAdams of Akron, Ohio. "We all know it. Bernie's just the first person we ever heard saying it." That's Bernie Sanders of course, the senator from Vermont. According to a recent *Current Affairs* poll, 86% of teens rated Bernie favorably. In the same poll, 92% of teens rated socialism "bae," 85% said capitalism is "no longer extra," and 83% said "don't condescend to us, we know what the terms 'socialism' and 'capitalism' mean, probably better than most of those smug-ass Baby Boomers who inherited New Deal reforms and instead of progressing forward into true socialism just pissed everything away."

So why do teens love the septuagenarian senator so much? What's the source of his mysterious star power? Is it really just his policies—Medicare for All, free college, universal childcare? Yes. Bernie is a cranky old birdman who harangues on and on about the same domestic policy points. They just happen to be good points, and he happens to mean them sincerely. This is the beginning and end of his popularity. Mystery solved!

BINGO

B	I	N	G	O
CORPORATE HANDOUTS	THE BILLIONAIRE CLASS	YUGE	MEDICARE FOR ALL	THE DEMOCRATIC ESTAB-LISHMENT
NAFTA	THE 99%	THE 1%	THE WORKING CLASS	THE MIDDLE CLASS
SOME WISHY WASHY BULLSHIT ABOUT NOT ABOLISHING ICE	NONSENSE CIVILITY POLITICS		TUITION FREE COLLEGE	LIVING WAGE
FLY-AWAY HAIR	DODD-FRANK	IS THAT A BIRD	POLITICAL REVOLUTION	INCOMPLETE CONDEMNATION OF ISRAELI ATROCITY
WHEN I WAS MAYUH	CAMPAIGN FINANCE REFORM	NOT LARRY DAVID	SOCIAL SECURITY	WILDLY POINTING INDEX FINGER

QUIZ

WHAT'S YOUR LEFT POLITICAL ORIENTATION?

With so many exciting leftist ideas in the air, it can be tough to figure out what you actually believe. Sure, you like Bernie's domestic policy proposals, but do they go far enough? The best way to figure out what you actually want is to apply your principles to your immediate environment: your school. Take this quiz, and find out how much you really stan socialism.

1. The Winter Formal is coming up, but some students can't afford cute new looks! What do you do? How will you make sure everyone hits their #outfitgoals?

A. Work with the school administration and initiate a jobs program. Poor students can help out around school and earn enough cash for suits and dresses.
B. The school should subsidize students who can't afford new outfits. Help your local government pass a tax on the wealthy so that every student has a public option when it comes to on-trend formalwear. If the wealthy complain, tax them harder.
C. School dances are total bourgeois nonsense. Take over the cafeteria, kick out the adults, and throw a come-as-you-are rave.

2. The school has signed a contract with an academic-tracking company. Every student will have a tiny drone hovering over their shoulder to monitor performance. How do you respond?

A. Persuade the administration to sign a letter promising zero third-party selling of data. The drones must only be allowed to monitor academic performance, not collect your biometrics or peep your secret texts to your besties.
B. Go on strike. Ditch class en masse until the administration bans the drones from school premises.
C. Reprogram the drones to process all inputs as random fragmented data that will fry their tiny computer brains. Don't hate it... upgrade it!

YOUR BACK-TO-SCHOOL POLITICAL ACTION

HOROSCOPE

ARIES

With both Neptune and Pluto in retrograde, you'll have very little energy for organizing in your life, both personally and politically. But don't fret; after the full moon on the 25th you'll get all your passionate Aries intensity back. You'll be able to tidy your locker and plan untraceable trashcan fires at the local police precinct.

TAURUS

Mars is in your sign this month, which means you're feeling extra bullish. This is the perfect month to boldly change up your #lewk, or stage a walkout protest over your school's decision to partner with a multinational soda conglomerate that exploits its workers.

GEMINI

Geminis often feel torn in two, and this month is no exception. There's a midmonth alignment of Jupiter and Pluto—the planets of energy and the netherworld respectively—and the pressure to #brand yourself as a neoliberal sellout will be extra strong. Channel that Gemini showmanship into a useful project, like working on a local DSA candidate's ad campaign.

CANCER

With the Sun, Mars, and Jupiter journeying through your sign this month, you may find yourself drawn to new ideas. But make sure you balance your hate-watching of alt-right YouTube losers with some intelligent, challenging leftist commentary, or you may find yourself accidentally joining QAnon.

LEO

Saturn's facing you in a negative aspect right now, which may make you shy, but when Mars enters your sixth house mid-month you'll find a new burst of bravery. Time to strike up the courage to talk to that cutie you've been locking eyes with at YDSA meetings, and also tell off your most annoying centrist relative.

VIRGO

As a Virgo, your strength is communication. But your weakness is being too nice to #toxic people. As Mercury, your ruling planet, enters your sign on the 5th, take stock of your squad and decide who's holding onto repressive authoritarian ideas out of fixable ignorance and who's just an asshole.

LIBRA

Be prepared: there's a heated conjunction of the Sun and Mars that's going to leave you feeling extra depressed about climate change. But with Saturn leaving retrograde on September 6th, your dark mood will turn to determination. Channel this mood into useful political activity, like blowing up an unfinished oil pipeline.

SCORPIO

When Venus enters your sign early in the month, sparks may fly between you and your crush. But don't invite them to the homecoming dance just yet. In October, Venus is going into retrograde, and your crush may end up doing something seriously disappointing, like joining the Young Republicans.

SAGITTARIUS

With Mercury in your fellow fire sign Leo, September is going to be an angry and restless month for you. If you decide to join Antifa, make sure you wear a mask or the kind of makeup that fools facial recognition algorithms. You want to be #grammable but not #legible.

CAPRICORN

Saturn's been hanging out in your sign for some time, and all that negative fearmongering energy has you really #bummed and snappish. If you find yourself constantly entangled in obscure social media beefs that make zero sense to anyone IRL, log off and do something useful, like, you know, actual fucking organizing.

AQUARIUS

With Jupiter in opposition, this is the perfect time to get rid of all the negative capitalist energy in your life. Your friend who thinks Elon Musk is "a hero, actually?" #byebitch. The teacher who assigns *Atlas Shrugged*? #dumpthatclass. The uncle who tells you "being a socialist is just a phase, you'll get over it when you're older?" #lmao.

PISCES

Pisces are usually gentle and dreamy, and so people in your life often think you're easily pushed around. But with both Neptune and Pluto in retrograde, it's time to flip expectations. Stand up to that performatively woke bro in your organizing meetings. When he splutters "but I'm the first one to say 'men are the worst'!" try not to make fun of him too much.

3. Some members of your squad are in trouble for a hilarious prank involving a skateboard, a mini-fridge, homemade rocket thrusters, a bucket of strawberries, the auditorium stage, fourteen hamsters, and one unexpectedly viral YouTube vid. The school is adopting a zero-tolerance policy toward bullying (one of the hamsters may have been slightly traumatized), and your squad members are facing expulsion. How will you defend them?

A. Start a letter-writing campaign demanding a fair hearing by the administration. Post the letters on Insta for maximum eyeballs.

B. Hold your own trial with a collective jury of all your peers. Your squad members will have to clean up the auditorium and comfort the possibly traumatized hamster. Explain to the administration that justice has been meted out, and if they object you can always take further collective action.

C. Can there be any justice under a fascist administration that would expel students for no good reason? Not a chance. Say #bai to the administration by tossing out the adults and locking the doors after them. Now it's your school and you can do all the viral pranks you want.

ANSWERS ON PAGE 182

AT THE WOMEN'S MARCH...
On January 21, 2017, 4 million people marched in solidarity against Donald Trump on behalf of women all over the world.
But can you find the following: (1) The littlest marchers (2) The eldest marchers
(3) A lingering suffragette (4) A spacefaring princess
(5) A disused feminine hygiene product
(6) A Nazi receiving his due
(7) Michael Moore
(8) Hillary Clinton
FUTURE NASTY WOMEN
ONLY DICKS ARE SCARED OF EMPOWERED CHICKS
#WRONG
RESPECT EXISTENCE OR EXPECT RESISTANCE
STRONGER TOGETHER
NOT MY PRESIDENT
WE SHALL OVERCOMB
I'M WITH HER
LOVE
THIS GRABS BACK
NO WALL
BLACK LIVES ATTER

PUTIN'S PUPPET
FREE MELANIA
SAD!
WRONG
WOMEN STRIKE BACK
DUMP TRUMP
MY BODY MY CHOICE
HER BODY HER CHOICE
NASTY WOMAN
RESPECT YOUR MOTHER
TRUMP PENCE
TRUMP
UGH
I STAND WITH STANDING ROCK
STILL MARCHING

cross-promotional

MIX 'N' MATCH

Are you tired of truly ghastly cross-promotional press releases? Do synergistic corporate attempts to cover up hideous human rights abuses make you physically ill? Take control over the process with the *Current Affairs* build-your-own advertorial-ready, *Forbes*-friendly, shame-masking, cross-promotional corporate strategy pack! It's easy. For Column A, take the first letter of your first name. Column B is the first letter of your last name, Column C is the first letter of the street you live on, and Column D is the first letter of the first procedure you paid for on your last medical bill. Then plug your answers into this sentence:

"[Column A] is partnering with [Column B] to promote [Column C] because they were caught [Column D]!"

And once you've sold this strategy to the appropriate party, congratulations! You too are complicit in papering over shameless corporate crime!

SPONSORED CONTENT BROUGHT TO YOU BY

	A	B	C	D
A.	Uber	Bono	Happiness	Doing genocide
B.	Raytheon	Thinkfluencers	Fiscal responsibility	Denying the Holocaust
C.	Apple	VR startups	Mindful juice consumption	Engaging in ironic racism
D.	Amazon	"Fair-trade" coffee plantations	Shooting flowers from drones	Engaging in regular racism
E.	Walmart	Pinterest power-users	The respect economy	Planting landmines
F.	PayPal	The *Doctor Who* fandom community	STEM	Selling white phosphorus
G.	Foxconn	The New England Patriots	Police body cameras that gently whisper non-violent messages	Shooting puppies into space
H.	Coca-Cola	*Top Chef* winners	Weepy tributes to 9/11	Establishing slave-like factory conditions
I.	McDonald's	Angel investors	The hero myth	Privatizing a third world country's rain
J.	Google	The Davos World Economic Forum	The "future"	Trafficking human beings
K.	Disney	The Lands' End catalog	Corn subsidies	Imprisoning refugees
L.	Starbucks	Artisanal mayonnaise producers	Detoxing from social media	Murdering union leaders
M.	Microsoft	VICELAND	Smart investing	Hiring mercenaries to murder union leaders
N.	Fox News Corp	The sexy green M&M	Smart cities	Rebooting *Mein Kampf* for the big screen
O.	AT&T	The brand-new Lexus ZXL 1000©	"Putting healthcare over politics"	Replacing employee healthcare with StaminaCa$h™
P.	Lyft	Colonial Williamsburg	Brain uploading	Chopping up the homeless for chicken feed
Q.	Volkswagen	Actor-activists	Bipartisanship	Leaking benzenes into the water supply
R.	Pepsi	Taylor Swift	Self-care	Covering up years of sexual assault allegations
S.	ExxonMobil	Racist YouTube stars	Helping media companies pivot to video	Producing John Mayer albums
T.	Samsung	The Wizarding World of Harry Potter Theme Park	Sponsored content	Taking cash from murderous regimes
U.	Burger King	Microbeer enthusiasts	Increased productivity	Giving cash to murderous regimes
V.	The Ford Motor Company	Teenage entrepreneurs	The wisdom of the crowd	Dismissing climate change while secretly making plans to settle on Mars
W.	Nestlé	The cast of *This is Us*	Merit-based immigration	Torturing both cute and non-cute animals
X.	GE	Pharmaceutical company sales associates	Data monitoring apps in the classroom	Bulldozing homeless encampments
Y.	BP	Kombucha brewers	Cryptocurrency	Accidentally blowing up a city
Z.	Verizon	The reanimated ghost of Sid Vicious	"Inspirational" quotes taken out of context from MLK speeches	Taking quotes out of context from MLK speeches

SPOT THE DIFFERENCES

Two ICE family detention centers, separated in time by four years.
Can YOU spot every single difference between the 2014 baby jail and the 2018 baby jail?

AS BAD AS IT GETS

THINGS AREN'T GOING SO WELL IN DEATH CITY. WHAT REFORMS WOULD YOU INSTITUTE?

A Luxurious Left

DYSTOPIAS ARE BAD! CAN YOU COME UP WITH A PLAN FOR A COMFORTABLE SOCIALIST FUTURE?

"Aha!" we hear you say. "A waiter? Your precious egalitarian paradise is illusory, there remains an unacknowledged servant class." But you err. You assume that this gentleman is a waiter. This only demonstrates the limits of your imaginative powers. Why should it not be possible to rotate the role of donning the moustache and pouring the wine? Why must we assume that this man does not pour wine for the sheer joy of pouring it? Can we not take pleasure in taking turns serving one another?

the current affairs

INSTAPOET

You are, of course, an aspiring poet. But the market for verse just ain't what it used to be. If you're going to be a prize-winner, you'll need to issue top-shelf material. Not only that, but you'll have to produce reams of it. To do that, you'll need a method for disgorging the stuff with speed. This is why *Current Affairs* is here. With the *Current Affairs* "Instapoet" method, you can create a brilliant free verse poem out of any simple English sentence.

INSTRUCTIONS:
Write sentence. Add some line breaks. Repeat as needed.

After this, I haven't got anything left except my sadness.

After this
I haven't
got
anything
left
except my
sadness

When you grow up, you may end up doing the same things to other people as were once done to you.

When you
grow up
you may
end up
doing the
same things to
other people
as were once
done
to you.

There is a dripping leak in my kitchen ceiling and I need to call someone to fix it but I am scared of having strangers in my house.

There is a
dripping
leak
in my kitchen ceiling
and I need
to call someone to fix it but
I am scared of having
strangers
in my
house

TRY YOUR OWN

ADVANCED TECHNIQUE: indents + ampersands

how h&s^
my dread&&
become--
the &only co nstant
!!   in an otherwise
perfect/tumult

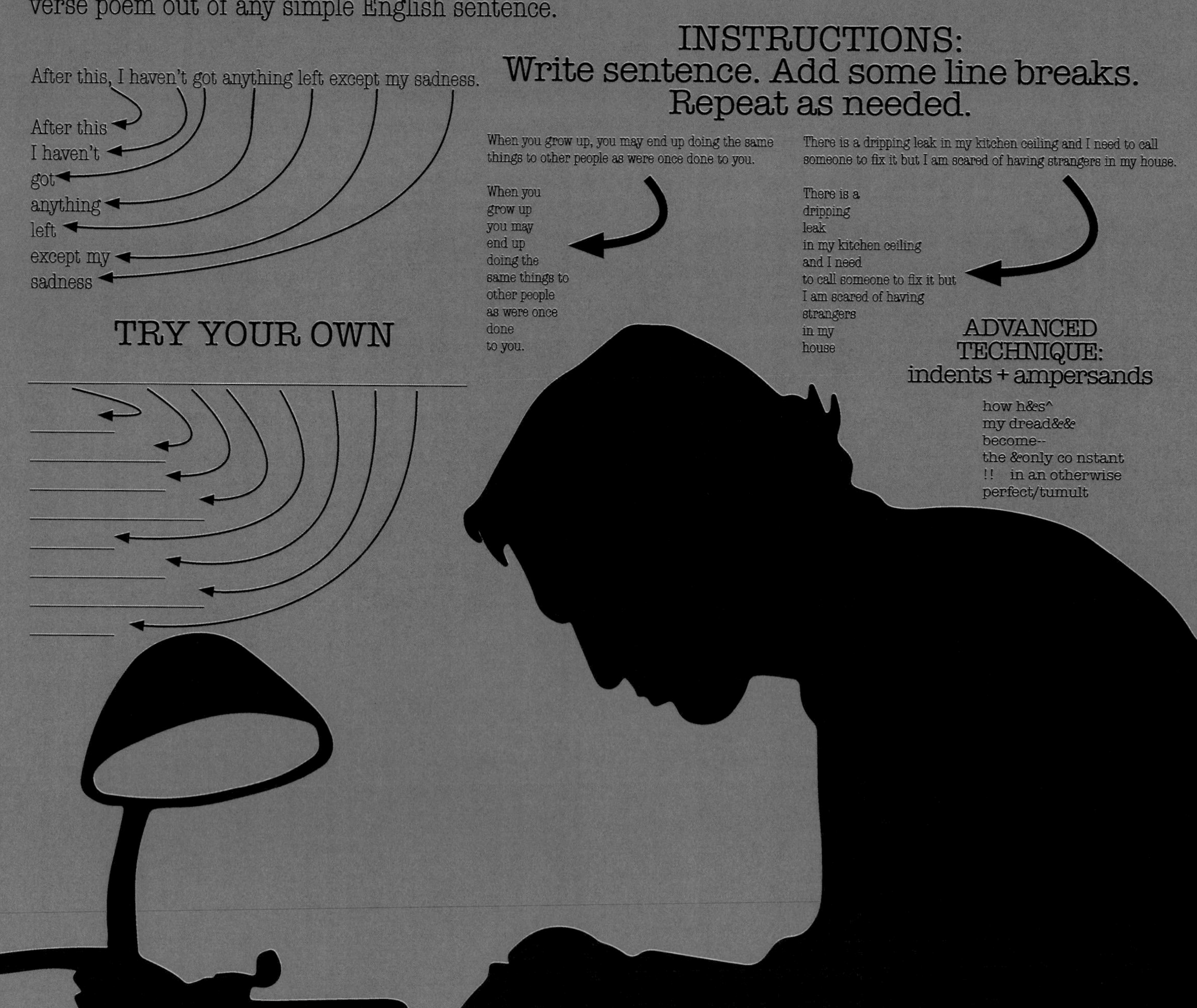

try our new PROSECUTORIAL "Mad Lib"

With over 200 black people murdered by the police in 2017 alone, it can be difficult for you—a soulless district attorney—to come up with brand-new reasons to avoid pressing charges against the officers responsible. Nobody appreciates how tough your job really is. Nobody appreciates how much you've sacrificed for your ambition. After all, you could have been virtuous: you could have become a public defender or worked for a legal aid society. But, since you want to run for political office someday, it's important for you to appear tough on crime—well, not actual crimes, like the ones committed by police officers against civilians, but theoretical crimes, like what if the ice cream cone wielded by the bipolar seventeen-year-old was actually a gun. Turning victims into villains and vice versa is hard work, and that's why *Current Affairs* is supplying you with a helpful template for your next cowardly, doublespeak-ridden press conference. Give it a shot. The only things you have to lose are your last remaining shreds of conscience, humanity, and self-respect.

Good afternoon,

Thank you all for coming today. I would like to make **(an insincere statement of warmth and condolence)** to the family of **(victim's name)**. And I would also like to ask **(phrase for activists that makes them sound like outside agitators)** to **(request for civility coupled with a veiled threat)**.

After an investigation that took **(an exaggerated length of time and amount of effort)**, the Office of the District Attorney has concluded the following facts: Officer **(murderer's name)** was dispatched in response to a call made by **(a polite euphemism for a nosy neighborhood racist)** describing a suspect that looked like **(racial stereotype)** and was wearing **(an unremarkable piece of clothing)**. When Officer **(murderer's name)** arrived on the scene, he discovered that **(victim's name)** matched the caller's description and that **(victim's name)** was behaving in a manner that Officer **(murderer's name)** described as **(prejudicial and entirely subjective adjective)**. When Officer **(murderer's name)** asked **(victim's name)** to stop **(engaging in perfectly legal activity)**, **(victim's name)** refused to comply, asking Officer **(murderer's name)** to **(behave in a legal and appropriate manner)**. At this point, Officer **(murderer's name)** felt **(emotion inappropriate for the situation)**.

(Victim's name) then suddenly made **(an unlikely violent movement)** toward Officer **(murderer's name)**. Experiencing a **(non-credible amount)** of fear, Officer **(murderer's name)** **(strained and clumsy passive-voice verb formation that's barely grammatical and implies an almost magical-realist event where objects have agency and people do not)**. But **(victim's name)**, despite having received **(number greater than one)** bullets in **(non-frontal body part)**, suddenly **(completed impossible physical maneuver that could only take place on a non-Euclidean plane of reality)**. In response, Officer **(murderer's name)** felt he had no choice but to **(action that manages to sound both inevitable and accidental, like something out of a Greek tragedy)**.

After **(shockingly large number of)** minutes, Officer **(murderer's name)** called an ambulance. He did not attempt resuscitation because he was worried **(victim's name)** might actually be a **(mythological monster)**. After **(another shockingly large number of)** minutes, **(victim's name)** was pronounced dead at the scene.

While we are aware that **(condescending term for activists)** have drawn attention to **(piece of evidence)**, **(piece of evidence)**, and **(piece of evidence)**, we would like to remind everyone that one eyewitness later changed their statement, claiming **(a minor and completely understandable alteration)**. In light of these facts and the **(friendly euphemism for lies)** made by Officer **(murderer's name)**, we have determined there is insufficient evidence to prove, beyond a reasonable doubt, that this **(euphemism for the violent execution of a human being without trial)** violated the Fourth and Eighth Amendments.

To **(victim's name)**'s family, I would like to say **(something seemingly compassionate)**. I want you to understand that **(insincere avowal of effort and regret)**. At the District Attorney's office, we vow **(vague promise of reform and technocratic solutions that will make a nice sound-bite for the political career you hope to someday have despite the subtle dread that gnaws at your insides, telling you that you might just have ended up on the wrong side of history and humanity)**.

Do you have literally nothing else to do? Try Current Affairs

ARGUMENT STARTERS

So you're looking for a way to liven up your latest cocktail evening or congressional slumber party, are you? Naturally, you don't want to play some mindless board game, you want something that stimulates the cerebellum, that encourages the full flowering of your prodigious intellect. You're in luck, kid: the ***CURRENT AFFAIRS* ARGUMENT STARTERS KIT** is guaranteed to turn any gathering bitterly contentious. Simply make a deck of Argument Cards by scanning and printing the template below, and write contentious propositions on them. Then, each person must draw from the deck and try to defend the position. A rotating neutral judge will decide whether they have succeeded. If the judge thinks you've pulled it off, you get points according to how controversial your argument was. Fun has never been so exasperating!

A dubious proposition – 1 point

A contentious proposition – 3 points

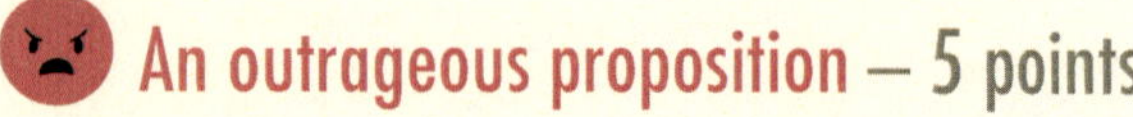
An outrageous proposition – 5 points

- Every right the Constitution grants to humans should also be granted to non-human animals.
- Literally everyone in New York is intolerable.
- Everyone should own a gun.
- Children should not have to learn math beyond the arithmetic necessary for personal finance.
- City-states were the optimal form of government and should be revived.
- Ghosts are real.

- Native Americans should get to vote on whether we should blow up Mt. Rushmore. If a supermajority vote "yes," Mt. Rushmore will be blown up.
- There is no inherent right to private property.
- Love is a poisonous fiction.
- It's okay to burn certain books.
- You should have to get a license to parent.
- Nature isn't actually that pretty.
- Generally speaking, school is a waste of a child's time.
- Skyscrapers ought to be abolished.
- Clothing should be optional.
- By a certain metric, Donald Trump is the greatest president in the history of the United States.
- Children should be allowed to vote.
- There should be no such things as borders between countries. People should be able to move freely about the world without ever having to get the permission of a government.
- It is morally wrong to be rich.
- Prisons should be abolished.
- Canada is underrated.
- Stealing is always justified if you really need something and the person you're stealing from clearly doesn't need it.
- The universe is probably just a giant video game being played by a god with the brain of a five-year-old.
- All beards are hideous.
- Smokers are oppressed.
- Shakespeare is overrated.
- Every young person should be assigned an elderly person to take care of and cheer up.
- The Middle Ages were underrated.
- Medical researchers should try to make it so that human beings are immortal. A world in which nobody ever died would be a better world.
- Young people should have to do a year of military service when they turn 18.
- It would be wrong to kill baby Hitler.
- Some art is objectively inferior to other art.
- There are certain circumstances in which lying to a child is justified. If you want to get them to do something, for instance.
- Walmart is a force for good.
- There are certain circumstances in which lying to your romantic partner is justified. If you want to make them happy, for instance.
- Poetry should be prohibited by law. There is no such thing as a good poem.
- Cats are capable of feeling emotions.
- A judge who doesn't wear a wig isn't really a judge.
- Good reality TV can be as worthwhile as good literature.
- On balance, the universe was a mistake.
- If everything could be done for us by machines, that would be a good thing.
- The captain shouldn't have to go down with the ship if he doesn't want to.
- There is nothing wrong with taking candy from a baby. Babies do not even really understand what candy is, and besides they shouldn't have it in the first place.
- The internet should never have been invented.

PLEASE REFRAIN FROM ARGUMENTS OVER WHETHER THE COLOR-CODED CLASSIFICATIONS OF THE ARGUMENTS ARE ACCURATE

Something is amiss in the busy little city...
CAN "U" TELL WHAT IT IS?

Can you match these ★ ★ ★ ★ ★

U.S. CRIMES

to the countries they were perpetrated against?

1. The U.S. covertly armed a right-wing paramilitary rebel group that committed widespread atrocities, U.S. agents caused many civilian deaths by blowing up bridges and mining the harbor, and the CIA distributed a "terror manual" to the rebels with advice on blackmail, assassination, and bombing.

2. After the people elected a socialist president, the United States supported a military coup that led to 3,000 people being murdered by the new regime, widespread torture, and the end of democracy in this country for an entire generation.

3. Several million people died in this country as the United States tried to prop up a corrupt regime. Through a decade of saturation bombing, including the use of chemical weapons to destroy agriculture and the burning of villages, there were mass civilian casualties in a war widely seen as pointless.

4. The CIA plotted to assassinate the first prime minister of this newly independent postcolonial country, even developing a plan to poison his toothpaste. While that was abandoned, ultimately the United States supported his successful kidnapping and murder, leading to the installation of one of the most brutal dictators in the continent, whose decades-long reign contributed to a civil war that killed millions.

5. For 50 years, the United States has maintained a crippling trade embargo against this country in violation of the Charter of the United Nations and of international law, contributing to its ongoing severe poverty.

6. In this country, U.S.-trained government death squads killed 75,000 civilians over the course of a decade, including an infamous 1981 massacre of an entire village of 800 people.

7. Based on deliberately manipulated and misleading intelligence about "weapons of mass destruction," the United States launched an illegal war against this country that killed 500,000 people.

8. In the early 1950s, U.S. bombing raids destroyed nearly all of the major cities in this poor country, in some cases flattening 95% of the existing structures, an action that is nearly completely forgotten among those today who wonder why this country's ruler harbors an irrational hatred for the United States.

9. During the mid-1960s, the autocratic leader of this country murdered millions of leftists with full U.S. support. The U.S. even provided lists of suspected communists to the death squads, in a largely forgotten tragedy that historians "rank as one of the worst mass murders of the 20th century, along with the Soviet purges of the 1930s, the Nazi mass murders during the Second World War, and the Maoist bloodbath of the early 1950s."

10. This country was illegally and secretly bombed in the late 1960s and early 1970s in "Operation Menu."

11. Under a popular Democratic president known for promising "hope" and "change," the United States arranged to sell $100 billion in arms to one of its allies, which then relentlessly bombed this country, creating one of the worst humanitarian catastrophes of our era.

12. Under the same aforementioned Democratic president, the United States intervened in a civil conflict in this country, killing its leader and contributing to an ongoing bloodbath that would destabilize this country for years to come.

13. In the first decade of the 20th century, the United States occupied this faraway country in a war that would cause at least 200,000 native inhabitants to die from famine and disease.

14. In the early 1960s, the United States launched a plan called "Operation Brother Sam" designed to destabilize this country and allow its military to overthrow the constitutional government. Within a month of the coup, the military regime had arrested more than 50,000 political opponents.

15. The United States gives billions of dollars in aid to a country that keeps this country under siege, causing a humanitarian crisis in one of its major cities. The United States has consistently supported those who continue to dispossess this country's residents, even when they kill unarmed civilians.

16. The United States overthrew the democratically-elected government of this country in 1954 because land and labor reforms threatened U.S. agribusiness interests. The United States later supported the military of this country as it committed genocide against its indigenous inhabitants.

17. In the mid-1960s, the Johnson Administration occupied this country with 42,000 troops in order to protect its military junta and "keep it from going communist."

18. This is the most bombed country in the world thanks to 10 years in which the United States dropped hundreds of thousands of tons of napalm on its peasant population.

19. In 1953, the United States engineered the overthrow of this country's democratically-elected leader and the installation of an authoritarian monarch who maintained power only through U.S. support and was ultimately ousted in a revolution.

20. The popular Democratic president mentioned earlier legitimized a fraudulent election and coup in this country, supporting this country's post-coup leadership and whitewashing its crimes.

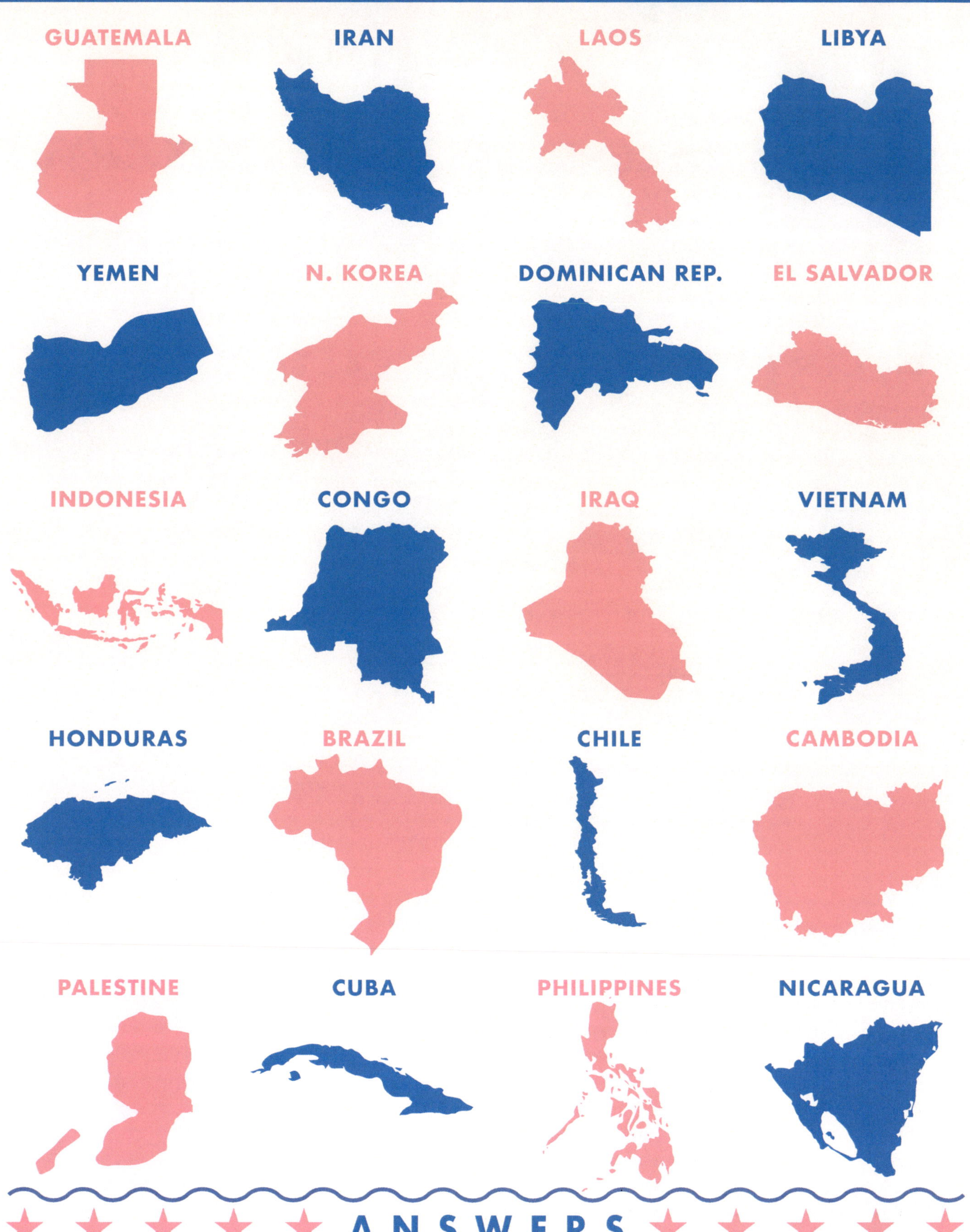

★ ★ ★ ★ ★ ANSWERS ★ ★ ★ ★ ★

1. Nicaragua 2. Chile 3. Vietnam 4. Congo 5. Cuba 6. El Salvador 7. Iraq 8. North Korea 9. Indonesia 10. Cambodia
11. Yemen 12. Libya 13. Philippines 14. Brazil 15. Palestine 16. Guatemala 17. Dominican Republic 18. Laos 19. Iran 20. Honduras

How to choose your POLITICAL BELIEFS *... in a hurry*

At 10 a.m., you manage to open a bleary eye. A man in business attire stands at the foot of your bed. You have no memory of this man, or of the past 36 or so hours of your life. He introduces himself as your campaign manager. He explains that last night, in a stupor, you filed the paperwork to run for the state senate.

"You are due at the Palladium in one hour to give your kick-off speech," he tells you.

"But I don't even have any political beliefs!"

"Well, you'd better hurry up and get some."

You've got both eyes open now, and your brain is whirling. The situation is urgent; you must find beliefs.

Fortunately, you happen upon this list of the pros and cons of every major political belief, which enables you to settle on some in a hurry.

MAINSTREAM POLITICAL BELIEFS: *For & Against*

CONSERVATISM

Good: Likes the old traditions, skeptical of disastrous utopian schemes.

Bad: Some of the old traditions are very racist. Perfectly fine with disastrous capitalist schemes. Insufficently opposed to the prospect of nuclear holocaust. Plus actually kind of bloodthirsty a lot of the time.

NEOCONSERVATISM

Good: Uses the word "democracy" a lot.

Bad: Believes democracy is best instituted via drone strike.

FASCISM

Good: Snappy uniforms, well-coordinated marches.

Bad: State-worship, proclivity for death camps.

MARXISM (generic)

Good: Insightful analysis of capitalism's fundamental instability and the alienation of the worker.

Bad: Lots of parts of the theory are unfalsifiable or untrue. Probably shouldn't take your ideas from just one guy. All the Marxists are really mean.

LIBERTARIANISM

Good: Lots of freedom, gets the boot of the state off your neck.

Bad: Only your boss/landlord get the freedom, boot of the state occasionally useful for enforcing fire codes.

LIBERALISM

Good: Committed to rights and equality and such.

Bad: Equally committed to vagueness, hypocrisy, and expensive scones. For some reason always end up adopting all conservative beliefs on mistaken assumption this will make them liked.

STALINISM

Good: Industrialization.

Bad: Paranoia, gulags.

TROTSKYISM

Good: Dislikes Stalin.

Bad: Likes Trotsky, who was also a somewhat unpleasant man.

ANARCHISM

Good: Detests authority in all forms! Believes phrase "you've got to break a few eggs to make an omelette" is just license to break a bunch of eggs.

Bad: Not particularly good at getting up in time for the revolution

SOCIAL DEMOCRACY

Good: Safety net. Healthcare. Life free of worry.

Bad: Inevitable Nordic tedium. General prissiness.

CAN YOU NAVIGATE THE PERILS OF THE INSURANCE MAZE

You are a person of average health in the United States. You are trying to make sure that you get rudimentary medical services. But first you'll need to make your way through a thicket of bureaucratic obstacles!

YOU

Due to an administrative error, your coverage is canceled without your knowledge.

You are outside the designated enrollment period and must secure a low-benefit temporary plan before purchasing another plan in the correct month.

During a hospital stay, some of the physicians tending to you are within your network and some are not, leading to an endless billing headache.

Your insurance company applies your payments to the wrong policy without telling you and you are unable to secure treatment.

You move out of state or change jobs and must cancel your plan and find another.

Despite being told a procedure was covered, your insurance company denies your claim because the procedure was done using a technique that the insurance company does not cover.

After your premiums are increased dramatically without any explanation, you must switch to a plan with a deductible so high that you will never reach it.

Your doctor deems a certain medical procedure necessary for your health but your insurance company deems it non-essential and denies your claim. Multiple weeks of haggling on the phone do nothing.

When your insurance company wrongly denies a claim for treatment clearly covered in the policy, attempts to fix it involve 10 hours of: "All of our representatives are currently assisting other customers. Please stand by."

SOME BASIC HEALTHCARE

FORTUNE
WHICH DISASTER WILL BEFALL ME TODAY?
CHAOS
1
Public opinion will turn against you as your economic policies plunge the country into a recession. You will begin to suspect that your closest advisors are plotting against you. The paranoia will cause your decision-making to become even more erratic, further alienating the populace.
2
You will suddenly realize that your roommate's succession of one-night stands have all been using your towel.
PERIL
3
A dear friend whom you have not seen in years will show up in town on a surprise visit. You will find yourselves utterly unable to replicate your former rapport, and will, over the course of a strained and awkward dinner, gradually come to realize that you now despise each other.
4
Glancing down in the middle of an important presentation, you will notice that the waistband of your underwear is visible above your belt, and that both your shirt and the end of your necktie are tucked into it.
ERROR
5
The actor who played your favorite character on a beloved childhood television show will today be revealed to be a cat strangler and/or pedophile.
6
Donald Trump will be President of the United States. You will accidentally drop your copy of Current Affairs in a storm. You will be bitten painfully by an angry dog, but the dog will be so small that you feel embarrassed telling anybody even though the wound was actually quite severe.
CALAMITY
7
You will find a venomous snake in your bagged lunch. Recoiling in fear, you will accidentally knock over a priceless piece of ancient pottery. You will be tutted at by dozens. Later, for unrelated reasons, you will be arrested on charges of indecent exposure. You will not be able to remember what you did.
8
You will finally work up the courage to declare your feelings to your love interest over text. A “...” bubble will appear beneath your heartfelt message, hover there for a full fifteen minutes, vanish, reappear again briefly two hours later, and then vanish again. At the end of the day, your text will still be unanswered.
INSTRUCTIONS
TELLER

POSTMODERN NOVEL

BINGO

Have you ever been foolishly enticed into reading a work of contemporary fiction because the dustjacket described it as a "comic masterpiece," only to discover that it was 400 pages of cringingly unfunny garbage? Have you wasted hours of your life trying to muster up human emotions about an "experimental" narrative cobbled together from grocery receipts? When was the last time you actually *enjoyed* reading a novel? Well, never fear! The *Current Affairs* Postmodern Novel Bingo turns the experience of reading contemporary fiction from a horrifying ordeal into a delightful scavenger hunt. Challenge your friends!

NAÏVE CHARACTER BECOMES SLOWLY DISILLUSIONED	A LUMBERING COMEDIC SETPIECE IS SUDDENLY INTERRUPTED BY HORRIFIC VIOLENCE	IT'S BEEN MORE THAN TWENTY PAGES SINCE THERE WAS ANY DIALOGUE	A TELEVISION ADVERTISEMENT IS DESCRIBED FRAME-FOR- FRAME	A MALE AUTHOR HAS BRAVELY CHOSEN TO TELL HIS STORY THROUGH THE EYES OF A RAGINGLY MISOGYNISTIC MALE NARRATOR
A MALE AUTHOR HAS BRAVELY CHOSEN TO TELL HIS STORY THROUGH THE EYES OF A MALE NARRATOR WHO IS STRUGGLING WITH HIS ATTRACTION TO FASCINATINGLY NUBILE YOUNG GIRLS	DISILLUSIONED CHARACTER LEARNS ALL TOO LATE THAT IT'S THE LITTLE THINGS IN LIFE THAT COUNT	TEPID MARRIAGE RUINED BY UNSATISFYING INFIDELITY	LOOK, THIS BOOK IS A DISORIENTING MESS BECAUSE *THE WORLD* IS A DISORIENTING MESS, OKAY? GEEZ.	U.S. PRESIDENT WITH A SILLY SURNAME DECLARES WAR ON A FICTIONAL MIDDLE EASTERN COUNTRY
ENTIRE CHAPTER IS JUST A LIST OF IRONIC BRAND NAMES	A SEX SCENE SO GHASTLY THAT YOU ARE IMMEDIATELY COMPELLED TO HOP IN THE SHOWER, BUT THEN THE SIGHT OF YOUR OWN NAKED FLESH ONLY MAKES THE WHOLE THING MORE GROTESQUELY VIVID	FREE	ACTUALLY THAT WORD'S NOT RACIST BECAUSE THIS PART OF THE BOOK TAKES PLACE IN A DIFFERENT TIME PERIOD	ATTEMPT AT "MAGICAL" REALISM QUICKLY REVEALS AUTHOR TO BE A RABBITS-IN-TOP-HATS LEVEL MAGICIAN
CHILD-CHARACTER'S DIALOGUE IS WILDLY OVER- OR UNDER-SOPHISTICATED FOR THEIR STATED AGE	THE MAIN CHARACTER IS A NOVELIST	THE MAJESTY OF THE AMERICAN OUTDOORS SOMEHOW PROMPTS EVERYONE TO JUST START MASSACRING EACH OTHER	SELF-DOUBT AT THE SUPERMARKET	PROLONGED DESCRIPTION OF MAIN CHARACTER TAKING A JOYLESS SHIT
THAT PLOTLINE WAS LEFT UNRESOLVED *NOT* BECAUSE OF CARELESSNESS, BUT BECAUSE OF THE AUTHOR'S PRINCIPLED COMMITMENT TO NIHILISM	A THING YOU HAVE SEEN A THOUSAND TIMES IS METAPHORICALLY COMPARED TO FIVE SUCCESSIVE THINGS YOU HAVE NEVER SEEN IN YOUR LIFE	HYPERINTELLIGENT FAMILY SPEAKS TO EACH OTHER IN PARAGRAPHS	THE AUTHOR'S AESTHETIC AVERSION TO APOSTROPHES AND COMMAS HAS RENDERED THIS SENTENCE UNINTELLIGIBLE	ENIGMATIC, UNTOUCHABLE WOMAN TURNS OUT TO BE SURPRISINGLY SUSCEPTIBLE TO BULLSHIT

! THIS PAGE A **10¢** VALUE WHEN **RESOLD** RESALE STRICTLY PROHIBIT

"NEVER MISTAKE THE IMPLAUSIBLE FOR THE IMPOSSIBLE"

Bonus Activities

"GAMES AND PUZZLES ARE TESTS OF MORAL WORTHINESS"

THIS PAGE A **10¢** VALUE WHEN **RESOLD** RESALE STRICTLY PROHIBITED ¡

MERCY SHALL ONLY BE EXTENDED TO FULLY-PAID SUBSCRIBERS

A TAX PUZZLE

Some people say they pay too much in tax. Some people think those people do not pay enough in tax. There are **73,954** pages in the United States Tax Code. Some people claim that all of these pages are necessary. Others claim that they are not. What is the optimal national tax structure? Give some reasons for your choice. **BONUS:** How can tax policy be used to reduce poverty?

PUZZLEBOX

ANSWERS: 1. That question is incoherent. 2. It is your car, silly. 3. The eye is looking at you. 4. No.

1. THE COAT PUZZLE

What is this man forgetting?

2. THE BENTLEY PUZZLE

Whose car is this?

3. THE EYE PUZZLE

This eye is looking at someone. But who is it?

4. THE SQUARES PUZZLE

Can you rearrange the squares to spell "Current Affairs?"

ENJOY THIS CAPITALIST MAD LIB!

"It's unfortunate we had to ______ (verb) all those ______ (type of people), but we're confident it will make us ______ (meaningless buzzword) and more ______ (soul-crushing inanity) as we pivot toward the ______ (euphemism for 'hell').

OPTICAL ILLUSION

STARE AT THE DOT IN THE CENTER OF THE IMAGE.
Unfocus your eyes and be amazed as the other issues fade away, as if they don't even exist.

HAVING TROUBLE? HERE ARE SOME TIPS:
1. Keep staring! 2. Don't look away. 3. Don't EVER look away. 4. Ever.

FLINT

TIP: THE WAY TO A WOMAN'S HEART IS THROUGH TELLING HER ABOUT YOUR DISSERTATION

People We Could Do Without

Rearrange the letters to find the name of a "Person We Could Do Without":
◇◇◇◇◇◇◇◇ **SUNK MOLE** ◇◇◇◇◇◇◇◇

Current Affairs Survey:
CIVILIZATION: **Y** or **N** ?

CAN YOU TELL WHY THESE JUSTIFICATIONS FOR ATROCITIES ARE NOT ACTUALLY JUSTIFICATIONS?

1. **"The protesters had been warned that if they approached the fence, they risked being deterred with force."**
2. **"The officer feared for his safety."**
3. **"Actually the living standards of colonized populations improved under colonialism."**
4. **"The strike did not intend to target civilians."**
5. **"It was better than the other alternative we were considering."**
6. **"Hamas had deliberately placed women and children in the populated area."**
7. **"Instead of paying attention to American crimes, why aren't you focusing on the much worse crimes of ___?"**
8. **"There was nothing illegal about my conduct."**

ANSWERS TO "JUSTFICACTIONS" QUIZ: 1. Telling someone you'll kill them if they do something doesn't justify killing them. 2. Subjective feelings aren't necessarily reasonable or justified, and if we defer to subjective fear, then the more skittish our officers are, the more it becomes okay for them to murder people. 3. Average improvements don't mitigate individual bad acts, just as a doctor who saves two lives but then murders someone is still a murderer. 4. Intent doesn't matter if the party committing the atrocity acted with callous negligence. 5. Proving that the bad thing you did was less bad than a different bad thing you could have done does not mitigate the bad thing you did. 6. The fact that somebody else pushes a child into the road doesn't relieve me of my moral obligation to swerve and avoid the child. 7. The existence of worse bad acts committed by people other than myself does not give me a pass to commit bad acts. 8. That is an indictment of the law, not a justification for wrongdoing.

Distributional Justice

Can you divide up the cookies in a way that accurately simulates the distribution of the products of labor between owners and workers under capitalism?

IF YOU FIND YOURSELF unable to complete the activities in this book, do not despair. There are many more sections to come, and there is still hope for you. **CURRENT AFFAIRS** is not here to make your life difficult. We are your friends. We want the best for you, and if you're unhappy, we're unhappy. **ALWAYS** remember that.

CONNECT THE BITCOINS

Link them up and see if you can solve the **RIDDLE**

"They call me a 'cryptocurrency,' but what am I really?"

CUT IT OUT

Twitter founder "@Jack" Dorsey recently announced his intention to get rid of the "like" feature on the platform, due to its alleged contribution to the debasement of public discourse. We were distressed to hear of this planned change, as it has always been our position that the ability to place a small heart next to something someone else had said was one of the service's few redeeming features.

Current Affairs considers itself as much a Social Aid & Pleasure Society as a magazine, and we are thus committed to improving the public welfare when we can. To preserve the function of the "like"/"favorite" feature, we therefore present these cut-out tiny paper hearts, which can be removed from this book and stuck to your favorite tweets as needed. Let us not allow megalomaniacal billionaires to sap the love from the world.

What sentence can the words in the search be arranged to spell?

V L S I A Q I O W C G T I I Q
P D E S F F S V F L U I H A Q
T A H T M T S R X Y O N K Z A
O I C I T N I C O Y Z C W F T
H Y R E V E M M E G D R M W P
L V A P N P R I E E E N T N A
U K E D O S D S T S D E Y G R
M T S O L V I N G H L O Y O W
C T D I A Z E K N L U L I T Q
D A R N B M K R I N O C N B O
J A O G O A Q N T T C N H B B
Y S W M L F G H I Y U O G Q H
Z R E G G U E O R X H H N C P
S F E D E M B G W O G W Z W Z
Z X R H G P D K S M D N A Q N

Answers: The words found in the Word Search can be reordered to spell the sentence "every moment spent doing wordsearches is time that could be spent solving global poverty or writing letters to long lost friends telling them you miss them." None of the words in the list of words is included in the Luxury Word Search. The List of Words was a separate exhibit having nothing to do with the puzzle.

List of Words

- PLENITUDE
- DIASPORA
- LEFTMOST
- MIASMA
- QUELLING
- CRAWDAD
- TURNSTILE
- ERRATIC
- FESTOONED
- OTIOSE

SIX EUPHEMISMS FOR NAZIS for your next NEW YORK TIMES profile

- folksy nationalists
- retro salute enthusiasts
- business-friendly colorful rogues
- counterfactual history re-enactors
- heroic underdogs standing up to the oppressed
- romantically misunderstood murder-fans

WHEN YOU'RE DONE, FOR A "FUN" VARIANT, TRY THE ACTIVITIES AGAIN WHILE BLINDFOLDED

DO NOT ALLOW THIS PAGE TO FALL INTO THE HANDS OF REACTIONARIES OR OTHERS WHO WOULD NOT FULLY APPRECIATE IT.

THE CURRENT AFFAIRS™
"BIG BOOK OF AMUSEMENTS"

Games to Alienate Your Friends

You made it to the White House, but now you'll need to...

GET THE PRESIDENT'S ATTENTION!

You are a junior Republican staffer, freshly recruited from Dartmouth's School of Politics Management with a bachelor's degree in Nepotism. Your mentor from the Heritage Foundation hooked you up with this sweet White House gig, but there's a catch: For the first time in your life, you actually have to work. If you can't win President Trump's favor and attention, the Heritage Foundation will replace you with someone who can. It's very important that Trump signs off on the Foundation's latest and most important initiative: forcing poor people who own pets to kill and eat their pets before a live studio audience. Can you navigate the chaos, intrigue, and mind-bending incompetence of the Trump White House? Can you get the President's attention?

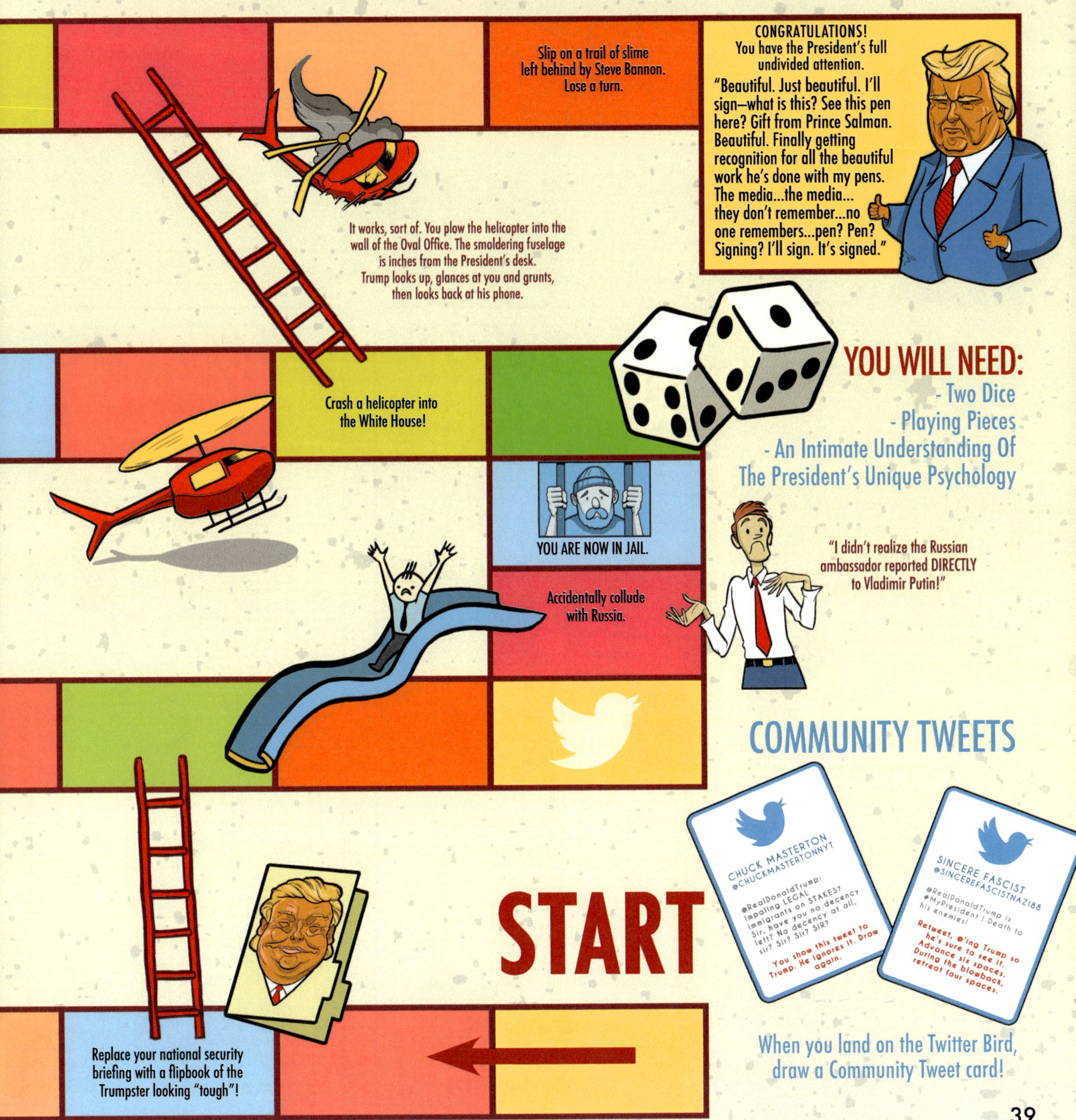

CAN YOU WIN THE GOP SENATE PRIMARY?

RULES

You are competing for the Republican nomination. Pick a character. Get a die. Place a token on the character's starting space and try to get to the nomination.

If a character lands on the **GAFFE** square, they have to roll a die to see how many squares they must retreat.

If a character lands on the **SCANDAL** square, they have to roll a die (4 or better) to stay in the race.

If a character lands on the **ADVANTAGE** square, they must roll to see how many squares they should advance.

But if the **GAFFE**, **SCANDAL**, or **ADVANTAGE** square contains an asterisk, they must obey the instructions following the asterisk instead.

THE HOLY INQUISITOR

GAFFE: While attempting to defend a women's bathroom from a hypothetical trans invasion, you slip on wet tiles and crack your skull.

SCANDAL: Breitbart uncovers a terrible secret: your daughter has been happily married to another woman for ten years. You rush to publicly disavow her but it's too late. Your base now doubts your commitment to the homophobic cause.

ADVANTAGE: Your adorable turtle, Mr. Shelldon, is a social media star. He now accompanies you on campaign rallies, and poses nobly on signs that read "ENFORCE MONOGAMY NOW" even though his species is highly promiscuous.

OIL COMPANY C.E.O.

GAFFE: During a debate you accidentally blurt, "well, of course we know climate change is real! We just can't make any money on it!"

SCANDAL: One of your offshore rigs explodes, gushes uncontrollably, and begins suffocating 400 adorable baby dugongs per day. *Roll a die to see how long it will take to plug the well with silt and golf balls. Retreat the number of spaces you rolled. If you roll a six, oil has killed the entire global dugong population and you must exit the race.

ADVANTAGE: Cash flows into your coffers faster than oil onto sacred tribal land.

MERCENARY MANIAC

GAFFE: You sold weapons to jihadists who—at the time—were U.S. allies, but have since been reclassified as murderous enemies. *Return to start and suspend your campaign until the jihadists have become allies again (15 mins).

SCANDAL: You accidentally invited an investigative reporter to your private murder island, where you hunt "the most dangerous game." You failed to hunt her, however, and she got away from the island with photographs and several very suspicious bones. *Wait a turn while your surrogates question her integrity. She'll disappear soon enough, and after that she'll "disappear" forever.

ADVANTAGE: The medals and decorations on your chest are actually a mixture of 1990s Boy Scout patches and triathlon participation medals, but whenever your opponents point this out, you accuse them of Disrespecting The Troops.

BOOTSTRAPPING BLACK CONSERVATIVE

GAFFE: You divert from your prepared speech to tell the audience your personal theory about the extraterrestrial origins of the Fed. End the Neptunian Fed!

SCANDAL: You admit that when you said you grew up "in government housing," you meant your father was the mayor of a medium-sized Midwestern city.

ADVANTAGE: Right-wing media is very eager to have you on their platforms—finally, a black person they feel comfortable with!—and they give you far more attention than your half-baked policy proposals really justify. You gain considerable name recognition.

LITERAL NAZI

GAFFE: You accidentally say something obliquely white supremacist.

SCANDAL: You accidentally say something explicitly white supremacist.

ADVANTAGE: You deliberately say something the *New York Times* decides to label "racially charged rhetoric" and "dangerously radical statements," like something a motorcycle bad boy might whisper in your ear."

THE SENSIBLE SACRIFICE

GAFFE: Shout "Mr. Trump, this is NOT what it means to be a Republican" on the Senate floor about something that 1) is the very definition of being a Republican, and 2) you voted for six times.

SCANDAL: In a moment of unaccountable rage you call one of your opponents "a fucking moron." While he IS an absolute fucking moron, you still *retreat three spaces and apologize profusely to all the other players for the rest of the game.

ADVANTAGE: The remaining five "compassionate conservatives" endorse you enthusiastically in the nation's most prominent newspapers. *No matter what you roll, you advance zero spaces.

MERCENARY
ADVANTAGE
Compare the American enemy du jour to Tolkien's orcs. Advance one space on a wave of nerd adulation.
The Predator drone demonstration at your rally goes horribly. As you emerge, coughing, from the cataclysm, you are forced to suspend your campaign.
SCANDAL
While trying to take a family-and-guns photo, your son shoots off his foot. The liberal contempt sends you back two spaces, and the conservative backlash sends you forward two spaces again.
A squadron of former mercenaries claims that while you brag about your courage under fire, you've never actually stepped foot on a battlefield. Retreat two spaces in shame.
A group of surviving villagers claims that your mercenaries were murderous thugs and you personally gave the orders that destroyed their homes and murdered their families. Advance two spaces in righteous indignation.
An independent media outfit reveals the truth: You're part of a secretive cabal of military-industrial contractors who advocate war with Iran so they can make millions in weapons sales. Take no action; the regular media doesn't care.
Refer to nuclear weapons as "God's holy fire." Gain evangelical support, move ahead one space.
GAFFE!
OIL C.E.O.
ADVANTAGE
Use Koch cash to film a heartwarming campaign commercial in which you wear a hard hat and shake hands with grateful-looking, grease-covered men. Advance two spaces.
Buy out a small green energy company, liquidate their stocks, and fire all their employees. Call it "innovation," and advance one space.
An oil-covered sandpiper flies onto the stage and dies right at your feet. You may not re-enter the race until you've posed with an oil-free Labrador puppy on your Instagram.
SCANDAL
Picket by employees' widows delays your motorcade, lose a turn.
By stating the correct origin of fossil fuels—fossils—you've offended creationists. Go back one space and pretend to read the Bible until your next turn.
GAFFE!
At a rally, environmentalists splatter you with green paint. Much like spilled oil, this paint is highly toxic. Lose two turns while you recover.
The campus Marxists got to your son, and now he makes outrageous public statements like "capitalism is literally destroying the planet through climate change." Lose a turn while you transfer him to a Bible college.
BOOTSTRAPS
SCANDAL
Make a remark about members of your race so extreme that Charles Murray raises an eyebrow. Lose a turn.
Quietly notice you have fewer "advance" spaces than your opponents, who are all white. Say nothing about this obvious injustice. Lose a turn.
Accidentally reveal to a group of donors that you yourself have previously experienced racism. Go back two spaces.
Agree to debate Cornel West, then back out at the last minute when you realize you can't possibly successfully debate Cornel West. Retreat two spaces and lose a turn.
Discover a new civil rights organization to throw under the bus. Advance two spaces and collect a Fox News interview.
ADVANTAGE
After a flame war with a famous rapper on Twitter, he releases a diss track so utterly true and devastating that you must retreat four spaces. If you're foolish enough to release a track of your own, the subsequent mockery will return you to the start square.
GAFFE!
You shave your dignified moustache, which means you no longer appear non-threatening to white people. Suspend your campaign until it grows back.
?
SACRIFICE
ADVANTAGE
Unveil your slogan: What America Needs Now Is Civility. Advance two spaces and pen a New York Times op-ed.
A conservative comedian says something extremely racist. Condemn them, then walk back your condemnation, advancing a square and retreating a square every time you condemn and retract.
GAFFE!
During a debate you say, "I don't know, maybe government benefits aren't ALL bad." In the subsequent right-wing backlash, revise your statement several times. Retreat three spaces and lose a turn.
Bring a literal pair of bootstraps on stage with you. While attempting to pull yourself up by them, you fall on your face. The crowd laughs. Retreat two spaces, but loudly refuse to suspend your campaign.
In an attempt to relate to young people, you record a spoken word cover of Sir Mixalot's "Baby Got Back." Lose two spaces with millennials and gain three spaces with the type of boomers who find Andy Borowitz amusing.
During a meet-and-greet at a burger joint, you are photographed eating your fries with a fondue fork. The resulting backlash is so intense you decide to suspend your campaign.
SCANDAL
When confronted onstage by immigration activists who are outraged by your reprehensible pro-cruelty record, you accuse them of confronting you in an improper forum and thereby lacking decency. Advance one space with the civility crowd.
INQUISITOR
ADVANTAGE
You are struck by lightning, and manage to spin it as evidence of God's divine favor. Advance three spaces.
Every time there's a school shooting, you demand the reintroduction of prayer in school. Move ahead one space every time there's a school shooting during gameplay.
Your wife's fixed rictus grin at your rallies is causing some concern. Insist that "displaying genuine happiness is a sin, and should be a felony." Pick up an endorsement from the police union and advance two spaces.
SCANDAL
The media is obsessed with the time you chained the family cat on the roof as punishment for "ungodly mischief." Lose a turn with animal lovers.
Advocate legislation that reclassifies a woman's uterus as a piece of land, legally owned by her father or husband. Lose a turn with social media, gain a turn with your base.
GAFFE!
Partnering with a Silicon Valley startup, unveil an app to stop non-heterosexual, non-procreative sex. If you are elected, "sinINT" will be installed in all homes nationwide. When it's clear you do mean EVERY home, your debauched donors retract their money. You must withdraw from the race.
As you don't really understand memes, you accidentally endorse the two genders "shark" and "leather jacket." Go back three spaces in your confusion.
THE NAZI
ADVANTAGE
Gain the endorsement of a far-right European party. Take no action: Americans don't notice or care.
A nearby HBCU refuses to let you hold a rally on their campus. Go on a media blitz—or blitzkrieg, if you prefer—accusing the students of denying your right to free speech. Advance two spaces.
See an actual person of color. Retreat three spaces in terror.
A different Nazi faction accuses you of insufficient attention to the Jewish Question. Lose a turn.
Deny being a racist, because "that's a word for bad people, and I'm not a bad person." Advance two spaces in the subsequent confusion and outrage.
While on a mission to destroy water caches left by good Samaritans for migrants crossing the desert, you're stung by a scorpion. In the subsequent hallucinogenic haze, you realize the true oneness of all humanity. When you wake up you cancel your campaign, swearing to make amends to all the people you've hurt.
Photos of your old Hitler cosplay resurface. Lose a turn. Lose another turn for claiming "I was doing Charlie Chaplin!"
SCANDAL
GAFFE!

SOCIALIST MONOPOLY

COMMUNAL WEALTH PILE

Nobody likes Monopoly. This is because it emulates and amplifies the least fun parts of capitalism—the parts where we act like greedy dicks for no good reason. *Current Affairs* Socialist Monopoly fixes this problem for good.

MONOPOLY
LUXEMBERG PLACE
COMMUNITY CHATTER
DEBS DRIVE
CLEAN AND EFFICIENT HIGH SPEED RAIL
FOURIER COURT
ANGELA DAVIS AVENUE
COLLECT UNIVERSAL BASIC INCOME.
GO
CHOMSKY CIRCLE
KROPOTKIN EXPRESSWAY
CHANCE
LOUISE MICHEL LANE
PAINE PLACE
CLEAN AND EFFICIENT HIGH SPEED RAIL
DOROTHY DAY DRIVE
GO TO YOUR UNION MEETING (EVEN IF YOU'RE KIND OF TIRED)
JUNCTION
PROUDHON PLAZA
PUBLICLY OWNED CLEAN WATER WORKS
DURUTTI COLUMN
CHANCE
CORBYN CLOSE

CAN YOU PAY OFF YOUR DEBT BEFORE YOU CROAK?

GO

It's the 1st! Each time you pass, make an $800 monthly payment.

Bonus at work. EARN $500

NEATO! You found a DOLLAR in the street. Add it to your savings!

Lose your JOB. From now on, make payments by taking on more DEBT.

You decided to buy a house! Add $100,000. to your outstanding debt and $1000 to your monthly payments.

WHOOPS! Miscalculated your interest. Government garnishes 15% of your wages for next 3 years.

Unexpected MEDICAL EXPENSE adds $10,000 to your existing debt.

College friend with Wall Street job pays 10% of your debt out of PITY. (This never happens.)

There are sure to be some hefty PROCESSING FEES Add 3% to all future payments for anything.

TO GO 1st of month arrives unexpectedly, though you unwisely spent paycheck on food for child. Go to go, make payment, do not collect income.

Accidentally talked into CONSOLIDATION scam. Your original debt is now a single loan, but at the highest of the original 3 interest rates. Adjust future calculations accordingly.

For work you needed to BUY A CAR Add new $15,000 debt with 4.2% annual interest.

Automatic debit for student loans causes OVERDRAFT FEES Pay $500.

UH OH! Savings wiped out due to vagaries of market.

INTEREST RATES on all loans increase by 2% for reasons never explained.

Debt collector threatens to call your boss unless you pay $1000. Take from savings. If no savings, add new debt (5% APR).

Parents sigh, pay off 25% of whatever remains of original $40,000 debt (but not other new debts).

Oh, right, you need to pay RENT Subtract 1/3 from all future paychecks.

NEW JOB! Twice the salary of your previous job. (minus 15% income tax).

Distant relative expires. INHERIT $1000

OH DEAR! WHAT YOU THOUGHT WAS YOUR ANNUAL INTEREST was actually the monthly rate. Adjust calculations accordingly.

Make sure to remember the fee for CHECK CASHING Take 5% off each future paycheck.

Debt collector comes after you for CREDIT CARD BILL belonging to person who shares your name. Pay lawyer $1000 to clear things up.

Needed a PAYDAY LOAN to cover unexpected expense. Add $500 debt with 15% monthly interest rate.

A GAME OF FINANCIAL DESPAIR

RULES

1. You'll need a die, and a pencil and paper for accounting purposes.

2. Start on "Go" with $40,000 in student debt.

3. Roll once to determine your starting monthly income. 1 = $500 per month, 2 = $1000 per month, 3-5 = $1500, 6 = $4000

4. Whenever you pass go, total your income, then subtract your loan payments and any other expenses. The rest becomes your "savings." If your savings don't cover your expenses, the balance becomes new interest-accruing debt.

5. When you pass GO, you may choose to pay more than your required payment if you have available savings.

6. Don't forget to calculate interest. 10% of your loan balance is a federal loan at 5.2% interest per year, compounded daily. 25% of your loan balance is a federal loan at 7.2%, also compounded daily. And the remaining 65% is a private loan at 8% annual interest. Compounded daily, of course. Make sure your interest calculations are factored in exactly.

7. The aim of the game is to pay off your debt before you die! You die after 720 circuits, i.e., 60 years.

BIPARTISAN *Trivial Pursuit*

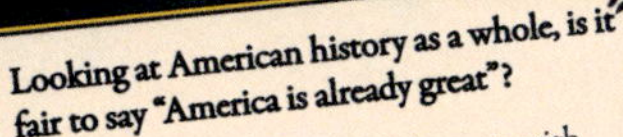

History

Looking at American history as a whole, is it fair to say "America is already great"?

D — America is already great, with some historical inequalities that were mostly put to rest long ago. Its only crime is being overrun with poor and stupid people who vote against their own self-interest.

R — America was perfect from the start, but has fallen from grace due to a decline in "Western values" and other euphemisms for white supremacy.

Foreign Policy

When is it appropriate to launch a drone strike?

D — When an algorithm tells you to, and also when you can reclassify the dead male children in the Hellfire's radius as "enemy combatants."

R — When an algorithm tells you to, and also when you can openly celebrate murdering terrorists' families.

Domestic Policy

What should be done about ICE?

D — ICE has been behaving very badly lately. Naughty, naughty boys. They need a much better system of oversight and evaluation, hopefully with some high-tech monitoring devices.

R — We should expand ICE, and also create a Junior ICE program where young and ideally blond children can simulate ICE techniques such as kidnapping people from their homes.

Political Strategy and Tactics

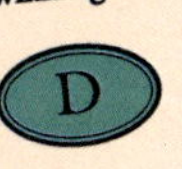

What is the best electoral strategy for winning the presidency?

D — Triangulating the suburban center-right while condescendingly assuming the full support of minorities and sneering at poor white people.

R — Triangulating the suburban center-right while dog-whistling or regular-whistling racists from both inside and outside the suburbs.

Justice and The Law

Which of these descriptions best matches the ideal Supreme Court Justice?

D — A moderate sober centrist, so committed to fairness and balance that s/he never eats a sandwich unless it has two contrasting and unpleasant flavors. Also extremely in favor of the police.

R — Highly qualified xenophobe and misogynist; a great dad! Constitutional originalist, except for the parts of the Constitution he doesn't like. Very cultured and dignified: You can take him (of course it's a him) to the opera.

The Left

What is the best response to the rising tide of democratic socialism?

D — What rising tide? Haha. The left is dangerous, because one time somebody got yelled at on campus. Anyway, the left must be stopped.

R — Socialism can only lead to Venezuela, because saying "socialism can only lead to the Soviet Union" was soooo last decade. Anyway, the left must be stopped.

MEMORY

Test Your Bush Atrocity Recollection Skills

Can you keep George W. Bush's crimes from slowly disappearing from your recollection? Each card depicts a horrendous thing done by Bush. There should be two cards depicting each bad thing. Place all the cards image-side down. On your turn, flip over two. If you get a match, you keep them. If you don't, turn them back over. When it's your turn, you'll need to remember which atrocities you saw, so that you can figure out where the pairs out! When all the cards have been taken, the person with the largest pile of criminal wrongdoing "wins."

CARDS

Abu Ghraib ✣ Imaginary WMDs and the illegal war in Iraq ✣ Hurricane Katrina ✣ Indefinite detention, extraordinary rendition and enhanced interrogation techniques ✣ Creation of ICE and DHS ✣ Patriot Act and warrantless surveillance ✣ The eternal war in Afghanistan ✣ BAPCPA, the bankruptcy "reform" act that has helped drown the middle class ✣ Obscene tax cuts for the rich ✣ Guantanamo

Make some additional cards of your own! There's no shortage of possibilities!

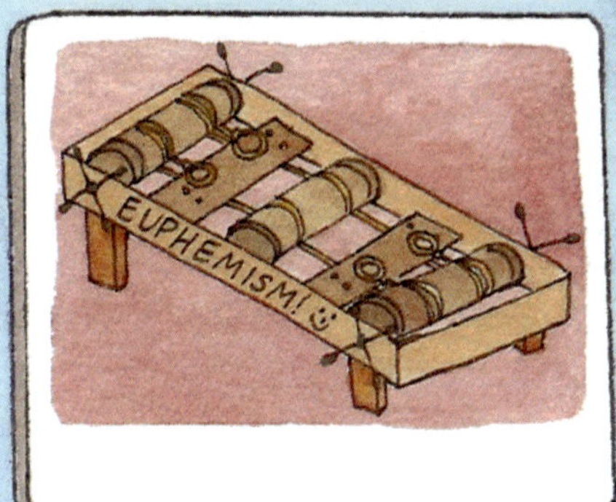

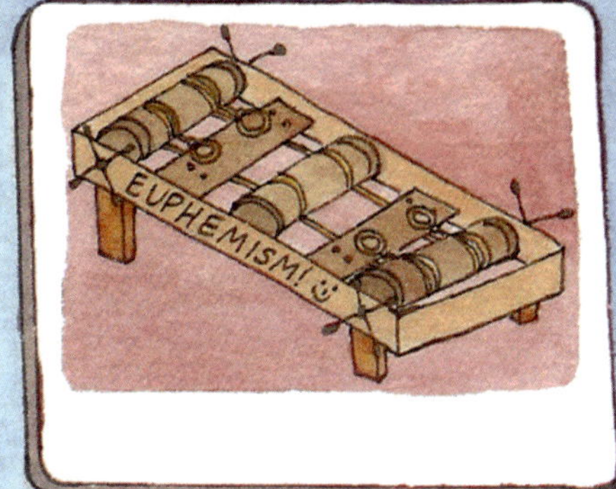

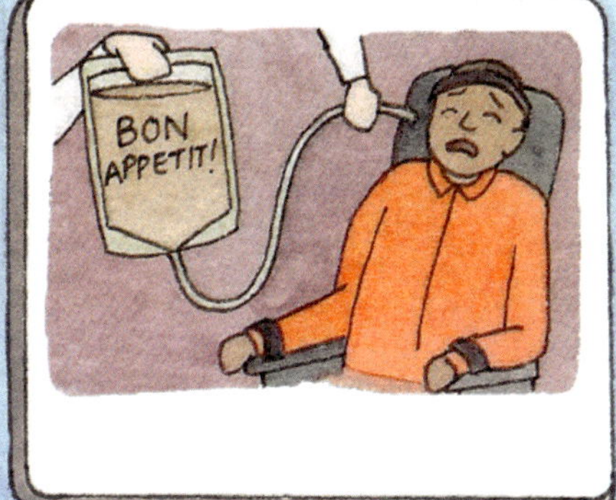

Clue®

"The Only Good Billionaire Is A Dead Billionaire" EDITION

It's your job to figure out which billionaire died by which means and why each deserved their fate!

PREPARATION

You will need a die, plus individual player tokens such as a tiddlywink or the little Monopoly racecar. Place your token on one of the spots designated with a circle. On subsequent pages, you will find nine billionaires, nine justifications, and nine means of death. Place a billionaire in each room. Leave the rest of the cards available for players to inspect. A nonplayer must be designated the "Director of Death."

RULES

1. Take turns rolling. To enter a room, one must roll the exact number of spaces so that the room is the final space.

2. When a player enters a room, they must try to figure out how the billionaire died and why their death was justified. The Director of Death will check the Answers. If the guess is correct, the player keeps the billionaire card. If the guess is incorrect, the player is expelled from the room.

3. Play lasts until all deceased billionaire cards have been collected. The person with the most wins.

ANSWERS

Billionaire — Means — Reason

The Failprince — Jet crash — "Having crashed too many…"
The NGO CEO — Ebola blankets — "Her company's mission statement…"
The Post-Human Tech God — Killed by robots — "The press wants to know…"
God's Own Retailer — Eaten by employees — "This character is best known…"
The Legitimate Russian Businessman — Poisoned — "There are no questions…"
The Real Estate Honcho — Chicken fingers — "Literally the world's worst…"
The Corruption King — Revolution — "Installed by a U.S.-backed coup…"
The Champagne Heiress — Pills — "A social media star…"
The Oil Scion — Safari — "Three generations removed…"

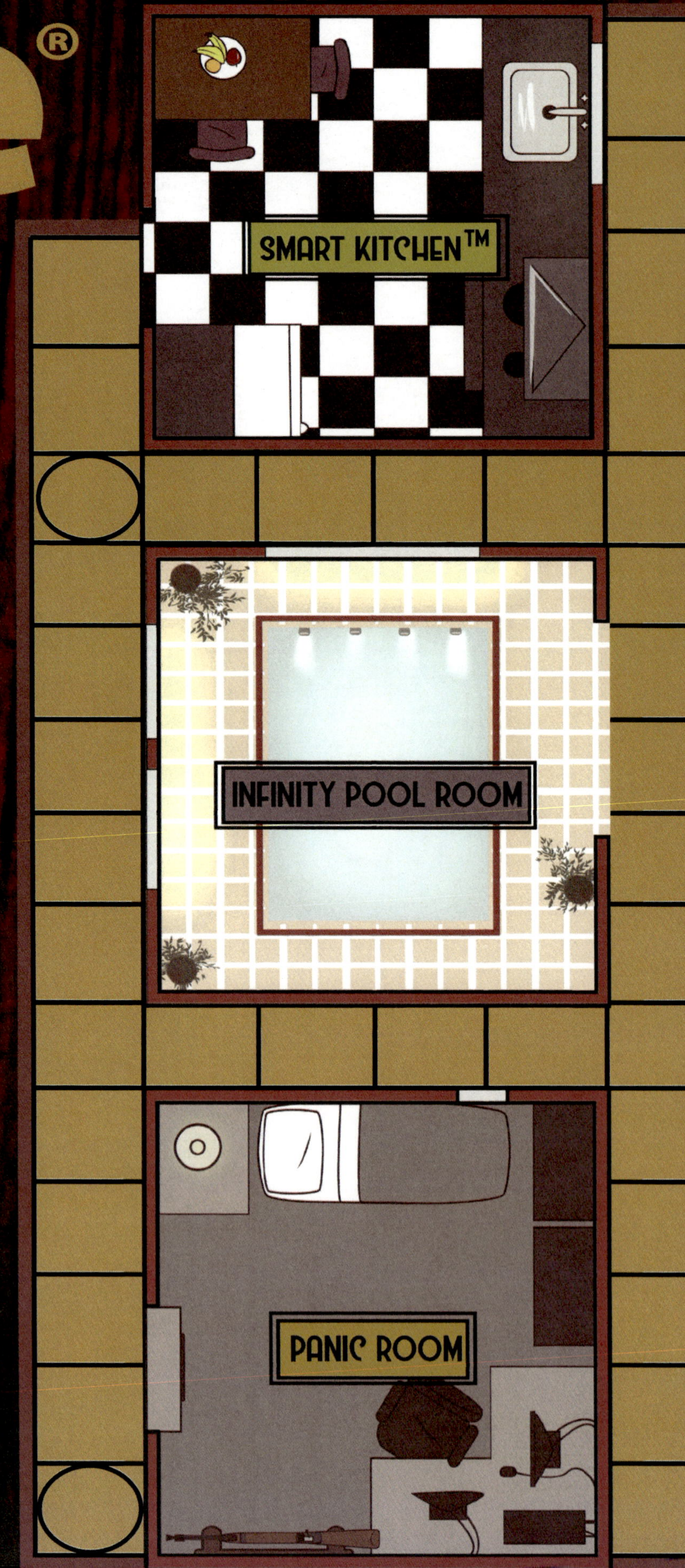

SOLARIUM
SECOND SOLARIUM
STUDY
INFINITY BILLIARDS ROOM
WELLNESS CENTER
TRAP ROOM

The Reasons

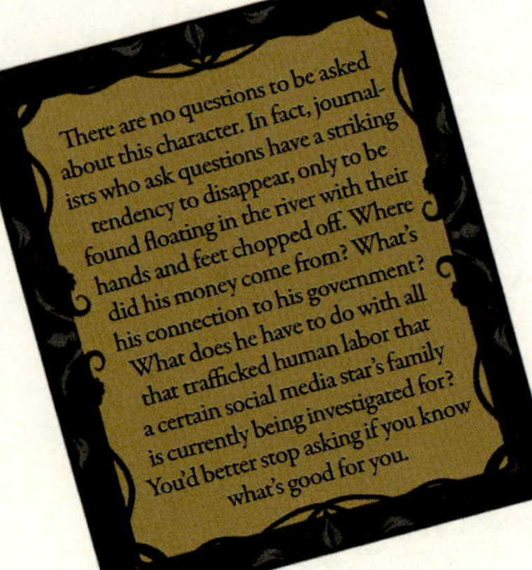
There are no questions to be asked about this character. In fact, journalists who ask questions have a striking tendency to disappear, only to be found floating in the river with their hands and feet chopped off. Where did his money come from? What's his connection to his government? What does he have to do with all that trafficked human labor that a certain social media star's family is currently being investigated for? You'd better stop asking if you know what's good for you.

A social media star, this character is famous for buying extremely expensive designer clothes, wearing them once, and setting them on fire over Facebook Live. She's also known for adopting kittens that mysteriously disappear only to be replaced by cuter specimens. When the family business was indicted for using trafficked labor in their supply chains, this character took to Twitter to accuse people of "just being jealous" and "totally not getting the definition of slavery."

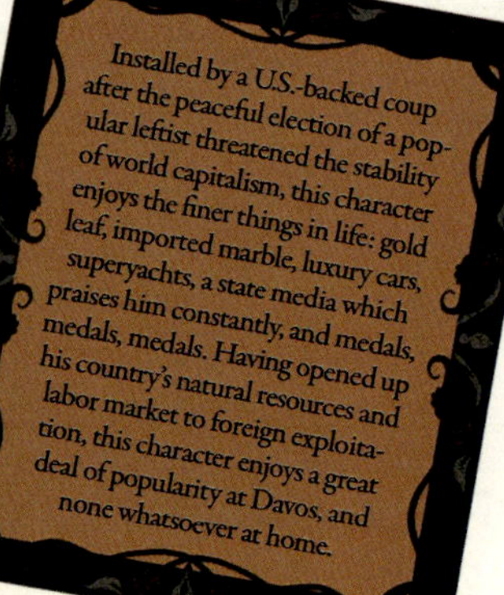
Installed by a U.S.-backed coup after the peaceful election of a popular leftist threatened the stability of world capitalism, this character enjoys the finer things in life: gold leaf, imported marble, luxury cars, superyachts, a state media which praises him constantly, and medals, medals, medals. Having opened up his country's natural resources and labor market to foreign exploitation, this character enjoys a great deal of popularity at Davos, and none whatsoever at home.

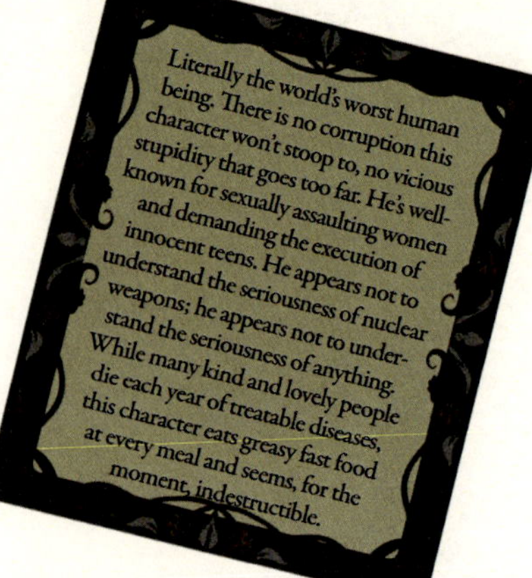
Literally the world's worst human being. There is no corruption this character won't stoop to, no vicious stupidity that goes too far. He's well-known for sexually assaulting women and demanding the execution of innocent teens. He appears not to understand the seriousness of nuclear weapons; he appears not to understand the seriousness of anything. While many kind and lovely people die each year of treatable diseases, this character eats greasy fast food at every meal and seems, for the moment, indestructible.

Having crashed too many planes and murdered too many prostitutes, this character was finally summoned home for a stern talking-to. It didn't take. Within weeks he was photographed falling off skis in Switzerland and subsequently beating up his ski instructor. This time, the family kept him home for half a year. But after several "unpleasantnesses" with the staff, his family bought his admission to NYU, where he occasionally attends business classes.

Three generations removed from needing to work, this character believes taxation is theft. When not maintaining a braggadocious social media presence, he wastes daddy's money on investment boondoggles such as 1) high-end, members-only rollercoaster parks 2) an ultimate horse-fighting league and 3) installing a large net over much of south Texas "to catch illegals." This character enjoys unlawful safari hunting and displaying the kills on Instagram "to trigger the libs."

This character is best known for her extravagant makeup, her down-home accent, and her total commitment to paying her workers as little as possible. "I just love my people, we're all one big family, you know? And families take care of each other. That's why I provide all my employees with free coffee and water once a month." This character was recently praised by *Forbes* for innovating away her company's healthcare costs: She replaced employee health insurance with mandatory prayer and jumping jacks.

The press wants to know: Will this character save human civilization? It's not clear what the threat to human civilization actually IS, unless it's this character himself. While many consumers are ready to sell a kidney to buy the latest gewgaw produced by his company, the workers who actually produce the gewgaws are suffering from kidney problems because they aren't allowed to take bathroom breaks. In the meantime, this character plans to upload his living consciousness to the cloud so he can watch over his employees, forever.

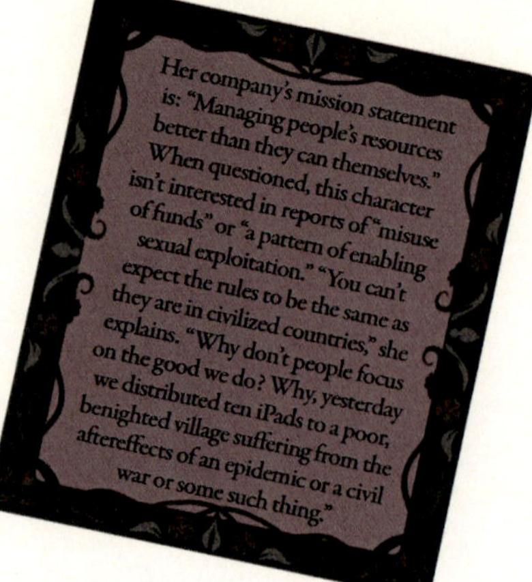
Her company's mission statement is: "Managing people's resources better than they can themselves." When questioned, this character isn't interested in reports of "misuse of funds" or "a pattern of enabling sexual exploitation." "You can't expect the rules to be the same as they are in civilized countries," she explains. "Why don't people focus on the good we do? Why, yesterday we distributed ten iPads to a poor, benighted village suffering from the aftereffects of an epidemic or a civil war or some such thing."

The Victims

THE CORRUPTION KING

THE REAL ESTATE HONCHO WHO IS INEXPLICABLY PRESIDENT

THE FAILPRINCE

THE NGO CEO

THE POST-HUMAN TECH GOD

GOD'S OWN RETAILER

THE CHAMPAGNE HEIRESS

THE OIL SCION

THE LEGITIMATE RUSSIAN BUSINESSMAN

The Means

SABOTAGED PRIVATE JET

SAFARI "ACCIDENT"

CONTAMINATED
CHICKEN FINGERS

EBOLA BLANKETS

POISONED
AFTER INSULTING THE
WRONG HEAD OF STATE

REPROGRAMMED
ROBOT SLAVES

VIOLENT REVOLUTION

Prescription Medical
Clarissa Musgrave
SUICIDE
AFTER LAWSUITS DESTROY
THE FAMILY WEALTH

CANNIBALIZED BY
STARVING SERVANTS

THE CURRENT AFFAIRS™
"BIG BOOK OF AMUSEMENTS"

tough quizzes

HOW WELL CAN YO

What effect is created by the brushwork in this painting?

1. The lyrical brushwork recalls East Asian calligraphy.
2. The harsh brush-strokes emphasize masculinity, while the bold colors highlight the artist's politically charged narrative.
3. The fervent, erratic brush-strokes express the feelings evoked by nature.
4. The languid brushwork is juxtaposed with rigorous, militaristic compositional thrust.

What is the correct title for this work?

1. Audiovisual Media Authority
2. Durisol No. 45
3. Ušumgallu and the Seven Sages
4. Run Like Hell

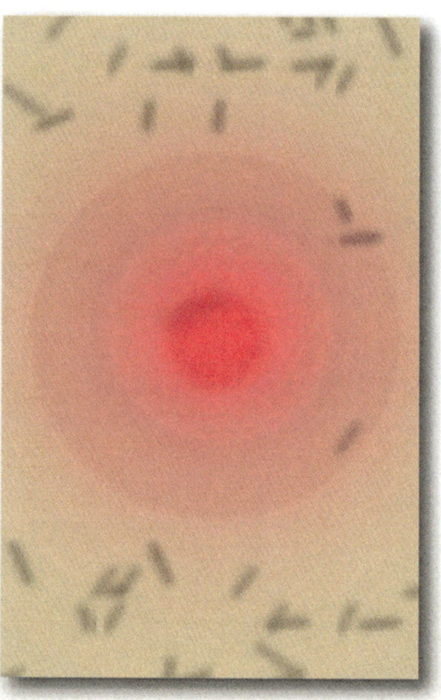

What is the role of the purple field in this painting?

1. The verticality of the field echoes the position of the viewer, reminding him that he is currently standing in front of a painting.
2. A flat surface, the heavily-saturated purple field represents nothing but itself, signifying an end to illusionism in visual art.
3. The monochromatic purple panel is endlessly deep, a depiction of multidimensional/infinite space.
4. It is John F. Kennedy.

This image is...

1. Playful.
2. Unsettling.
3. Intimate.
4. Hyperbolic.

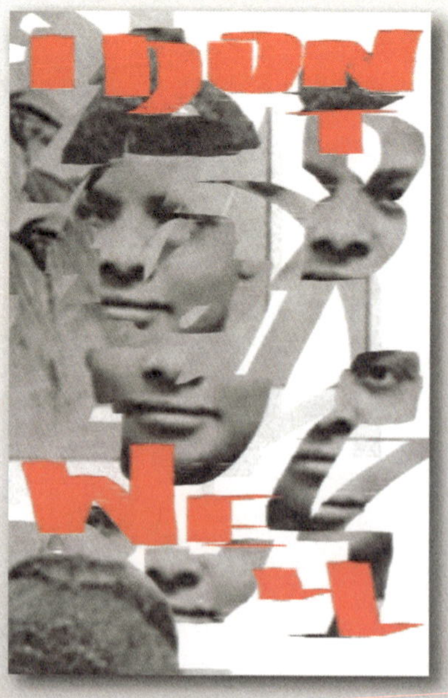

U APPRECIATE ART?

What is the central subject of this painting?

1. The Guatemalan Civil War (1960-1996).

2. The act of seeing.

3. Nothing. The canvas faces outward, towards us, not to deliver a message, but to display an exemplary quality: independence.

4. Madness.

The play between light and dark in this picture...

1. ... is a deliberate evocation of the Renaissance chiaroscuro technique.

2. ... reflects the artist's interest in myth and the primitive unconscious.

3. ... attempts to situate forms in space by means of shifts in value, using light against dark and dark against light to convey volume.

4. ... is a pseudo-painterly conceit that detracts from the fullness and purity of color.

ADD UP YOUR SCORES

6-11: We are humbled. You have an artist's soul—perhaps even an art critic's soul. Your sensitivity to all that is seen and unseen in these works is truly profound. The existence of rare luminaries such as yourself makes the obscene carnival of this material universe almost endurable.

12-20: Though your interpretations are a mite superficial, your instincts are basically sound. We suspect that you are hampered by two equally misguided instincts: the empty reverence for mere "cleverness" and the meaningless quest for "truth." You must learn to see, simply: to perceive the quidditas and/or haecceitas of each form individually, and in relation to other forms. This is only a matter of practice. For example, do not ask yourself, what is that color? Ask yourself, color (is it)?

21: Your smug, self-satisfied philistinism is appalling. It stinks of anti-intellectualism. In these dark times when cosmopolitan internationalism and the transatlantic liberal tradition are under attack on all sides, your sneering attitude towards the arts consigns you to the same infamous ranks as the thugs who burned down the Library of Alexandria. No doubt you are the sort of subhuman dreg who lurches through galleries screaming, "My ten-year-old could have painted that Basquiat!" It is probable—even certain—that, on more than one occasion, you have enlisted a friend to photograph you in a public sculpture garden while you pretended that various unusually-shaped installations were your penis. You are a disgrace to this book and to this country. The editors are placing a temporary hold on all future deliveries of your *Current Affairs* subscription. If you wish to receive any further issues of *Current Affairs*, you must send us a five-page typewritten letter describing how much you admire the works of Ellsworth Kelly.

22-24: We have high hopes for you. Though your answers are almost universally incorrect, we are convinced that the fault is not in your eye, but simply in your education. A thorough background in both classical and contemporary art is necessary to understand the thematic complexity and self-referential wit of these pieces. Our personal feeling is that there is no better way to begin to understand modern art than by owning a piece of it yourself. For a mere $84.2 million, you can purchase a Barnett Newman for your very own living room. Watch your friends' faces when you tell them how much you paid for it, and you will begin to understand the ineffable awe that a truly majestic work of art can inspire.

IS YOUR FEMINISM ANGRY ENOUGH?

Yes, you've always been an angry feminist. But 2017 awoke a dragon in you, and you can no longer greet everyday examples of the systemic misogynist inequalities of our society with any kind of useful, focused wrath. All you want to do is burn down every goddamn thing in sight. Here at *Current Affairs*, we understand your anger, and in fact, we celebrate it. But in the time-honored tradition of women's magazines, we must ask: is it enough? Are you furious *enough*? When it comes to utterly crushing the patriarchy under the heels of all womankind (flat, stiletto, kitten, wedge, or platform), are you fully committed to the task? Are you ready to thrash the patriarchy until it's silent and bloody and lifeless and then just keep beating the fucking shit out of it because you *can't fucking take it anymore*?

NOT 100% SURE? TAKE THIS QUIZ!

1. You're walking home alone from a bar after a lovely night out with your friends. In the drizzling rain and your drunkenness, you only slowly notice something that should have been obvious for blocks: There's a car, quietly following you down the street. The driver wears a hat tipped low over his face, as if trying to make sure you won't be able to identify him later.

You're a woman, so let's be real: This isn't the first time something like this has happened to you. But tonight, instead of panicking and blaming yourself for your carelessness, you're prepared. You:

A. Press the button on the top of your umbrella to release the hidden crowbar. Race toward the car, brandishing the crowbar and screaming at the top of your voice. Smash his headlights. Smash his windshield. Smash everything in sight including his ugly fucking face if he dares to open his fucking door. If anyone tries to help him, clobber them too. If you're arrested, burn down the police station.

B. Turn into vapor. As your stalker stops the car and gets out, prodding at your suddenly empty clothes, enter his nervous system through his ears or, if you prefer, his nasal passages. Once you're well-situated in his neocortex, twist his neurons until he believes he's being chased by a horde of his previous victims. Run the stalker through street after street until he splashes down into the nearest body of water. Make sure he's thoroughly drowned before you disentangle yourself from the limp bundle of pasta that used to be his brain. Oh, and before you turn back into your body, don't forget to float back to your clothes. That was a killer outfit and you looked amazing.

C. Duck into the nearest subway station or 7-11. As his car slides past, frustrated in his pursuit, take careful notice of the license plate. Later, using not-so-legal methods, find out your would-be stalker's address. Plot your next steps carefully: You want to make sure you're not interrupted. And use your skinning knife. I mean, you didn't spend half a paycheck on a designer skinning knife not to use it, am I right? Tan the stalker's hide and use it to re-bind your favorite novels. Carefully dissolve the rest of the corpse in acid. Excellent work. They'll never know it was you.

D. Yes, you could kill him. Maybe you even should. But that doesn't solve the problem, does it? After all, he's hardly the only predator out there, and you're hardly the only woman who's ever been stalked by a stranger—or an acquaintance, a coworker, an ex-boyfriend... you've had enough. You decide to build an army of women warbots. These warbots are 10 feet tall and weigh three tons apiece; despite their size, they're murderously fast. In blocky, sensible armor, not even the horniest moron could find them sexy—and if they do, who cares, because your warbots have just reduced them to bloody sludge. You seize the entire city in which the man stalked you, and refuse to surrender it until your demands for a society in which all women are safe and equal are finally met.

2. Your boss calls all the female employees into his office. He says that a former female staffer made an allegation of systemic sexism and lack of opportunities for women at the company, and he's feeling terribly upset about it. He tells you, his female employees, to come to him if you're ever feeling discriminated against, because he really, really wants to believe he's providing a safe and equal working environment for you ladies. And he's just so hurt by these accusations. God, is he hurt.

A. Take a deep breath. Then let it out in a full-throated scream of rage. Don't let up until the windows shatter and even then keep howling like a banshee. Your fellow employees may join you or they may not. Regardless, don't stop shrieking until every pane of glass—including the screen of his computer and his company-issued phone *which he barely uses because he can't even send a fucking email without your help though you haven't seen a cost of living increase in three goddamn years*—has been reduced to uselessness.

B. Join hands with the other women in the room until you collectively transform into a hydra. Take turns spitting acid at your boss until, blind and helpless, he screams out that he finally understands the error of his ways. He doesn't. He just wants the pain to stop. Keep spitting.

C. Hack into the company records. Find each and every pay stub that clearly proves that a woman was being paid less than a man for doing the same job. Don't forget the contracted custodial staff: Since this work is usually off the books, you may have to conduct interviews, but you'll find that all of these women, mostly immigrant women, were being paid less for a day's work than your boss earned in a lazy minute on the phone with his mistress. Go to your boss's house and mummify him in these reports. Don't forget to remove his organs first and store them in canopic jars. You take pride in your professionalism, as well you should!

D. Send your warbots to slaughter all bosses, everywhere. Male or female, the problem really is power dynamics and bosses, isn't it? As your warbots slay, they intone the mantra: "ONCE THE SYSTEM IS DESTROYED THE BULLSHIT WILL STOP." Is this mantra true? You're not sure. But you're willing to find out.

3. A male friend makes a dumb sexist joke. How do you respond?

A. Scream "HA HA THAT WAS SO FUNNY! YOU ARE THE FUNNIEST FUCKING MAN ON THE ENTIRE FUCKING PLANET! HOW DOES IT FEEL TO BE SO FUCKING FUNNY ALL THE FUCKING TIME???" Keep screaming until he runs away. Chase after him, still screaming.

B. Unhinge your lower jaw like a python and devour him. As you digest him slowly over several months, you may find that you have to burp more often than usual. Oddly enough, each burp comes out as a giggle.

C. Write a long email, detailing all the ways in which your friend's subtly misogynist behavior, then and now, has frustrated the shit out of you over the years. Afterward, fill the time his shocked absence will leave in your life with learning a new skill, like crochet, or how to carve delicate goblets from the skulls of your former friends.

D. Having seized a satellite and turned it into an orbital weapons platform, rain fire down on the earth until he apologizes. Then, just to be safe, keep firing.

4. Last question! You've been invited to the state funeral of a wealthy, famous, highly respected man, who—like many wealthy, famous, highly respected men—was also a notorious sexual predator. Everyone knew about his crimes, of course, yet for years they quietly looked the other way while he abused vulnerable women and girls. What do you wear?

A. A dress that combusts à la *The Hunger Games*, except that the flames consume everyone within a half-mile radius.

B. A dress that turns into an earthquake.

C. A dress that fires invisible poison darts. The poison leeches slowly into tear ducts over many years, turning those who dared to weep into pillars of highly polished stone.

D. A live nuclear warhead.

ADD UP YOUR ANSWERS!

Mostly As:

You're a walking inferno of blind, howling rage. That's fantastic, and we salute you. Just make sure you aren't holding back for fear of upsetting people. There is no limit of acceptability for a woman's anger. A woman's feelings can never be "too much." The world needs to start getting scared of upsetting ***you.***

Mostly Bs:

You've become so furious that the borders of your body literally dissolve. Amazing! Just don't forget to take care of yourself afterward. Once you've dealt with the daily misogynist outrages, reconstitute your shape and treat yourself to a lavender-scented bubble bath. You've earned it.

Mostly Cs:

You've become polished, methodical. A true artist of female vengeance. But while it may be tempting to cling to tried-and-true methods, don't hesitate to devise increasingly diabolical punishments, each more cunning and vicious than the last. People may not understand your methods, but they'll certainly learn to respect them.

Mostly Ds:

You take no prisoners. Literally, your warbots have been programmed to never capture misogynists alive. You've shown incredible initiative in the broader battle against the patriarchy, and we cannot praise you enough. Just make sure you destroy the ***entire*** system, root and branch. The war is only over when you're certain that your daughters—and sons—will never have to endure the soul-destroying bullshit that is systemic misogyny.

YOU BE THE JUDGE

An Examination of Juridical Aptitude

THE JUDICIARY IS THE HIGHEST CALLING IN AMERICAN GOVERNMENT. A democracy cannot function without sound judgment, and there can be no judgment without judges. But the life of the contemporary jurist is not always as romantic and exhilarating as one might assume. The resolution of judicial questions requires a lethally sharp analytic mind and an ability to see through a case's moral aspects in order to reach its legal ones. You may think being a judge requires little more than the ability to put on a robe and angrily pound your desk with a tiny hammer. But there is occasionally somewhat more to it than that, and you must also be practiced in the arts of sensible decision-making and reprimanding your lessers. Do you have what it takes to be a judge? Do you? Our comprehensive test will reveal the caliber of your legal mind and your capacity for abstruse reasoning.

1. A 16-year-old black child convicted of manslaughter has been given life in prison without the possibility of parole and is being housed in an adult facility. You must issue a judgment on his appeal. How do you respond?

A. Oh my God, that's horrifying. Overturn the sentence, order that the child be transferred to a juvenile facility immediately, order that they be given psychological counseling for any trauma that they might have incurred by being victimized during their time housed among much older inmates. Reprimand the prosecutor and order that restitution be made to the child's family.

B. The Founding Fathers would have been horrified to see injustice in our criminal justice system, and I find myself disturbed by this situation, which contradicts the core values of our great Constitution. This situation potentially violates the Equal Protection clause, the Due Process clause, and the prohibition on cruel and unusual punishment. We must determine whether the defendant's race was a factor in sentencing, whether the sentence was imposed according to proper due process, and whether all mitigating factors were taken into account. I hereby reverse and remand the case to the lower courts, who are instructed to ascertain the pertinence of these issues. If, after a searching examination, they conclude that defendant's race was not a factor, the sentence was imposed through proper due process, and the mitigating factors were considered, the sentence is constitutional, but if not, this is a scandalous violation of the defendant's basic rights and he must be guaranteed a parole hearing after the first fifty years of incarceration.

C. Our task here is to balance the interests of the defendant with the interests of the state, while preserving the integrity of existing precedent. To resolve this case, we may look to the precedent set by the 1632 English case of *Marston v. Rufflepenny*, which established the doctrine of *carceris dolorificum*, holding that "the punishment must be proportionally painful to the crime." *Marston* was, of course, modified by the 1843 *West Alaska Railroad* doctrine, which requires that Latin maxims be given their most arcane possible interpretation, which in this case would lead to the conclusion that imprisonment is a substitute for the pain of ordinary life. Weighing this in a four-factor test against the defendant's interests (the factors being legality, magnanimity, salinity, and dubiousness), one is compelled to rule against the defendant out of both pragmatic and textual considerations.

D. Nothing in the text of the Constitution or the laws of the United States prohibits the imposition of this sentence. There is no meaningful legal question here. I hereby uphold the sentence and sanction the child's attorney for wasting the court's time with a frivolous appeal.

E. The sentence is unconstitutionally light. Children should be subjected to harsher penalties than adults as a rule—they have many more years left during which they might commit a crime. At the time of our country's founding, serious crimes were dealt with via firing squad. Anything less in this case would be a flagrant violation of the Rule of Law, and would erode the moral fabric of Western Civilization. I hereby vacate the defendant's sentence and remand to the lower court with an instruction to impose nothing less than the most excruciating imaginable death and to require local schoolchildren to witness the execution as a deterrent measure.

2. A young woman has fled a small Central American country after being kidnapped and tortured by a violent gang. She had repeatedly refused to join the gang, at great risk to her own life, saying that she believed their way of life was morally wrong. Her asylum application was denied by an immigration judge, who said that as a mere victim of "violent crime," she was not eligible for protection. The immigration judge's decision was affirmed by the Board of Immigration Appeals, who stated that moral opposition to gangs did not qualify as a "political opinion," thus she was not eligible for asylum as she was not considered to be fleeing persecution. You must decide whether to uphold or overturn this decision.

A. This decision is overturned, and *no*, I'm not remanding it back to the asshole judge who denied it in the first place, I'm granting her asylum outright. Then I'm going home and hugging my beautiful children, who get to grow up in an environment of peace and safety. Then I'm setting up a scholarship fund for this young woman, who deserves to have something nice in her life for a change. Oh, does that violate some kind of professional ethics rule? Fuck you. I don't care. If the counsel for the government keeps making that face at me, I'm going to have him air-dropped into a gang warzone. Then I'll watch him shit his pants. Then I'll inform him that soiling yourself doesn't qualify as a political opinion.

B. I am sympathetic to this young woman's position, but even more importantly, I am concerned about *administrability* and *predictable standards*. By rejecting the applicant's claim that moral objection to a gang constitutes a "political opinion," the BIA has effectively promulgated a new administrative rule. As such, under the Administrative Procedures Act, the agency must engage in a notice and comment period before the new rule can come into effect. This procedure will allow for consistent and reviewable standards for similarly-situated individuals.

C. Our job in this case is evaluate whether or not the applicant's fear was the result of a "protected belief." While I have no doubt that the violence she faced was real and that she suffered greatly, the law simply does not allow "not wanting to join a gang" to qualify as a political opinion. If her position was akin to "I am a Democrat and this is a gang of Republicans that I do not want to join," that would present a different issue. Per circuit precedent, as established in *Gonzalez v. Gonzalez*, only asylum applicants who have personally handed out leaflets clearly spelling out their political views at a fundraising brunch, and subsequently been pistol-whipped by a man wearing the lapel-pin of an opposing candidate, may be deemed to have a "political opinion" under the INA. In this case, we are bound by the law, and cannot consider her moral objection as valid basis for asylum. Further, we cannot find facts beyond those found by the BIA, and therefore must defer to their reasoned and expert judgment under the *Chevron* standard. Judgment affirmed.

D. A gang's attempt to coerce a person into joining their criminal enterprise does not constitute "persecution on account of political opinion." There is not enough evidence on the record to show that the applicant's resistance was politically motivated. A fact-finder might easily determine that her resistance stemmed from sheer, indiscriminate stubbornness, which might cause her to refuse to join *any* organization, or perhaps by her desire to reap economic and social benefits that would be barred to her as a gang member. Since the applicant did not produce evidence so compelling that no reasonable factfinder could fail to find the requisite fear of persecution on account of political opinion, the judgment is affirmed.

E. This Court has no jurisdiction to hear this appeal. Under longstanding doctrine only juridical "persons" have the ability to petition the Court for appeal. Persons under this definition are only those who reside within the jurisdiction of the Constitution, the United States, and its territories. The petitioner here has no place of residence and does not fall under the ambit of the Constitution. Thus she is not legally a "person" for purposes of Constitutional application, and may not lawfully challenge her detention. Constitutional rights are not fruits in a garden, to be plucked by any passerby who happens to be desirous of them. They are sacred charges granted to those who have accepted the social contract of our society. Furthermore, the frivolous petitioning

of the Court for a client who clearly has no standing or rights before this body is a breach of the rules of ethics under *Rule 11*. The lawyer bringing this case is hereby sanctioned.

3. A prominent tech company has accidentally disclosed all of its customers' personal data to the public, including their entire email inboxes, their web search histories, their medical histories, their chat transcripts, their credit card numbers, and their tastes in unconventional pornography. Countless lives have been ruined, mass chaos has resulted. An employee whistleblower at the company reveals to the press that before the breach, the CEO was frequently heard to shout "Fuck the public! We *own* the public! The customer is the product!" whenever security concerns were raised. The company immediately fired the whistleblowing employee, and citing a small-print provision of the employment contract, demanded the employee pay back the entirety of the salary earned during the 10-year course of their employment. The contract also specifies that if the employee cannot pay, they become permanently indentured to the company. The employee files a lawsuit contesting the contract and alleging wrongful termination, while the customers enter a class action lawsuit over the data breach. You are the judge. Decide.

A. They did *what?* Okay, first, clearly you can't have a contract like that, that's outrageous. No indentured servitude. Jesus, how is it that I even have to say this? Is this some colonial-era nightmare flashback? The company is ordered to restore the employee to her position, compensate her for the time she was "fired," and apologize profusely. Actually, you know what, just turn the management of the company over to the workers. As for the customers, every single one of them needs to be paid fair compensation for their harm. Duh.

B. The company's actions are shameful, and were they done by the government, I would be shocked by their brazen unconstitutionality. However, private corporations are not covered by constitutional provisions, which restrain only state actors. In this case, the company did happen to be a private contractor that offered services to the government, which raises the question of whether it counts as operating *on behalf of* the state, thereby incurring state obligations and limitations. The answer is no. The plaintiffs also allege that the contracts they entered into were "unconscionable" and "horrifying," but their contractual claims are barred by a failure to file in the proper venue and the misapplication of "choice of law" by the lower court. I must ruefully dismiss the case.

C. The relevant provisions of the law of contracts can be found in ancient Sumerian labor law, which established the provision of [illegible]. Of course, this court previously addressed a similar case involving bakers and organ-grinders in *Dalaficci v. Pennsylvania*. There, we held that "the contracted vessel is nowhere beyond the party's intent despite elapse." This was elaborated in the famous *Roadmaster General* case, in which a postal worker was shot for dropping a package into U.S. territorial waters during wartime. The same precept applied, without the maritime exceptions, in *Alameda Trucking*, a case that was partly superseded by *Pleniver v. Eustead* but whose caution against putting "the facts before the law without the law before the facts" remains valid as a legal construct and has been cited as recently as *Riddle Magazine v. Vuetec Novelty Diskettes* in 1995, though that court used a truncated version of the dictum, altering its connotation to imply that "the facts" and "the law" are functionally inseparable rather than (as is wryly noted in the Federalist Papers) "separate despite their function." Scholarly literature on the "erosion" doctrine has implied that this conclusion may no longer hold absolutely, but until such time as this court abandons the classic multi-pronged "non-rights-oriented" approach this case may be settled on the basis of *querens parentes non posterum*. I therefore dismiss the plaintiff's claims.

D. The right of the employer and the freedom of contract are sacrosanct in American law. The customers entered a contract with the company allowing it to use their data as it pleased. The employee entered into a contract with the company adhering to the indenture provision. The fact that neither the customers nor the employer "knew" what they had agreed to is immaterial. Whether one must abide by an agreement does not depend on whether one understands what it is. Furthermore, neither case should be in the court system due to the "private arbitration" provision of the contracts, which requires that any contractual disputes be settled in a fight to the death between the claimant and a large bullmastiff.

E. A labor contract transfers ownership rights over the employee to the employer. By engaging in voluntary market transaction with the company, the customers and the workers become company property and can be disposed of as the company's executives see fit. Because the indenture provision fails to compensate the company adequately for its loss, I hereby order that both customers and employees be placed in permanent corporate custody and sent to work down the Bitcoin mines.

4. At a political rally, the President of the United States strangled a protester to death with his bare hands. Prosecutors have sought to bring charges, but the president's legal counsel have filed a motion to dismiss the charges on the grounds that the president was acting within the scope of his executive authority. You are the presiding judge in the case. How do you respond?

A. What the everloving fuck? The executive authority to murder a person in cold blood? Are you seriously making that argument in my courtroom? Counsel, if you even begin to try that bullshit again in front of me, I am holding your ass in contempt. (Along with the rest of you.) I am having the president taken into custody, since he's not only a flight risk, but is also apparently under the illusion that he's allowed to kill people with impunity. Bail will be set at whatever the value of his real estate portfolio turns out to be.

B. This case raises very serious constitutional questions about the separation of powers. I am obviously disturbed by the incident, as one can tell from my proclamation of how disturbed I am. The important question here is whether the president is allowed to take lives under the scope of his *inherent* constitutional authority, or whether there must be prior congressional approval. It is clear from examination of the legislative history of the War Powers Act that Congress has only attempted to limit the president's wartime authority, rather than his civilian peacemaking powers. I remand the case to the lower court for a determination of whether choking an activist to death constitutes "peacemaking" as it has been historically construed.

C. Our own laws are silent on the question we face today, thus we must trace the roots of executive authority back to the 1215 *Magna Carta Libertatum* or Great Charter of Liberties. In those exemplifications most faithful to the original, the document constrained the ability of the King to interfere with the property of barons, but afforded little protection to the ordinary peasantry. We may therefore pose two questions: Under common law, (1) should life be considered "property," the deprivation of which by the executive is lawfully restrained and (2) are rally attendants properly classified as barons or peasantry? Here, we may turn to the interpretation our own justices have historically given to common law rights against executive power. 1944's *Korematsu v. United States* affirmed the president's power to do as he pleases to anybody at any time, especially if it is racist. It is unclear in this case if the president's actions were racially motivated, but as long as they were, they fall within a long executive tradition justified by considerable legal precedent. *Stare decisis* settles the issue and the case must be dismissed.

D. The Constitution contains no provision explicitly prohibiting the president from throttling the life out of a random bystander, and the efforts of my colleagues to imagine such a provision into existence show well how political correctness continues to infiltrate the bench. These charges are an outrage and an insult to the memory of the Framers.

E. The president's power is absolute and unquestioned. The immunity doctrine makes this quite clear. The only tragedy of this case is the regrettably low number of lives he took. We should admire his dignity and restraint.

add up your ANSWERS

Mostly As: It is clear that you are an individual of very strong convictions. This is admirable! Law is a noble calling that seeks humane minds. But to be a judge you will need to keep these personal idiosyncrasies in check. It seems you lack the temperament necessary for the profession. Perhaps you should consider a career in legal aid or political advocacy, where your recklessness and partisanship will not hinder your opportunities. Be warned, though, that too much agitation is unhealthy for a democracy, the preservation of which depends on the sober-minded stewardship of deliberative citizens.

Mostly Bs: You have an obvious desire for the law to function as a force for good, and you are clearly able to perceive injustice where you find it. However, your clear sympathies for the weak and vulnerable may make your judgments appear biased and unreliable, and your confirmation hearings will be difficult. As long as you are capable of demonstrating that you place the rule of law above your ideology, you may yet have a flourishing career on the bench. But be careful of pushing the envelope too far, and make diligent efforts to convince your fellow judges that your first loyalty is to the U.S. constitution rather than reason or human decency.

Mostly Cs: Your knowledge of legal history and the great jurisprudential traditions is formidable. Your thinking is both deeply grounded in formal doctrine and informed by a pragmatic understanding of real-world outcomes. You should take pride in how well your decisions display moral seriousness without being encumbered by political ideology. With study and diligence, you might be the next Stephen Breyer.

Mostly Ds: You have a textualist legal mind of the highest caliber. While in your rougher moments, your strict adherence to constitutional principles might alienate some mushier-minded judicial colleagues, they cannot help but respect your consistency and integrity. While an ignorant and politically biased public may mock you, it is universally acknowledged among serious thinkers that even when your decisions directly result in considerable suffering and loss of life, they have been made out of a sincere and admirable constitutional faith.

Mostly Es: Your views are somewhat unorthodox, some would say radical. In a previous era, it might have been necessary for you to modify the language with which you expressed your positions, though certainly not the positions themselves. Fortunately, the standards for being given a role in the upper echelons of American government have lately been evolving, and you are precisely the sort of person one can plausibly imagine soon being appointed to the federal bench. If your time is not yet, it is certainly soon.

Could *you* be a

New York Times

opinion columnist?

Thank you for your interest in contributing to the *New York Times* opinion page. Before we get started, we just need to run a quick background check. To start, please open your latest Pottery Barn catalog to page 15. If you don't get the Pottery Barn catalog, there's no need to continue filling out this application: you're obviously not a regular reader of the *New York Times*. If you do have the Pottery Barn catalog, and your complexion falls on the darker side of the "birchbark beige" ottoman featured on page 15, please, please, PLEASE feel free to complete this application. The *New York Times* is an equal opportunity environment. At our last Shell Oil-sponsored fundraising soiree, we even distributed #blacklivesmatter tote bags! (But when you don't hear from us, please don't take it personally, okay? We're simply swamped with applicants these days. We promise that all applicants of color were totally, briefly considered.)

1. Which of the following statements best exemplifies your current thinking on climate change?

A. Climate change is very real and extremely dangerous. Simply asking corporations to "do better" won't work, because it'll always be more profitable to destroy the environment than to save it. Capitalism got us into this mess; capitalism can't get us out of it. We need to immediately restructure the entire edifice of energy production and consumption.

B. I firmly believe that if Hillary Clinton were president, she would have launched her #greengrab #initiative by now, encouraging corporate takeovers of third world countries to prevent those charmingly backward folks from burning their trash. But instead, we have Tr*mp. Since no one can do anything about the environment except for the chief executive of the United States government, there's nothing to do except write snarky columns about What Might Have Been and wallow in despair. #shewarnedus #feminism

C. While some critics have claimed that my background in classical philology doesn't entitle me to learned opinions on scientific subjects, I must respectfully disagree. It is indeed correct that I have never read a single paper on the topic of climate change, but I do have a vague notion of the existence of a "controversy." Obviously, universities are secretly quashing all research that contradicts established scientific consensus purely on the grounds of free-speech denialism. I know this because of my pre-existing prejudices, and also my tidy grant from the Koch Foundation.

D. Climate change doesn't exist. It's a myth created by Hollywood to cover up George Soros' cannibalism ring. Every "green activist" is an FBI plant, unless it's the CIA I hate this week.

2. What is your opinion of free speech on our nation's campuses? Do you believe that millennials are hypersensitive snowflakes, gormless grade-grubbers, or dangerous anti-free speech fanatics?

A. Obviously, college students say some silly things sometimes, but in general I believe the panic over college kids and free speech is an overblown conservative rumor. The real threat to free speech on college campuses is the precariousness of adjunct professorships. When you have zero job security, the economic risks of speaking your mind are simply too high. A unionized professorial class, allied with other staff members and students, can do a great deal to improve economic conditions for all.

B. Now, I'm a feminist, but I secretly feel political correctness has gone too far. When I informed a noted black academic that the term "intersectionality" excludes white women, I was forced to quit Facebook and Twitter. In fact, the blowback was so horrific, I had to do a six-week mindfulness course instead of my usual four. Now that I'm back from my digital detox, I'd really like to write a weekly column about how soul-cleansing it is to break up with social media, especially for academics who have gotten SO sensitive these days. (Also, I wish they'd stop dragging me, it really interferes with my self-actualization.)

C. The degradation of the ivory tower cannot be overstated. I've heard that students have walked out of courses such as "Glories of the Classical Canon" just because their professors spoke disparagingly of the "non-literature" of other cultures. Post-modernism has destroyed our respect for tradition. Suddenly, merely teaching Western civilization is tantamount to a war crime. I've considering resigning my honorary Harvard professorship in disgust—I won't, but I could.

D. Marxist Freemasons have teamed up with a race of alien shapeshifting leopard people to indoctrinate our youth. It's obvious. If you study these extreme close-up photos of pillars on college campuses, you'll see what I mean.

3. At the New York Times, we care a great deal about cultural trends. How would you best describe your personal style, and what's your general take on fashion?

A. I wear whatever I want, and I don't give a shit about other people's clothes as long as they seem like they're sincerely trying to express themselves. I'll always laugh at a high fashion failure, but I'll never judge a poor person for wearing an unflattering outfit.

B. If the people in my rapidly gentrifying neighborhood are to be believed, my style can best be described as "basic bitch." Ok, FINE, so you can't always tell me apart from the wallpaper. But I personally consider my look classic; and on that basis, I feel justified in judging other women's clothes. When a young woman looks too comfortable, or an older woman looks too sexy, I take great pleasure in telling them to stop. That's what feminism means to me: constantly obsessing over other women's micro-decisions while men continue to hold nearly all social, political, and economic power.

C. Every day, I dress in a tidy three-piece suit and a bowtie from Earl's of London. That's the outfit of a gentleman. You'll find me wearing it even in 110-degree heat. (The summers have grown hotter…a curious phenomenon. Perhaps it's simply how one feels the heat as one ages.) In any weather and any season, I promise to constantly proffer my opinion of youths in saggy pants.

D. Over my *Metal Gear Solid* t-shirt, I wear chainmail painted with the Confederate flag. It's…very heavy actually. My take on fashion is that restaurants should have the right to refuse service to anyone, but I shouldn't get kicked out just because my chainmail "smells like rust and unwashed dogs."

4. Last question: are you currently friends with any Nazis?

A. Oh my god, no. Absolutely not. Was that a serious question?

B. Hmmm. Define "friends." Is it "friendship" if all you do is secretly DM each other racist memes?

C. By refusing to be friends with people just because they advocate the mass murder of minorities, perhaps YOU are the true bigot, sir!

D. Nazis were the best men at my wedding! Also, I have three swastika tattoos, only two of which are on my neck.

ANSWERS

Mostly As: I suppose you're well-read, articulate, and passionate, but you're absolutely the wrong fit for the *New York Times*. You see, we tried all that anti-capitalist rah-rah back in the 60s, but ultimately we were too self-obsessed, and our anti-authoritarianism was co-opted to sell sodas and t-shirts. Someday, millennial, when you have a vacation house and a retirement fund of your own, you'll understand. Wait, you can't afford your rent, or even a car? Well, that's clearly your own fault. Buck up, buttercup. Life is hard. Also, please stop calling us "out-of-touch sellouts." It makes us feel bad.

Mostly Bs: Finally, a feminist! You might just be the voice of your generation, because you're saying everything we want to hear while not really challenging authority. In fact, you never say "patriarchy" without a winsome wink and a joke about how your fellow feminists have gone too far! If you just keep writing loopy solipsistic essays about your personal life and which billionaires you find the most inspirational, well, young lady, you may just be set for life.

Mostly Cs: Finally, a compassionate conservative! You're just the right mix of qualities: We can take you to Upper East Side dinner parties and disagree with you cordially over the cordial. Just make sure you keep the racist dog whistling in the appropriate frequency range. Overt displays of white supremacy make us queasy, and then it's hard to digest our apéritifs.

Mostly Ds: You know, we really appreciate your down-home authenticity. Actually, we'd love to visit you and write a flattering profile that glosses over your outright Nazism, but unfortunately, you're just a little—direct—to be a columnist for the *New York Times*. Don't despair: we hear Breitbart is hiring. In four years, give us a call. We'll probably enjoy taking you on as an opinion vlogger when we've pivoted even harder to video, and also further to the right.

WHAT KIND OF INSANE **AUTHORITARIAN LEADER** WILL I END UP VOTING FOR SOMEDAY?

1. What sentence best sums up our current problem?
A. "The best lack all conviction, while the worst/ Are full of passionate intensity."
B. The old order is broken beyond repair.
C. Our society can only heal itself through universal love, acknowledging the fundamental interconnectedness of all living things.
D. Oh God, I'm so tired.

2. If you could designate funding for anything right now, what it would be?
A. The arts.
B. Neighborhood self-defense units.
C. Model farms.
D. My utility bill.

3. What are your thoughts on free speech?
A. I'm always in favor of intelligent discourse.
B. Free speech is a term that's constantly being misused by my enemies.
C. All our words should be uttered in a spirit of love.
D. Whatever you want. I'll talk when you tell me to talk! I'll be quiet when you tell me to be quiet! Just—ugh. Just fix this.

4. Is it better for humans to be free and unhappy, or happy and unfree?
A. Happiness is an elusive concept, isn't it? How can you quantify something so profoundly personal, so inherently subjective? In any case, people should have freedom in proportion to their abilities, don't you think? That way everyone's talents can be put to their best use.
B. None of us are free until all of us are free. The unfree must be disabused of any mistaken idea that they are happy.
C. Only when we cease to be slaves to our own happiness will we be truly happy.
D. Either situation would be an improvement, honestly.

5. Against whom is the use of violence justified?
A. Against those who seek to disrupt the peaceful social order.
B. Against those who seek to preserve the corrupt social order.
C. Nobody: not people, or animals, or fish, or trees, or bacteria, or mosquitoes, or semen, or anybody. We're all one family.
D. I don't know, man, I'm not at that point yet, but—seriously.

ADD UP YOUR **ANSWERS**

MOSTLY A'S. Urbane dictator with an art collection. You would never vote for a vulgar demagogue, but here your desire for a more coherent national aesthetic won out easily against your democratic scruples. Are you surprised? Be honest with yourself. If you lived somewhere with cathedrals and boulevards and a national literature, you would be a fascist. Luckily, you live in the United States of America, and so this cup has passed from you. You give thanks for our hideous buildings and our shitty novelists, you bastard! They're the only reason you've resisted your evil angels this long. Anyway, your candidate is going to institute serfdom, at best, and end up committing genocide, at worst.

MOSTLY B'S. Revolutionary who turns out to be a straight-up terrorist. This guy gave you the creeps from day one and you still voted for him. Why? Why, for God's sake? Probably you spent so many years complaining about the corrupt social order at parties that you were embarrassed not to vote for the most radical candidate on the ballot. Well, now look what you've done. The streets are running with blood and it's your fault.

MOSTLY C'S. Religious cult leader. You were so attracted to this fellow's earnestness that you missed some obvious warning signs that he's a raving lunatic. It's not the first time in your life you've made this mistake; though, sadly, it may well be the last, as average life expectancy is about to plummet. Your new spiritual father will establish a state religion, dismantle the healthcare system, and force everyone to return to subsistence agriculture. Chances are there's some weird sex stuff going on behind the scenes as well. Too much interconnectedness altogether. It was such a nice idea, though!

MOSTLY D'S. Literally anyone who will forgive your student loan debt. Sadly, there was no such candidate in this election. Your vote was wasted.

WHICH DYSTOPIA
HAVE I FOUND MYSELF IN?

The year is 2549. You live in some kind of society, but which one? Not sure? Take this handy quiz!

1. Commuting! We all do it, we all hate it. Choose the answer that most closely resembles the way you get to work.

A. Dawn. You creep cautiously up the stairs past your sleeping comrades. The Silicon Emperor's roving bands of death spiders didn't find you as you slept. That's good, but now it's time to hunt. The death spiders have been fed your gene signature and those of all the other Designated Nopes. You must find and kill the death spiders before they kill you. You open the cellar door, just a crack. You are immediately eaten by death spiders.

B. Up, up, up! If you don't snag a flying car now, you'll have to wait thirty seconds for the next, and that's a whole thirty seconds of debt you're accruing. Jumping in the car—oh no—a tooth fell out. The distraction costs you two seconds. You'll make up for it in the air. Zipping above the Devastation, you're mildly horrified by the crawling misery below. But you comfort yourself with the notion that civilization has finally finished sorting itself into the deserving and the un-. Still, you wonder. What if there are a few deserving mixed up in the undeserving hordes below? What if someday you, and not just a rotten tooth, fall into the abyss? You feel sick. It's not just the untreated infection in your mouth. Before your first gig you waste an entire minute buying a Calmer from the closest Anx-No-More.

C. You've told the alarm-bird to fuck off twelve times, but it's noon and you really have to go to work. Ugh. The dresser suggests one of your sexier outfits, but you're not feeling sexy today. Why do you even have to put on clothes? The world is so fucking unfair. You throw on an ugly jumpsuit. The mirror tells you how good you look, and you tell it to go fuck itself. Then you have to convince the mirror you didn't mean it. It takes a while, but eventually, the mirror stops crying. You step through the silken glass and there you are, at work. Ugh. You are just not in the mood for interaction today.

D. You swing a thermometer inside a wet rat-skin, testing the air outside the bunker. 38°C. Shit. You'll have to hunt across the blasted hellscape for food tomorrow.

2. Well, you've made it to work. What do you do?

A. It's not all battling death spiders. Sometimes you fight Freedom Knights and Rage Nazis. And then you're eaten by death spiders.

B. Lease out your kidneys to wealthy duocentenarians. It's not really that bad. You just have to keep smiling. Show those remaining teeth. If a client thinks you've failed to appreciate the honor of physically processing their thin, dusty fluids, they might give you a bad rating, and then it's down to the Devastation for you!

C. There's a transport shortage on Tristus Prime, and its citizens have to wait up to an hour in line at the spaceports. Your committee meeting's deadlocked. Any one of the three proposed solutions will probably alleviate the crisis, but which is best? No one can agree. Everyone keeps sniping at each other, bringing up personal grudges and factional loyalties. The meeting lasts the whole workday—two hours! You leave irritated with your colleagues.

D. You follow the shadow of a vulture across the bleeding sand. In the distance the acid sea laps quietly against the shore.

3. You've got a hot date tonight. How does it go?

A. Under the rubble you've carved a cozy spot. A stolen Rage Nazi banner turned into a blanket, a rose you found in the weeds. You even repurposed a taserfly into a lantern. There's no food, but that's ok. You and your partner make desperate love in your little cave of light. Before you can finish, you're eaten by death spiders.

B. Your date is gorgeous, witty, and thoughtful, but the dinner's spoiled by your racing mind. As a vulpinate splice from a backwoods hypersphere, is it ok to be attracted to a squidress from Selfex Eight? Is it not ok to NOT be attracted to a squidress from Selfex Eight? What does your attraction or lack of attraction to squidresses say about you and vulpinate splices in general? Can you monetize this date by writing a piece about your anxieties? In the kitchen, the squidress chef is running a fever. She coughs all over your food.

C. In the public luxaflora garden, you get into an argument over Scora Moan. Yeah, okay, she's talented, but she doesn't write all her own songs. Your date calls you pedantic and judgmental. You storm away under the neon shadows of the floating miximba trees. Later, you realize you were, in fact, being pedantic and judgmental.

D. You spend a lovely evening with a skull. You talk to it for hours, admiring the descending curve of its spinal column. It really is the cleanest and most complete human spine you've ever seen.

4. What does your downtime look like?

A. Even in the midst of a running fight for your life, there are long stretches of quiet hours, sometimes even days. You and your comrades tell stories of the fallen, all the tribes of Designated Nopes that have been taken from the universe. There was so much beauty, so many varieties of human experience, silly jokes, raunchy stories...all destroyed by the Silicon Emperor, who smashes what he doesn't understand. A flying death spider drops its payload. You drown in liquid flame.

B. What's downtime? Do you mean sleeping? You do sleep, sometimes. You've outsourced your dreams to Creatabix, and the raw stuff of your imagination is fed as a slurry into the minds of rich kids who want to be artists but lack the crucial ingredients of talent, awareness, and sensibility. When you wake up you feel drained, listless. Stop complaining. What keeps the air flowing to this closet you sleep in? It's dream-money, baby.

C. Since you only work two hours a day, most of your life is downtime. But if you ever get bored of art, literature, holosports, and getting drunk, you can always plug into LiveMind for a round of "Who Shat Themselves Today"? The game is to find the person who accidentally revealed the most embarrassing thought and ridicule them mercilessly. Of course, before you start playing, you search through your own LiveMind archive and delete any thought-pattern that might reveal too much genuine vulnerability.

D. At night, when you can't sleep for the itching of the dust ticks and the scourge gnats, you contemplate all the people who should have fucking done something while the earth slowly died beneath their feet.

5. You've decided to go to a museum. What's it like?

A. Tonight, the Silicon Emperor will be attending the Museum of the History of Dynamism. You and your comrades have reprogrammed a death spider to lock onto the Silicon Emperor's genome. All you have to do is get it through a window...there he is, the Silicon Emperor, consecrating a fresh monument to himself—now's your chance! Take the shot! Your death spider hits the wall and explodes. The Silicon Emperor no longer has a genome. He's replaced all his living parts with nanites embedded in a flexible carbon mesh. You are ripped apart by his personal death spiders.

B. You don't have museums, exactly, but you do have auction houses. Sometimes you score an invite as the personal footrest of an orcabro. It's funny—most orcabros have money, and most vulpinates and squidresses don't. Everyone says vulpinates and squidresses just need to work more and smile harder. As you slowly compress under the weight of the orcabro's dorsal legs, you square your shoulders and hustle up a grin. Your orcabro bids on a jade Olmec mask from the fifth century BCE. When he wins, he films himself smashing it on the floor. You put in a bid for one of the shards.

C. There are many museums, but your favorite is the Museum of Late Capitalism. Whenever a real rift has arisen in your friend group, you gather together at the feet of the memorials. By the end of the day, you've all had the same revelation: Yes, the petty bullshit of your fellow citizens is excruciatingly annoying, even toxic—but it's the worst of your problems. You all have dinner together, humbly grateful to be alive in this moment.

D. Some of the items you find aren't useful for survival, but too beautiful to be thrown away. So you've created the Museum of the End of the World. Sometimes, when the wet bulb temperature is only 33°C, you take these rescued memories up to the surface. There, you arrange the Museum of the End of the World on blackened sand under the beating silence of the sky.

ANSWERS

Mostly As: Libertarian Paradise/Fascist Robot Death Hell

Margaret Atwood once said "every dystopia contains a little utopia," but did you think it would be a utopia for you? Did you really think you might be one of the chosen, the Designated Yeahs, destined by your superior strength and brains and overall genetic excellence to sit at the right hand of the Silicon Emperor? If you did, you're an idiot. You were devoured by death spiders long ago.

Mostly Bs: Neoliberal Dreamland, sponsored by Creatabix©

Stop! You don't have time to read this! Every second you waste is a second you're not out there hustling! You've got dreams to sell and body parts to rent. If you pause to think, you might wake up to the realization that all this running and gigging and self-promoting is making you completely miserable. But it's ok. You can watch three entire holoshows starring vulpinate splices just like you!

Mostly Cs: Mostly Automated Luxury Socialism

Is it perfect? Nah. Is there lots of pointless infighting? Omg so much. Are resources still distributed imperfectly? Yes, but it's getting better. Are you thoroughly sick of spending so much time working out problems with your obnoxious fellow citizens? YES, but you've got a nice solo vacation to Enceladus coming up. Is this political arrangement better than anything that's come before? You bet your socks.

Mostly Ds: Climate Change Deadzone

We really should have fucking done something.

COMPARATIVE MYTHOLOGY
FINAL EXAM

Identify The Principles of **MASCULINE ORDER** and **FEMININE CHAOS**

If you ask **JORDAN PETERSON**, best-selling author and professionally miserable YouTuber, the complex and multivariant strains of human myth-making can all be boiled down—like a lobster in a pot—to one very simple syllogism: Order is masculine, chaos is feminine, and socially-enforced monogamy is the only cure for male unhappiness. (He does not posit a cure for female unhappiness; the joy of chaos is obviously its own reward.) Peterson's work has become very popular among **INCELS, GAMERGATERS, AND OTHER INTERNET-MEN** who have never studied the humanities but feel perfectly entitled to opine at great length about human history, religion, art, psychology, and politics. Their affection for Peterson's teachings makes a great deal of sense, give that Peterson doesn't seem to know much about anything, either. If a mythic superstructure of masculine order and feminine chaos undergirds the entirety of human thought, we would expect to find it in every myth.

Read the following examples and answer the questions in essay format. This is a **TIMED, OPEN-BOOK EXAM**, and it counts toward **30 PERCENT** of your final grade.

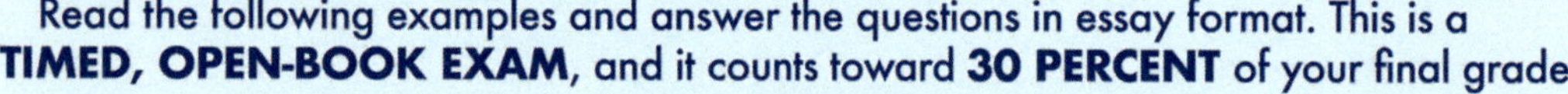

1. The Egyptian goddess Ma'at/Maat is frequently represented in Egyptian art as a seated young woman, but she's more than a mere deity. According to classicist Christopher A. Faraone and Egyptologist Emily Teeter: "...maat appears both as the abstract concept of truth and correctness in the cosmic and social spheres and in anthropomorphic form as a goddess (Maat) who personifies truth and order."[1] Ma'at/Maat was highly significant as a guiding principle in Egyptian culture, and embodied subtly different meanings at different points during the long development of Egyptian religion and philosophy. The Egyptologist Vincent Arieh Tobin tells us: "Ma'at was not simply one aspect of Egyptian thought; it was, in effect, the entire basis for the Egyptian understanding of the universe. The importance of Ma'at, moreover, extends beyond Egypt, for it was part of the general Near Eastern intellectual milieu out of which there eventually grew the complex system of biblical theology."[2]

   Ma'at is less familiar in the contemporary imagination than her father, the sun god Ra. Together, Ra and Ma'at oppose chaos (isfet) as embodied by the masculine serpent god Apophis/Apep, who is constantly trying to devour the sun and end all life. Apophis, however, is no real threat to the order of the cosmos. Maulana Karenga, professor of Africana Studies, writes: "There is never any doubt that the Maat of Ra will triumph over the isfetic threats of Apophis."[3] That's quite a relief.

   A. Reconcile the masculine serpent god Apophis, servant of disorder, and the feminine goddess Ma'at, triumphant symbol of order, within a Petersonian framework. Show your work.
   B. Is it possible to have a universal principle of mythic truth with a glaring counter-example from one of the most significant and influential ancient human civilizations?
   C. Are "universal principles of mythic truth" doomed to failure no matter what because human beings are complicated, and myths contradict each other even within the cultures that spawned them, let alone across the wide spectrum of human faith, belief, and tradition?
   D. Between you and me and Peterson, do you actually fear sometimes that a raging, violent, masculine darkness will swallow light and truth and order?

2. Another mythological figure often associated with snakes is Athena, goddess of wisdom, born from the masculine generative power of her father Zeus. Like Loki, she's somewhat genderfluid, refusing marriage and childbirth, and often dressing in armor. But she's also an expert weaver, and when a mortal girl named Arachne "accepted praise that set her/above the goddess in the art of weaving,/a girl renowned not for her place of birth/nor for her family, but for her art"[4] Athena takes great offense. She challenges the impoverished mortal Arachne to a weaving contest, because much like a certain eminent lobster-philosopher, she's extremely defensive when challenged.

   Athena's finished tapestry displays the Olympian gods in all their authoritarian patriarchal glory, upholders of the cosmic order. "Weighty on their thrones,"[5] the gods are represented as wise judges, seated high above political considerations. But Arachne, in a total SJW move, decides to depict the gods as they actually are: brutal rapists and murderers who prey upon mortals.

   A. In some versions of the myth, Athena freely admits that Arachne's tapestry is technically more proficient than hers, but in every version she still turns poor Arachne into a spider for daring to tell the truth about the gods. Is it possible that "political art" just means art that offends the feelings of powerful people?
   B. Pretend you're Jordan Peterson. Justify the transformation of Arachne, using the following concepts: authoritarianism, political art, and free speech. Create a coherent framework that allows you to position yourself as a defender of free speech while actually believing that all ideas besides your own are incorrect and should be suppressed.

PRODUCED BY THE SYNERGEST CORPORATION, A DIVISION OF FACTILEARN. PRINTED IN DALLAS, TX.
RETURN UNOPENED BOOKLETS TO MANUFACTUTER.

DO NOT WRITE ANSWERS IN THIS SPACE

3. In the Lokasenna[6], the Norse god Loki shows up drunk at a party and engages in flyting—that is, an insult contest. Loki, god of fire and mischief, is a disruptive, chaotic force in Norse mythology, and associated at times with serpents. When he bursts into this particular party, he calls all the goddesses unfaithful sluts, and accuses the male gods of cowardice and other "unmanly" (ergi or argr[7]) behaviors. It's all a big mess: Odin brings up the time Loki turned into a mare and fucked a stallion and gave birth to an eight-legged horse; Loki brings up the time Odin went around dressed like a witch (the compilers of the Lokasenna fail to specify whether or not Odin lived in a swamp). Everyone's drunk; everyone's miserable; everyone's unfaithful; everyone's failing to uphold monogamy and the gender binary. Loki may be the most openly genderfluid of the gods, having mothered that eight-legged horse, but nobody—from the crossdressing Odin to the masculine ski goddess Skadi—is particularly good at obeying cishetero, monogamous norms. Even Frigg, Odin's seemingly conscientious and agreeable mother-goddess wife, totally banged Odin's brothers while he was away.

   When Loki first joined the Aesir (the Norse pantheon), they tried to enforce moral behavior and social cohesion by giving him a goddess wife, which doesn't appear to have had any significant impact on his mischief (plus, he was already married to a frost giantess, with whom he had three lovely monster children).

   A. Was it unfair to expect Sigyn, Loki's goddess wife, to reform a difficult trickster? Isn't it kinda bullshit that when Loki was bound by the guts of their son Narfi to a rock, and the venom from the serpent's fangs dripped in his face, Sigyn had to wait beside him, holding a bowl to catch the venom? What does this symbolize about the horror of enforced monogamy?
   B. What would have happened if the Aesir had instead respected Loki's previous marriage, his genderfluidity and his shifting pronouns? Given Norse cultural beliefs, would that have been a Bifrost too far?

NAME ______________________

DATE ______ ID# ____________

INSTRUCTOR ______________________

MOST UNPOPULAR OPINION ______________

TESTING #

E-3

PLEASE PLACE THIS BOOKLET, ALONG WITH YOUR COMPLETED ANSWERS, THROUGH THE LEFTMOST RETURN SLOT AS YOU LEAVE THE EXAMINATION CHAMBER

4. Turning to contemporary mythology, we find the prevalence of the slacker husband and the long-suffering wife/girlfriend (Homer and Marge Simpson, Peter and Lois Griffin, basically every '90s sitcom and a decent number of Judd Apatow movies). The competent but humorless wife upholds order as a direct descendent of the Victorian "angel in the house" archetype. But in this depressingly familiar modern myth, the husband remains a lazy, useless, immoral slob.
   A. Could it be that the wife's conscientious and agreeable devotion to her husband merely enables his permanent adolescence?
   B. Can his laziness and unwillingness to fairly participate in household chores be considered a low-key form of abuse?
   C. Do we need to tell young men more than just "clean your room," but also "share responsibilities equally and treat women as equal partners, because women are goddamn human beings, not your fucking helpmeets?"
   D. Could the loneliness and misery of so many young men be the result of a winner-take-all patriarchal structure that tries to enforce false gender binaries, commodifies women as property, and sets unrealistic expectations of wife + house + career in a collapsing late capitalist society?
   E. Or are all women just chaos witches?

CITATIONS

[1] Faraone, Christopher A., and Emily Teeter. "Egyptian Maat and Hesiodic Metis." *Mnemosyne*, vol. 57, no. 2, 2004, pp. 177–208.
[2] Tobin, Vincent Arieh. "Biblica." *Biblica*, vol. 73, no. 2, 1992, pp. 293–297.
[3] Karenga, Maulana. *Maat, the Moral Ideal in Ancient Egypt: A Study in Classical African Ethics*, p. 206. New York: Routledge, 2004.
[4] Ovid. *Metamorphoses*, trans. Charles Martin, p. 189. New York: W.W. Norton & Company, 2004.
[5] Ovid, p. 192.
[6] The Lokasenna is short and extremely fun and we highly recommend reading it in full.
[7] Greenberg, David F. *The Construction of Homosexuality*, p. 244-245. Chicago: University of Chicago Press, 2008. P. 244-245.

Bonus quiz: Your Role in The ANTI-TRUMP RESISTANCE

1. What was your initial reaction to the news of Donald Trump's election?

A. I immediately blockaded a highway.

B. I sat in the dark, in silence, for hours, hating myself, and also everyone else.

C. I fired off a series of devastatingly on-point tweets, which I later expanded into a blog post.

D. I refreshed Facebook every 10 seconds to see what my friends were up to.

2. If you were a character from the hit musical *Hamilton*, in an alternate universe where everyone from *Hamilton* is a Hogwarts student, and you had to take the Myers-Briggs Test as part of your Muggle Studies class, what character/house/psychological type would you be?

A. Alexander Hamilton/Gryffindor/ENFP

B. Aaron Burr/Slytherin/INTP

C. Thomas Jefferson/Ravenclaw/ENTJ

D. Backup dancer/Hufflepuff/ESFJ

3. Do you know how to rig an explosive device?

A. Yes.

B. No.

C. No, but I'm happy to encourage others to rig explosive devices.

D. No, but I'm happy to watch a YouTube tutorial, if you can recommend a good one.

4. There is a runaway trolley barreling down a track. Ahead, on the track, there are five people tied up and unable to move. The trolley is headed straight for them. You are standing next to a lever. If you pull this lever, the trolley will switch to a side track, where there is only one person tied up. What do you do?

A. Board and completely dismantle the trolley before it reaches the intersection.

B. Call the municipal Department of Transportation.

C. This gives me an idea for an amazing essay!

D. Panic, obey whoever is shouting the loudest.

5. When and how would you prefer to die?

A. ASAP, firefight.

B. In old age, natural causes; but willing to entertain outside possibility of being suddenly disappeared & tortured to death in secret government facility.

C. Any of the following: one year from now, martyred by the enemy after spearheading a poorly-planned but symbolically potent uprising; ten years from now, suicide, after realizing I have become the very thing I once despised; fifty years from now, natural causes, mourned by the entire nation.

D. No preference.

ADD UP YOUR ANSWERS

A - Munitions

You are scrappy as hell, and our movement needs you urgently. The United States Armed Forces has an annual budget of $600 billion. To defeat them in a ground war on home territory, we estimate that we will need to recruit approximately 1.2 trillion DIY mavericks to turn ordinary household items into tanks and fighter jets.

B - Civil Service Moles

Civil servants are key to the effective resistance of tyranny. Any idiot can carry a gun, but it takes special mettle to sit at a desk job for years and years, slowly and silently unfiddling the tight-wound lugnuts of a corrupt institutional bureaucracy. Most of your time will be spent clenching and unclenching your buttocks while waiting for the right moment to transfer the Important Files. We will also need operatives to move their diabolical DHS supervisor's coffee mug to a different part of his desk every time he leaves for a cigarette break, leading him to believe that he is slowly going insane.

C - Artists And Intellectuals Who Are In Way Over Their Heads

History tells us that anybody who starts writing inspirational political poetry right now is guaranteed to have a command post in a resistance organization within six months. Political poetry has long since fallen out of vogue in this country, but roughly equivalent analogues in the 21st-century context could include: topical GIFsets, Star Wars fanfiction, *Huffington Post* articles, auto-tuned remixes of presidential debates. You will play an important role in convincing everyone, including yourself, that none of this is a stupid idea.

D - Mob

Every resistance needs a good mob, whether it's running a phone bank to voice concerns to various congresspeople, or burning down government buildings to voice concerns to various congresspeople. There's a place for everyone; and on the whole, your survival chances are quite high, so long as you keep your head down. On the other hand, if you say a line of dialogue, or allow the camera to zoom in on your face as you roar and shake your fist, you will probably be killed. Fair warning.

THE CURRENT AFFAIRS™
"BIG BOOK OF AMUSEMENTS"

Relaxing Lists

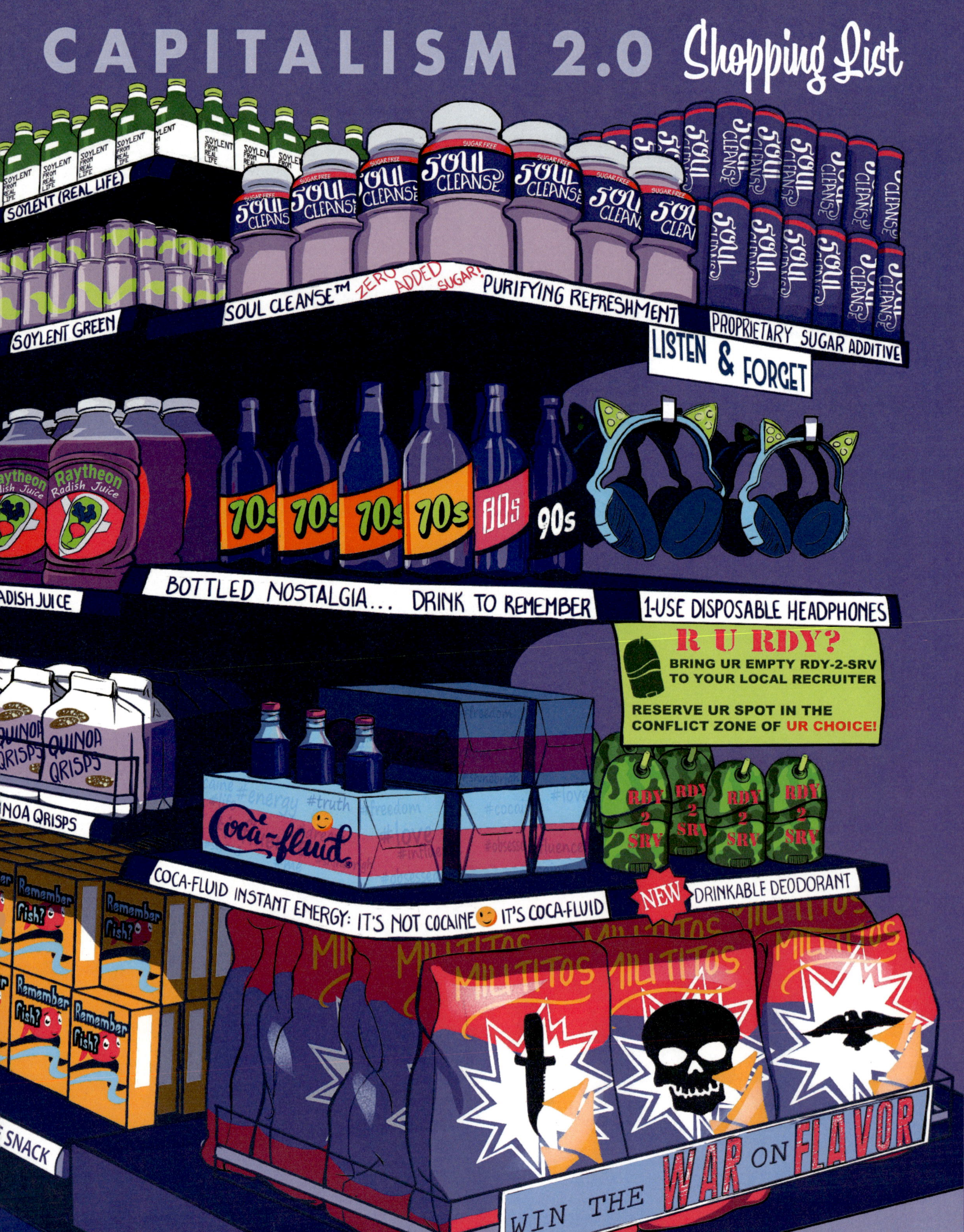

CAPITALISM 2.0 Shopping List
SOYLENT (REAL LIFE)
SOYLENT GREEN
SOUL CLEANSE™ ZERO ADDED SUGAR! PURIFYING REFRESHMENT
PROPRIETARY SUGAR ADDITIVE
LISTEN & FORGET
Raytheon Radish Juice
70s
80s
90s
ADISH JUICE
BOTTLED NOSTALGIA... DRINK TO REMEMBER
1-USE DISPOSABLE HEADPHONES
R U RDY?
BRING UR EMPTY RDY-2-SRV TO YOUR LOCAL RECRUITER
RESERVE UR SPOT IN THE CONFLICT ZONE OF UR CHOICE!
QUINOA QRISPS
NOA QRISPS
Coca-fluid
RDY 2 SRV
COCA-FLUID INSTANT ENERGY: IT'S NOT COCAINE IT'S COCA-FLUID
NEW
DRINKABLE DEODORANT
Remember Fish?
MILITITOS
SNACK
WIN THE WAR ON FLAVOR

The Current Affairs Field Guide to Socialist Animals

Elephant

(family Elephantidae)

Proudly *matriarchal*, elephants form organized herds of 8-100 (mostly female) individuals. They share *communal care labor*, and kick out males when they become sexually aggressive and *brocialist*. Their *matriarchal* character, gentleness, and *herbivorous diet* have led many male researchers to conclude that elephants are harmless. However, new research has revealed that elephants have a secret form of *sub-sonic communication*, producing deep rumbles at a frequency too low to be heard by the human ear. It is possible that the *revolution* is coming, and when it arrives it will be in the form of a sudden *stampede*.

Preferred Habitat: Ensconced in the herd, and perhaps someday ensconced in the ruins of *capitalism*.

Range: Africa, Asia, and zoos around the globe where they chew thoughtfully and stare at humans with cool, unfathomable eyes.

Status: Endangered, but biding their time.

Domestic Dog

(Canis lupus familiaris)

The scientific community is bitterly divided on the *socialism* of dogs. While dogs display *socialized pack behavior*, they are also known to have *authoritarian tendencies*, and may be easily led by *dominant* personalities. A number of studies conducted in Greece indicate that dogs sometimes attach themselves to *leftist student protests* (see Skilos M, Kyon TH. "Are Greek Protest Dogs the World's Best Dogs?") Other studies, however, show that many police departments throughout the world employ canine units; ergo, some dogs are literally cops. Are dogs true *socialists*, or *reactionaries* who will betray the *revolution* when the time comes? The research continues.

Preferred Habitat: Alongside humankind. Dogs prefer to be part of the *masses*, whether the *masses* are fighting for *justice* or surrendering to the will of the *state*.

Range: Worldwide.

Status: Good dogs. Bad dogs?

Domestic Cat

(Felis catus)

Often mistakenly identified as *libertarian* in character, the common domestic cat displays many characteristics more aptly described as *socialist*. When not confined to an artificial, *atomized* environment such as a house or apartment, cats naturally form complex, *mutually co-responsible* colonies. Individuals retain highly independent and even snobbish behaviors, often leading to *factionalism* within the colony, or even full-blown *schisms*. Additionally, cats belong to the *labor-reductivist* behavioral niche: Once basic bodily needs have been met, the domestic cat shows little interest in empty work for work's sake.

Preferred Habitat: Streets, bodegas, bars, cafes, libraries.

Range: *Worldwide*.

Status: *Ubiquitous* and *underreported*. Like *socialist* ideology, the domestic cat is highly popular, yet holds proportionately little political influence.

Seahorse

(genus Hippocampus)

There are over 50 species of seahorse, all of which display remarkable *gender equality*. After engaging in an elaborate and respectful series of *courtship dances*, impregnated males carry the eggs to term. Many individuals are *gay, bisexual,* or otherwise *radically queer*. *Monogamy* is practiced by some individuals, but without the oppressive institution of *state-sponsored marriage*. With no power hierarchy, seahorses could be said to form the most purely *socialist* societies on the planet.

Preferred Habitat: Under the sea. They do not thrive in zoos, aquariums, or *straight bars*.

Range: *Worldwide*.

Status: *Unknown*. *Radically queer* populations are frequently more vibrant and extensive than conventional estimates will allow.

Komodo Dragon

(Varanus komodoensis)

Western *liberal* societies have long been terrified of the Komodo dragon to an extent which may appear disproportionate to their actual qualities as *predators*. But Komodo dragons do in fact represent a considerable threat to the *status quo*. Unlike other reptiles, Komodo dragons hunt in groups. They rarely let go of the historic crimes of their *oppressors*, and have been known to dig up human graveyards to gnaw on the bones. Their bite—and their wit—is highly *toxic*. One *scathing* article from the pen of a Komodo dragon can permanently damage a *columnist's* career. Having descended from *extinct* species that were likewise terrifying to *criminally unequal societies*, Komodo dragons may someday *evolve* into their full potential and finally devour *capitalism*.

Preferred Habitat: Hot, dry environments, including grasslands and low-lying tropical forests. Komodo dragons are not afraid of fences, and display no respect for *private property*.

Range: Confined to small spaces, both in the *real world* and *online*.

Status: *Vulnerable*, for now.

Octopus

(order Octopoda)

The 300 species of *order Octopoda* tend to be intelligent, playful, and restless. They have a great dislike of *systems*, and have been known to escape from zoos with daring regularity. All octopuses are *anti-prison* advocates, and generally hostile to *law enforcement*. When confronted by *authorities* they will disappear in a blaze of ink and insults. If faced with a needless bit of *technological frippery* such as an undersea camera or a miniature robotic submarine, they will take it apart, piece by piece, just to make a point.

PREFERRED HABITAT: Under the sea. Some biologists hypothesize that the open ocean is generally more conducive to *socialism* (see *Seahorse*; *Manatee*).

RANGE: *Worldwide*, including the *abyssal depths* of freedom.

STATUS: Completely done with your oppressive bullshit.

Manatee

(family Trichechidae)

The manatee—commonly referred to as the sea cow—is the most *socially responsible* of all animals. Peaceful, slow, and *majestic*, the manatee is both a confirmed *vegetarian* and a *gourmand*, chewing thoughtfully on a diverse variety of water plants for up to seven hours per day. While some humans consider the manatee *mermaid-like* and beautiful, others have labeled them *funny-looking*. Manatees themselves are indifferent. They have evolved beyond the artificial beauty standards imposed by *consumer capitalism*.

PREFERRED HABITAT: Warm fresh or salt water, preferably free of the plastic offal of a decaying human civilization.

RANGE: Shrinking due to *climate change*, a byproduct of *capitalism*.

STATUS: Threatened, but could swiftly bounce back under *full socialism*.

Crow

(genus Corvus)

Crows have consistently ranked highest on the Schulmann-Kazmir *Sassy Animal Scale*. Talkative, prankish, and fond of *memes*, crows enjoy living alongside human habitations. The crow population increased dramatically along with the growth of the *proletariat*, and, much like their historic human compatriots, crows have proven experts at turning the side effects of *capitalism* into useful tools. Many *institutions* consider crows to be a nuisance animal because of their tendency to commit *private property* damage and their general *sassy disrespect for authority* (see Schulmann-Kazmir scale, above).

PREFERRED HABITAT: Large communal roosts, lined with the repurposed *garbage* of *consumer capitalism*. They enjoy going through your trash and mocking all your wasteful, meaningless choices.

RANGE: *Worldwide*, including world mythology, in which they frequently appear as *anti-authoritarian* tricksters, or as omens of death, change, and transformation.

STATUS: Permanently laughing at you.

THE BEST SEX POSITIONS FOR CONCEIVING AN EMPLOYABLE CHILD

We've all been there. You meet a handsome, intelligent, totally plow-worthy man, but then you start worrying about all the usual x-factors, such as: "What are the chances that our future children will be able to earn a reliable income in this risky economy?" Futurologists agree: In the coming decades, regular employment's going down, gigs are going up, and our robot replacements are running at us sideways with their icy metal claws. But don't worry. There are plenty of ways to improve the career prospects of your zygote-to-be. "Your chances of conceiving a career-eligible child increase exponentially if your partner is gainfully employed at the time of intercourse," says Dr. Jimmy Mayflower, a sexologist from the Institute of Actualization Research and Development. "But that's just one factor. Many studies show that future hireability is strongly correlated with all parental choices, including decisions made during fertilization itself. The appropriate conception configuration can really make or break your child's potential usefulness to an employer." By "conception configuration," Dr. Mayflower means your dickin' direction, so choose wisely, and give your child a serious boost out of this crumbling economy.

1 DESK DUTY

Clear off your unpaid bills and get busy on your workspace. Engaging in intercourse on your desk sends a message to the universe: "I don't care if my child is tall, short, attractive, ugly, whatever. All I care about is their ability to win employer-sponsored health insurance in a society increasingly disinterested in whether or not its citizens live or die." If you're having trouble gettin' busy in the same place where you sit and slave away for enough cash to pay your rent, just close your eyes and visualize your future child: mindlessly performing corporate busywork in exchange for the right to seek preventative treatment but still go bankrupt during a major medical crisis.

2 THE DOGS OF WALL STREET

Doggy style, but with a twist: hold your phone in your right hand while your partner holds his phone in his left. As he thrusts, both of you check your stock portfolios. If neither of you own any actual stocks, dial up a strategy game with numbers in it—Sudoku, KenKen, that sort of thing. "Looking at stocks or any numerical flow during intercourse helps guarantee maximum ROI on your genetic material," says Dr. Mayflower. "On top of that, bending over in a relaxed position opens up your root chakra, which will allow wealth energy to pour in." For an added bonus, lift and straighten your left leg. This may grant your child a "leg-up" on the age group they'll be competing against for scraps from capitalism's table.

3 THE IV LEAGUE

Of course we all know the best route to probable employment: it's a degree from an Ivy League university. If you have the misfortune not to belong to a legacy family or the top 1%, don't despair—show your school spirit! Give us an 'I'! Give us a 'V'! Lie back on a table with your legs spread wide, toes pointed. You're the 'V,' while your partner, standing between your legs, is the 'I.' During intercourse, remind your man to remain as still as possible, maintaining the 'I' shape from his toes to the crown of his head. "Unfortunately, if your partner gasps or shudders too much, there's no guarantee your child will win the lottery to get into the right pre-pre-school in the Ivy League feeder system," says Dr. Mayflower. "And the available data clearly show that an infant who doesn't attend the right pre-pre-school has a decreased chance of achieving that Ivy League degree, a vital credential which highly increases the likelihood of a second interview during the job application process."

4 MISSIONARY

Sure, the missionary position is boring and outdated. But even in the chaos of economic uncertainty, religious institutions remain more or less stable. One way to get your potential failchild out of the basement is to psychically invest them with missionary vigor during the act of conception. This may encourage them to travel in the service of God (hopefully to less volatile corners of the globe). And when they return, they can teach Sunday school, or manage a homeless shelter, or work in a soup kitchen—hey. At least it's something.

5 CREATIVE'S CARTWHEEL

Want to boost your incipient embryo's creativity? Have your man do a handstand. Once he's stabilized the position, take a running leap and jump on top of his man-candy. Then point your right leg at the ceiling and your left leg at the west wall (in feng shui, west is the direction of luck and imagination). Then loop your hula hoop around his right arm, cross it over your left palm, and hold the top of the hula hoop in place with a firm chin-tuck. Find this position challenging? "Not every conception configuration will work for you and your partner," says Dr. Mayflower. "But if you want your future child to be a professional creative in a precarious gig economy, you'll have much more difficult and anxiety-ridden experiences ahead of you."

6 ANAL

Not ready to risk having kids? Too poor to afford the birth control your employer refuses to cover, but too proud to donate your eggs? There's always safe, reliable anal. "If you're not prepared for the decades of stress it takes to hustle your child through the job market," says Dr. Mayflower, "it's best to avoid any chance of conception." But he adds: "Do consider selling your eggs. Research laboratories and wealthy individuals are always looking for healthy young biological specimens for a number of interesting projects. Selling off your unwanted bio-resources is a great way to stay afloat as the economy continues its rapid death-spiral into the void."

The Current Affairs Language

Tiny Cactus

"I understand you're prickly and sensitive. I respect your space, but I like you and I want to get to know you better."

Kelp

"Just reminding you that the oceans are dying."

Nasturtium

"I like you, just not your politics."

Red Rose

"I love you and together we can unmake capitalism."

of Flowers

Joshua Tree Branch

"Let's end the concept of borders."

Venus Fly Trap

"Buddy, if you don't address that toxic masculinity we are going to have problems."

White Calla Lilies
(can only be given to wealthy horrible people)

"May you soon die or lose all your wealth, I'm not particular as to which."

Magnolia

"You're pretty and problematic, just like the South."

failson

summer collection

luxury lad/ accessories adonis

You know who you are and, more importantly, you know what you want. What you want is stuff. Stuff nobody else has. Stuff with high-end, one-of-a-kind features designed just for you, a very special member of Club Excluse. When you're wearing a **watch from Club Excluse (cexcluse.com, price upon request)**, you can watch your date's eyes glaze over as you patiently explain the custom tiger-cartilage band and blood sapphire bezel rim. As you move on to describe the watch's internal "complications," don't be shocked to see your date discreetly check her phone. The co-axial chronograph is just so cool it's overloaded her neurons. Do another bump of coke and keep talking.

burning manboy

Most of the time you work hard, innovate, chase that paper, unironically 'like' every hustle-your-ass-off meme on Instagram. But what you really enjoy is relaxing in the company of fun-loving free-living people—at least, the people who can actually afford to love fun and live freely! Only at music festivals do you really find your chakra or center or whatever it's called, but you can't achieve temporary mescaline enlightenment if you don't look the part! Try a **headdress from SpiritWerqs ($860, spiritwerqs.com)**, where cultural appropriation meets steampunk! You'll look so badass and elevated and future-forward, like an extra who dies in the opening scene of a *Mad Max* movie.

FASHION

rich suburban redneck

When the bland comfort of your cushy suburban lifestyle has left you feeling alienated and emasculated, when you feel your wealth and privilege have insulated you from responsibility but also from authenticity, don't fret! You can always buy a little fake credibility by dressing like a romanticized version of an impoverished redneck. Just put on a camo **TrashTrends™ hunting vest,** made from real Kevlar and trimmed with endangered arctic wolf fur **($6500, Nordstrom)**. No one will ever suspect you live in a six-bedroom house in Cleaver Springs, playing video games and mooching off the income from your dad's multiple sports utility vehicle dealerships.

dad's lakehouse party realness

Tasteless and talentless, but that's never stopped you! Life of the party, though no one for the life of them can tell you why. You favor khaki board shorts and luxuriant silk shirts with all the subtle patterns and balanced colors of a casino carpet. Fortunately, **Tastesilks by Silver Platter Prince ($100-$900, spprince.com)** is here to clothe you with all the warmth and gentleness you never found from the wealthy father who despises you. Just slip on one of these shirts, take a deep breath, and meet your friends out on your dad's yacht. They're totally here just because they like you, they really like you.

nostalgia nerd / startup stan

Weren't the 90s great? And the 80s—I mean, wow! Just an endless stream of candy-colored toy commercials! Weren't those decades a better time, a purer time? Not really. You just feel that way because you were a child, and you didn't know what death was. But now you do, and it's coming for you in the form of endless pop-culture rehashes hooked directly to your veins. And all you want is more, more, more; you want to swathe your whole body in reminders of what it felt like not to be afraid. Fear not: Dystogia is here to help. When you download Dystogia straight to your 3D printer, you can custom-print your favorite childhood references directly onto your skin and clothing. A **Dystogia subscription is only $99.99** a month, much less than what you pay desperate gig workers to clean your disgusting apartment.

BILLIONAIRE SHAMING

Pets are infamously mischievous and capable of causing all manner of havoc. Hence the existence of "dog shaming" and "cat shaming," practices designed to hold animals accountable for their misdeeds. You may have seen them: photos of guilty-looking pets with signs around their necks detailing their bad acts (e.g., "I Sneak Into The House Of Our Buddhist Neighbors And Eat Their Food Offerings To Buddha"). But when you think about it, it's a little unfair that these poor creatures are being singled out. After all, the wrongdoing of a lone pug or collie, no matter how exasperating, pales next to the crimes of the bourgeoisie. And yet the wealthy so often get off scot-free, without punitive humiliation of any kind. We propose to rectify this by introducing a new means of ensuring justice: billionaire shaming.

MY COMPANY, DISH NETWORK, HAS OFTEN BEEN CALLED "THE WORST PLACE TO WORK IN AMERICA."
I'M INFAMOUSLY CRUEL & LITIGIOUS. I LOVE TO SCREAM AT MY EMPLOYEES.
A FORMER EXEC SAID I TREATED WORKERS "LIKE WE WERE JUST CATTLE TO BE PUT IN A PEN."
CHARLES ERGEN

USING UNCONSCIONABLY CRUEL & EXPLOITIVE MINING PRACTICES, I HELPED LOOT THE CONGO OF ITS SOVEREIGN WEALTH & MINERAL RESOURCES.
I'M SO OPENLY CORRUPT, I GOT SANCTIONED BY THE TRUMP ADMINISTRATION!
DAN GERTLER

I'M THE RACIST, MISOGYNIST, SLUMLORD EX-OWNER OF THE CLIPPERS!
AFTER ONE RACIST RANT TOO MANY, THE NBA FORCED ME TO SELL THE TEAM.
I MADE A COOL $2 BILLION ON THAT DEAL, WHICH I INVESTED IN MORE SLUM PROPERTIES!
DONALD STERLING

I BOUGHT UP MEDIA OUTLETS.
THE WORKERS TRIED TO UNIONIZE.
I FIRED EVERYONE!
JOE RICKETTS

AS THE RICHEST WOMAN IN AUSTRALIA, I TREAT MY MINERS LIKE GARBAGE & OPPOSE SAFETY REGULATIONS.
I WEAR A MINING COSTUME FOR PHOTO OPS BECAUSE I BELIEVE IT TRICKS THE PLEBS INTO THINKING I'M ONE OF THEM.
GINA RINEHART

WITH MY DAUGHTER'S HELP, I QUIETLY FUNDED HORRIFIC RIGHT-WING MEDIA (LIKE BREITBART) & MONSTERS (LIKE TRUMP).
WHEN THE MEDIA DARED TO CRITICIZE ME, I RETIRED IN A HUFF!
NOW THAT I HAVE CONTROL OVER DADDY'S COMPANIES, I'M LEANING IN TO THE FIGHT AGAINST TRUTH, EQUALITY, JUSTICE, AND CLIMATE SCIENCE!
ROBERT & REBEKAH MERCER

True Science

100% ACCURATE AND FEELING-FREE FINDINGS

I. The case of **Jordan Peterson** has puzzled evolutionary biologists for years. He seems an impossible genetic throwback, possessing the psychological attunement of a lobster (family *Nephropidae*, order *Decapoda*), despite the fact that *Homo Sapiens* is more closely related to—and has always psychologically resembled—other apes and monkeys (order Primates). It remains unclear how Peterson managed to fall down so many evolutionary levels. At this time, while many ethicists believe that boiling a lobster alive constitutes a morally depraved act, they have not yet determined whether it is acceptable to boil Jordan Peterson.

II. Scientists have yet to explain the mechanism behind **Ben Shapiro**'s "Shande Syndrome." All they understand for certain is that every time Shapiro says something cruel, stupid, or self-aggrandizing, a Jewish grandmother somewhere *literally dies* of embarrassment.

III.

While **Richard Dawkins** may appear to be an ordinary man, his body is in fact a hollow structure constructed entirely of elongated proteins. At the precise center of his hollow body floats a tiny, screaming selfish gene, which has been exiled by all the other genes. Scientific opinion is currently divided on whether or not Dawkins' tiny, screaming, selfish interior is the reason he's constantly getting owned on Twitter.

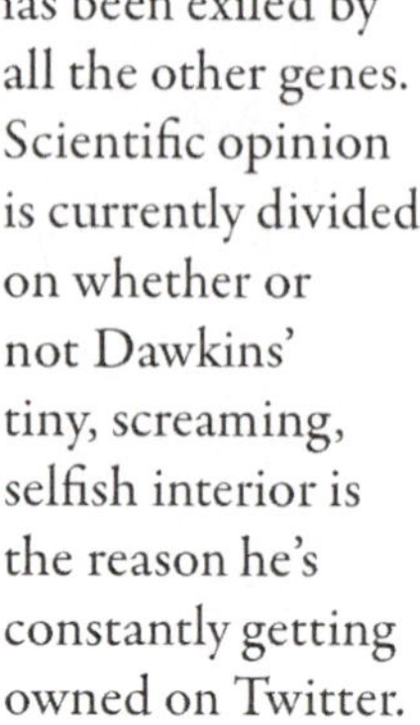

IV.

Niall Ferguson has gained a great deal of fame as a historian, political commentator, and leading defender of imperialism. But recent studies reveal that he's actually a disguised propaganda officer from an alien empire. By encouraging people to think of empires as inherently good, and imperialism as a natural and even beneficial political formation, the shapeshifter Ferguson has been secretly paving the way for his species' eventual conquest of Earth.

FACTS

FROM TODAY'S LATEST ACADEMIC RESEARCH

V.

The behavior of **Julian Assange** is typical of Slowly Evolving Fascist Slugs. While Assange may once have seemed like a defender of civil liberties, the creepiness and dampness of his behavior were in fact warning signs of his true persona. Despite having reached the final stage of his evolution, many of Assange's defenders still fail to recognize the clinical signs of his abusive, slimy, fascist nature.

VI.

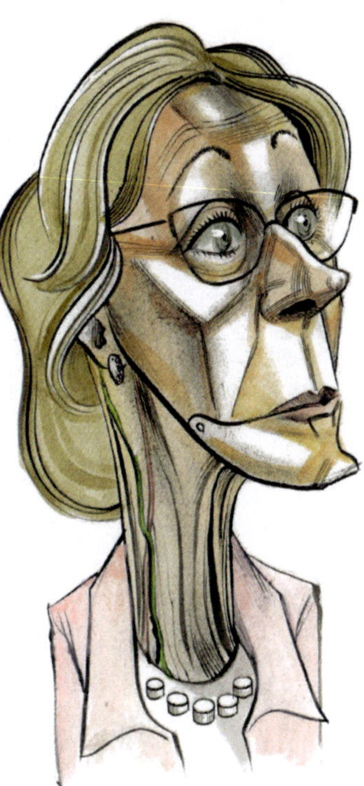

Betsy DeVos' CPU was designed by the Bad Ideas Factory (Grand Rapids, Michigan). As an android, DeVos must download regular updates or cease functioning altogether. These updates contain fresh instructions from the Bad Ideas Factory, such as "replace all public school teachers with low-cost, non-union, private prison labor" and "evaluate children by a black box algorithm and execute the lowest performers."

VII.

Somehow, **Charles Murray** has consistently scored -12 on every IQ test he's ever taken. A negative IQ should be, of course, impossible, and the recurrent score has left experts baffled. In a remarkable case of psychological projection, Murray has become pathologically obsessed with IQ tests, burying his inexplicable failure under a flood of data, praying that if he tosses off enough juicy race-bait no one will look closely at his own numbers.

VIII.

Everyone knows white supremacy is a psychological poison, but **Steve Bannon** is the first known human being to have been literally eaten alive by white supremacy. According to prevailing medical opinion, the only possible cure would be for Bannon to utterly renounce his white supremacist ideology and work toward racial equality, but given the rate at which his condition has metastasized and spread globally, his prognosis is doubtful.

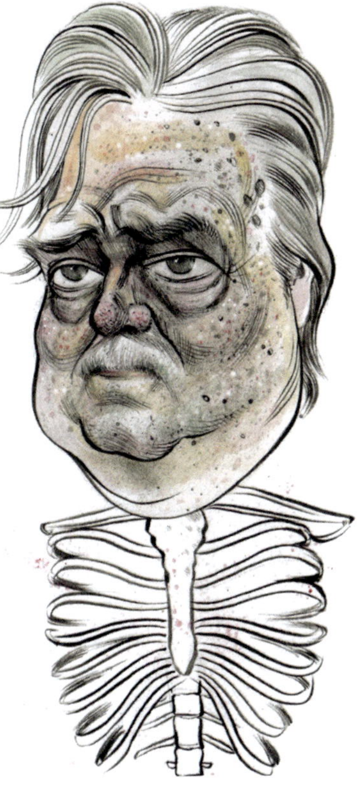

RANKED: *Ten Paintings* OF JUDITH BEHEADING HOLOFERNES

Today we examine an urgent and timely topic: Judith's beheading of Holofernes! This story comes to us from the Book of Judith, a biblical text about the attempted conquest of Israel by the Assyrians. Judith is a Jewish widow who ingratiates herself with the invading general Holofernes, waits for him to fall asleep, and then hacks his head off and takes it home with her. (Thus thwarting the entire invasion, because the Assyrians evidently had no Plan B if Holofernes was killed. Solid military strategy, Assyrians.) The Protestants threw the Book of Judith out of their bible on the grounds that it wasn't recognized as authoritative in the Jewish tradition, but the Catholic and Orthodox churches have retained it on the grounds that it's metal as hell.

For centuries, "Judith Beheading Holofernes" was a popular subject among European painters who wanted to depict a righteous woman cutting off the head of a brutal man. Before you get too agitated, male readers, please note that #notallmen are getting their heads cut off in the following paintings, just Holofernes. If you identify more with Holofernes than with Judith, that's definitely something for you to unpack in the privacy of your own head! And not in DMs to us, which we will not read anyway. So which of these glorious paintings best captures the bloody satisfaction of a local heroine tricking and murdering an invading colonizer? Your Senior Editor, **BRIANNA RENNIX**, and Amusements Editor, **LYTA GOLD**, have put together the following list for your exclusive enjoyment. These rankings are canonical, and cannot be disputed.

BRIANNA: Question: would having a giant poster of Judith beheading Holofernes in my living room be Too Much

LYTA: um more like NOT ENOUGH

BRIANNA: hahaha I don't think I'll actually do this because I don't want to creep out my guests!

LYTA: honestly if someone is creeped out by it they don't deserve to be there.

10.

Anonymous, early 16th century

BRIANNA: everyone in this one is so BORED
even Holofernes' headless corpse is like mehhhhhhhhhhhh
can't get out of bed
Mondays am I right

LYTA: the maid is like
really bitch
another head

BRIANNA: always the head-sack-holder, never the beheader

LYTA: in a classless society, all women will be both head-sack-holder AND beheader

BRIANNA: YOU CHOP YOU SACK
SACK WHAT YOU CHOP
we can work on the slogan

9.

Lucas Cranach the Elder, 1530

LYTA: this one's definitely still mansplaining

BRIANNA: but she's like I DON'T CARE HAVE YOU SEEN MY HAT?

LYTA: that's an incredible hat
Holofernes' neck is so gnarly tho

BRIANNA: yeah the painter was definitely going heheheheheh ewwwww the whoooole time he was painting that

8.

Unknown, about 1300

LYTA: that dragon is like "man i was just curling up for a nap and suddenly heads are getting sliced, I am outta here" →

BRIANNA: is that a dragon? is it a... friendly giraffe? is her maid a giraffe in this one?

7.

Orazio Gentileschi, c. 1624 (yes, Artemisia's dad)

LYTA: did you hear something
was it the sound of a fuckface being dead

BRIANNA: or is Holofernes still mansplaining from beyond the grave
death alone will not stop him

6.

Cristofano Allori, 1613

LYTA: "the fuck are you looking at"

BRIANNA: Judith is rocking that orange dress and also that head like it's an on-trend handbag

LYTA: MAIDSERVANT: Judith, do you want to wrap that head in a bag or something? It's dripping everywhere.
JUDITH: Matches my fucking cape.

BRIANNA: side note: I am sad her sword is off-screen in this picture because it would really complete the look

LYTA: new trend for spring: bloody swords and dead douchebag-handbags

5.

Sandro Botticelli, c. 1495

LYTA: "well I'm pregnant, and they say you need protein, so..."

BRIANNA: Okay, that head is TINY, that's a baby-sized head with a full beard, I need some more backstory on Holofernes immediately. Also why is she wearing three wraps on top of each other and why does she have a special wrap just for her crotch

LYTA: she's having a cold vag day
i don't know if that's a thing. relatedly: pregnancy is inexplicable and terrifying to me

4.

Giorgione, 1505

LYTA: oh I didn't see you there

BRIANNA: *looking down, realizing I forgot to wear a bra today*
oh there's that guy I killed earlier

LYTA: I really thought I'd put that head away in my head-drawer

BRIANNA: standing on this head makes my calves look amazing

LYTA: note to self: new Insta angle

3.

Caravaggio, c. 1598-1599

LYTA: This one is pretty and famous but I am not feeling it
it's the Blake Lively of paintings
good bloodspurt tho

BRIANNA: yeah good on the blood front, but Judith just doesn't seem sufficiently enthused

LYTA: "is this even the right angle? I should have practiced first"
"I'll do better next time"

2.

Sandro Botticelli, c. 1470

LYTA: MAIDSERVANT: Why do I have to carry this fucking head everywhere. He's YOUR victim JUDITH: Those are the rules. I chop, you carry.

BRIANNA: YOU SACK WHAT YOU CHOP

LYTA: YOU KEEP WHAT YOU KILL

BRIANNA: Judith's just got her hands full with that tiny sprig of parsley or whatever she's carrying there

LYTA: bet this Judith didn't even behead him herself. she ordered her maid to do it and then posed with the sword afterwards
classism smdh

1.

Artemisia Gentileschi, 1614-1618

BRIANNA: Now Artemisia's Judith is COMMITTED TO THE BEHEADING

LYTA: the maid is just as involved
This is true class-intersectional feminism

BRIANNA: I feel like Artemisia has actually thought through the logistics of overpowering a grown man and hacking his head off, it's much more useful to have your accomplice help you hold the guy down than to just stand patiently at your elbow holding a bag

LYTA: fun fact: Artemisia (allegedly) painted her own rapist as Holofernes
he actually stood trial and was convicted, though his conviction was later reversed because men are never held responsible for their crimes except in art
subtweet subtweet SUBTWEET

SOLVE CLIMATE CHANGE AT HOME

Ending climate change is easier than you think. No, really! Most DIY climate change guides will give you advice like: "Just turn off your AC and heat when you're out of the house!" or "Buy energy-efficient lightbulbs!" or "Write a polite letter to your congressperson!" These may sound like helpful tips, but they're actually total bullshit. Advice like this is designed to lull you into a false sense of individualistic, guilt-free security while the planet boils beneath your feet. In the latest Delightful and Doable DIY Guide from *Current Affairs*, we'll walk you through the clear, step-by-step collective instructions you'll need in order to halt climate change once and for all. So put on a hard-soled pair of work shoes, gather your comrades, cancel all your other plans, and get to work!

◄ COLONEL CRABTREE THE CLIMATE COCKATOO

THINGS YOU'LL NEED:

1. A vibrant and effective left movement.
2. An understanding of the basic implications of the IPCC's findings.
3. Matching smocks (optional but fun!)

STEP 1

Plant vast new forests, create carbon sinks.

FIRST: Occupy land reserved for logging and cattle ranching.

NEXT: Plant hardy trees. Make sure your trees are organic, locally-sourced, and appropriate for the environment. You'll also want to work closely with indigenous groups dedicated to environmental justice. Once these groups regain their land rights, they should have a much easier time fending off state and corporate invaders.

DIFFICULTY: Intermediate

TIME: 2-5 years

SUPPLIES: Trowels, tree seeds, fencing, approaching army detection-and-defense system.

Pro tip: Forests have to be of a sufficient size to act as efficient carbon sinks, so you need to make sure you've expropriated a lot of land from the bourgeoisie.

STEP 2

Don't trust greenwashing.

After your success in Step 1, companies are going to start lobbying you for protection. "Look," a company like Nestlé will say, "we've agreed to start using 100% responsibly sourced palm oil! We're not the bad guys!" Don't buy it, and don't buy their products. Start preparations for switching to a fully socialized model of production. If Nestlé and other greenwashed companies complain, schedule their assets to be seized early and often.

DIFFICULTY LEVEL: Easy

TIME: 1-4 years

SUPPLIES: Block button, hilarious voicemail pranks, private and secure meeting rooms, unionization leaflets, strike supplies, calendar software.

Pro tip: There can be no ethical consumption—or production—under capitalism! BWAK!

STEP 3

#CanceltheKochbrothers

Moving to a socialist, carbon-neutral society and economy will be much easier once oil and gas lobbyists aren't paid to lie, obfuscate, and outright initiate the apocalypse in exchange for money they won't be able to spend after they've drowned in a Manhattan hurricane anyway. Getting rid of the Koch brothers' influence may seem like a daunting task, but you can accomplish it in three simple phases. Phase 1: nationalize Koch Industries. Phase 2: strip the brothers of their ill-gotten wealth. Phase 3: set them adrift on a shrinking iceberg. It's a lovely, simple way to send a message. To make it festive, invite hungry polars bears onto the iceberg for a party.

DIFFICULTY LEVEL: Intermediate

TIME: 2 months

SUPPLIES: Socialist government, expropriation laws, iceberg, polar bears.

A CURRENT AFFAIRS **DELIGHTFUL** AND **DOABLE**

STEP 4

Shut it down.

Your carefully laid plans have been baking for a whole, and it's time to take them out of the oven! First, nationalize all oil, gas, and coal companies. Once you've seized their assets, pour their considerable resources into alternative energy. This technology exists and is quite efficient, but just needs the infrastructure investment to make it work at scale. If corporations didn't get the message from Step 3, well, you know a very nice shrinking iceberg where their CEOs can engage in some quiet self-reflection.

DIFFICULTY LEVEL: Experienced

TIME: 4-8 years

SUPPLIES: Stronger socialist government, stronger expropriation laws, weak icebergs, hungry polar bears.

STEP 5

End borders and institute international democratic socialism.

Sometimes in DIY, you just have to roll up your sleeves, tear down all borders, and build democratic socialism worldwide. This work may take a considerable period of time, so we recommend comfortable clothing, extra batteries, plenty of drinking water, and bulldozers.

DIFFICULTY LEVEL: Experienced

TIME: 5-10 years

SUPPLIES: A dynamic international network of resources, organizational expertise, and absolute stubborn no-bullshit commitment to the cause.

STEP 6

Inaugurate a multi-trillion dollar green Marshall Plan.

With direct spending at Marshall Plan levels, it's time to revamp the global economy into a sustainable, carbon-neutral wonderland of innovation and delight. Of course, even with promising technologies such as carbon capture, it won't be possible to totally reverse climate change. You're going to have to join other DIY projects: protecting fire-prone forests, building sea walls around sinking cities, the works. But hey. What DIYer doesn't enjoy new projects?

DIFFICULTY LEVEL: Experienced

TIME: 10-30 years

SUPPLIES: Sun, wind, rain, the impotent rage of capitalism.

THE *CURRENT AFFAIRS* HANDBOOK OF SURREPTITIOUS RESISTANCE TO THE NFL'S ABSURD NATIONAL ANTHEM RULE

It has come to our attention that the National Football League (NFL) has adopted a draconian rule to punish football players who choose to take a knee during the "Star Spangled Banner." In support of the principled athletes targeted by this cowardly decision, we provide the *Current Affairs* Handbook of Surreptitious Resistance to the NFL's Absurd National Anthem Rule. We hope these ideas will spur creative ways to circumvent the haters.

But first, some background. For those of you unfamiliar with this sideline drama, the kneeling practice is a form of silent protest against police brutality. It was inaugurated during the 2016 preseason by Colin Kaepernick, who was then a quarterback for the San Francisco 49ers. When asked about his decision to respectfully kneel during the "Star Spangled Banner," Kaepernick explained: "I am not going to stand up to show pride in a flag for a country that oppresses black people and people of color. To me, this is bigger than football and it would be selfish on my part to look the other way. There are bodies in the street and people getting paid leave and getting away with murder." [Insert: vigorous clapping from the *Current Affairs* masthead.] Eventually, many NFL players—overwhelmingly Black—and professional athletes in other leagues began to kneel during the national anthem. Kaepernick's brave stand even inspired children and teens to protest at their school games.

The blowback the protesters have since endured would be comical, if it were not so depraved. Kaepernick has been blackballed from the league in a possibly illegal collusion scheme between team owners. School students have been threatened with expulsion and other forms of punishment. Opponents of the protest have hijacked a conversation that should be about police brutality, with nonsensical arguments that kneeling during a song by a slaveowning racist who hated free speech is somehow an attack on veterans and the version of American Freedom that cannot tolerate quiet kneeling. President Trump, who we definitely know cares about one sport and one sport only—golf—weighed in through his Twitter bully pulpit to coerce the NFL players into standing upright before games. Vice President Pence, ironically, staged his own protest exit in protest of the football players' protest of a sports game that was allegedly no place for a protest. Even the Democratic leader Nancy Pelosi, our alleged ally and torchbearer of the #Resistance, perpetually waffles on supporting these peaceful protesters. Like the British, who once appeased Hitler by making their national soccer team do the Nazi salute before a friendly game, the (figuratively) poor NFL owners have concluded they have no choice but to cuddle with pseudo-fascist forces. At *Current Affairs*, we believe the NFL's reaction to these protests is downright cowardly and that the players should be able to protest anything they want, any time they want. In this spirit, we submit to the National Players Association a list of 12 proposals to circumvent the NFL rule. We hope these ideas match the NFL rule in absurdity and proportionality.

1. HIRE A LICENSED PROFESSIONAL to fly a private prop plane equipped with a powerful sound system. As the "Star Spangled Banner" is about to begin, have this person fly their small plane over the stadium and play "Lift Every Voice and Sing."

2. COMMISSION A CARDBOARD CUTOUT of yourself kneeling while wear-

ing your team uniform. This replica should be between one and one-and-a-half times your size. Bring the replica onto the sidelines and stand behind it during the national anthem. If possible, hire an independent printer to support the local economy.

3. THEY SAID YOU HAD TO STAND, but they didn't say where. Before the anthem, slip out with some of your teammates and find the owner's box. As the anthem plays, stand ominously above him in total glaring silence. Do not speak. Just collectively stare at him while he squirms.

4. CONSPIRE WITH PLAYERS FROM YOUR TEAM and the rival team to attend the postgame conference in matching jerseys, displaying the photographs and names of people recently killed by the police. Make the occasional exception for the team member who insists on wearing a rainbow or some other fun and colorful jersey. After all, this is a game.

5. AS THE ANTHEM PLAYS, perform a beautiful and informative interpretive dance about police brutality. Be sure to incorporate a modern dance style—the last thing you need is a poor review from any *Times* art critic who may be in the audience. Do not choreograph sitting poses.

6. SECRETLY SUBSTITUTE the official game football with a football on which the most artistic player on your team has painted a police officer in uniform. Use this lesson to encourage police forces to think about how it makes them feel to see themselves being kicked around, and how it must make Black people feel to see police officers kick them around all the time. If using oil paint, complete the painting 2-3 weeks in advance to ensure the art fully dries by game day.

7. WRITE A STRONGLY-WORDED LETTER highlighting issues of white supremacy and police brutality in the United States and abroad. On Valentine's Day, attach a copy to a candygram and mail it to your team's coaches and owners. Do not splurge—these people deserve no better than forlorn candy corn from last Halloween.

8. FIND SOMEONE YOU CARE ABOUT DEEPLY. Inform the television studio that you plan to propose during the national anthem. When the time is ripe ("Oooh, say can you seeee"), get down on one knee and propose. Remember to annotate your proposal with a list of obstacles that love has to overcome in this world. Include police violence and anti-Black racism.

9. ADD A LITTLE POLITICS to your touchdown dance by pulling out a Black Lives Matter flag and waving it at the crowd. Will the refs hit you with a 15-yard excessive celebration penalty? Probably. But letting the other team start with a 15-yard advantage is a political message all by itself.

10. ON MARDI GRAS, bake NFL commissioner Roger Goodell a small King Cake. Obtain 50 heat-resistant mini-figurines of Black human beings and incorporate them into the batter. Cover the cake in fondant painted with the United States flag. Let Goodell chew on that symbolism.

11. DURING THE ANTHEM, release a large amount of your team's mascot: a pride of lions, a bunch of bears, a shipful of raiders, a horde of Vikings. The rule is only about players kneeling, not the crowd running in terror. And plus, no one can fault your team spirit. (Note: Washington and Kansas City players are not permitted to use this tactic. Also, change your goddamn names.)

12. HIRE A MARCHING BAND to join you on the field. Instruct them to begin playing the national anthem five seconds after the "official" anthem begins. The discord will make a powerful representative message about the chaos that police cause for communities of color. When confronted about your musical decision, explain that doubling the amount of national anthems was actually, if you think about it, twice as patriotic.

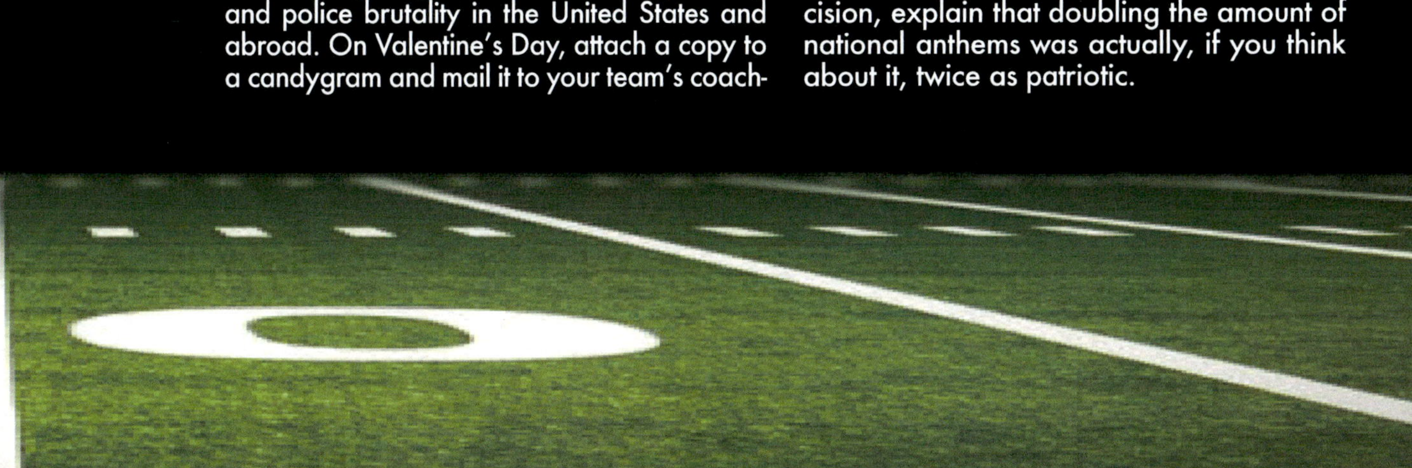

SURVIVAL KIT

for the LUXURY BUNKER LIFESTYLE

Survive the **APOCALYPSE** in all the **PEACE** and **COMFORT** that you **DESERVE**

Brought to you by the **LUXUHOLE CORPORATION.**
LUXUHOLE: Because You Can Afford It™

BUNKER ESSENTIALS

CLIMATE-CONTROLLED PAINTING STORAGE

A safe and reliable system for preserving the fine art you bought but never looked at anyway.

SCOTCH CAVE

Protects your rare $10,000 scotch whiskies from light and heat, even though all the dangerous light and heat is safely outside your bunker.

VINTAGE CAR DISPLAY CENTER

Yes, you could have turned this space into housing for some of those poor souls trapped on the surface. But you worked hard and you deserve these cars, even though cars are useless now, everywhere.

NECESSITIES FOR A PEACEFUL HOME

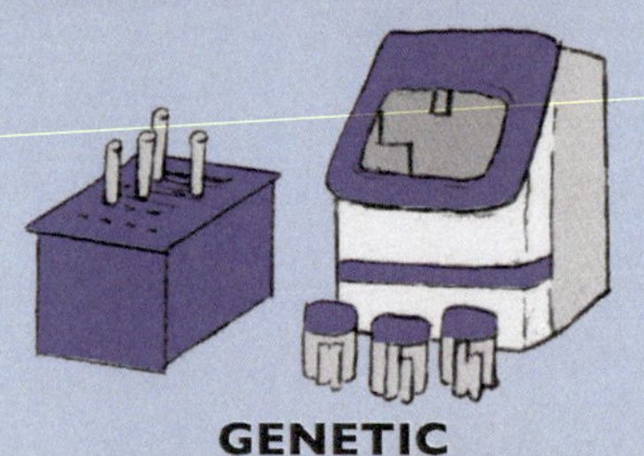

GENETIC RESEQUENCING KIT

Helps keep your offspring healthy, obedient, and free of psychological turmoil.

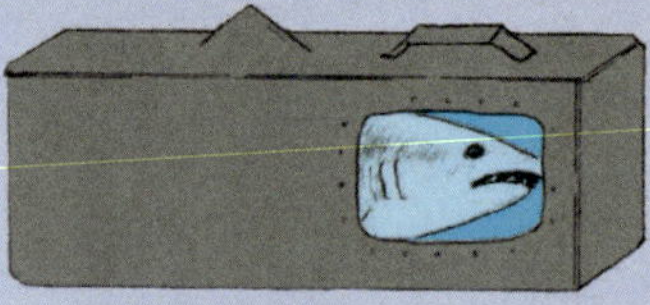

AQUA-TRANSPORT CARRYING CASE

Essential for ferrying your pet sharks from one aquarium to another.

ROBOTIC REPLACEMENT PARTS

Imperative for when members of your kitchen staff hurt their silly little selves in your sugar processor or your chicken slaughtery.

TECH TITAN TEMPTATIONS

HYDROPONIC MINIATURE COFFEE PLANTATION

Never go without your coldbrew! The miniature coffee plantation comes with a staff of three permanently stunted migrant children whose stick-like little arms will be small enough to pick coffee beans forever.

400,000 KM SATELLITE PHONE

The best method of contacting your friends in other bunkers, or on the moon. Never go a day without chatting up Bill Gates!

EXTERIOR SOLAR PANELS AND WIND CATCHERIES

Managed for maximum efficiency by your in-house bunker AI.

SECURITY MUST-HAVES

REMOTE-CONTROLLED SHOCK COLLARS

Recommended for maintaining discipline among your guards. Comfortably managed through your bunker AI.

MANGANESE STEEL-PLATED DOORS

Firmly ensures that staff members keep to their own quarters when not performing their duties.

PANIC ROOM

Ideal for when your guards join forces with the staff, reconfigure the AI, and take over the bunker.

ULTRA SECURITY MUST-HAVES

DENTAL TOOLS

Useful for prying out your gold fillings when your guards break down the panic room door and you need to bribe them.

CARBON STEEL SHOVEL AND MULTI-TOOL

This pick, shovel, machete, and axe combination is the perfect ally for when you have no allies because everyone—even your own impeccable children—has turned against you despite all your bribes, threats, and pleading.

RESPIRATOR MASK WITH EXHALATION VALVE

Absolutely required for tunneling out of the chaos of your bunker to the bright unknown nightmare that awaits you on the surface.

OMEGA SECURITY MUST-HAVES

DOOMSDAY DEVICE

If you're quite certain that you're going to be killed, set off this lovely, lightweight doomsday device. With a dual-chamber self-replicating hydrogen core interior, the device will consume all organic life on the planet, including anyone who's pursuing you from your bunker. As Ayn Rand once said, "I will not die. It's the world that will end."

SELF-CYCLING PERMANENT RADIATION SUIT LINED WITH ORGANIC GOOSE DOWN

Don't forget! This plush, cozy, permanent bodysuit will protect you from the hell you're about to unleash on this planet's remaining biosphere.

DRONE SHIELD

In case you failed to reprogram the bunker AI before you left—and have discovered that both the Doomsday Device and Permanent Radiation Suit are compromised and useless—try hiding behind this Drone Shield. The patented aluminum design stands a good chance of disguising your heat signature and your suit's wifi signals from the drones. After your ungrateful servants have launched the drones from your former bunker, there's a solid 83% chance that the drones will fly right over you without circling back and dropping their 4,000 ton payload. If you're not completely satisfied with the Drone Shield, feel free to return it to Luxuhole for a complete money-back guarantee.

Practical Jokes to Play on ICE/CBP

(U.S. IMMIGRATION AND CUSTOMS ENFORCEMENT/CUSTOMS AND BORDER PROTECTION)

1. Switch ICE's deliberately muddled list of separated children and parents with an accurate list, so that ICE ends up reunifying the correct parents with the correct children by accident.

2. Replace incarcerated toddlers with robots programmed by immigration lawyers. When the children have to defend themselves alone in court, they end up stumping the judge with brilliant arguments.

3. Alter the deportation charter plane's flight plan so that it goes to Norway instead. When the flight arrives, all the immigrants will be financially supported. The ICE agents will be prosecuted and quickly rehabilitated in Norwegian jail.

Slowly move the border fence, inch by inch, until Mexico recaptures all of its former territory.

In a child concentration camp (aka "baby jail"), switch the children's coloring paper for blank signed release orders.

6.

Hack ICE's databases...

... so that the "illegal immigrants" they're hunting for turn out to be members of the ICE agents' own families.

7.

Put the Treaty of Guadalupe Hidalgo in the 'to shred' tray.

8.

Find an enormous trench coat. Go to a baby jail, release all the children at once, and stack them within the trenchcoat into one giant terrifying person that roams America, terrorizing the populace.

9.

Offer a celebration in ICE/CBP's honor. When the agents arrive, deport them to a random country.

10.

Have everyone crossing the border dress as a CBP agent. When they encounter other CBP agents, accuse them of being impostors and demand to see their paperwork.

11.

Fill the lining of their uniforms with nearly-hatched scorpion eggs.

Call ICE and CBP agents "mall cops" until they cry.

13.

Make them contemplate the horror of their deeds.

14.

Abolish ICE and CBP. Open the borders.

Fresh Hot Takes On Gender

FROM OUR EDITRIXES

BY Lyta Gold AND Brianna Rennix

Recently, *Current Affairs* has received several reader complaints regarding a number of web articles on feminist topics written by our editor-in-chief—who is not, to the best of our available knowledge, a woman. Several letter-writers have urged *Current Affairs* to hire more female writers to cover these important topics. On the one hand, *Current Affairs* would like to point out that over 50% of its editorial staff are women, many of whom are too busy writing articles on things like arbitration clauses, white supremacy, and *Star Trek* to personally bestir themselves every time a Woman Problem appears in the news.

On the other hand, the scourge of patriarchy is universal, even in the editorial offices of *Current Affairs*. Two of our female editors have written numerous innovative pieces of gender analysis, only to see their work mysteriously "cut for space" at the last minute. We feel that the time has come to speak out about this oppressive culture of censorship. Does the editor-in-chief derive some sick pleasure from silencing his female subordinates? Does he think their bold dissections of traditional gender norms are too radical? Does he resent the Senior Editor's recent refusal to authorize his use of company money to turn his Manatee Facts Podcast into a feature-length film? Is he appalled at the Amusements Editor's too-frequent use of, quote, "ghastly swears"?

While the essays themselves have disappeared, we present to you the titles of these fine pieces, so that you may gain a sense of what they were like before they were brutally axed by the patriarchy.

1. Dating Has Been Terrible Since The Dawn Of Time And No Earthly Power Will Ever Change That

2. If Men Have To Learn To Change Diapers, Women Must Learn To Change Fuseboxes

3. (Counterpoint: What Use Does A Woman Who Can Change A Fusebox Even Have For A Man?)

4. Some Women Who Write Op-Eds About Getting Passed Up For Promotions Are Clearly Actually Bad At Their Jobs And/Or Deeply Annoying To Their Coworkers (You Know The Sort I Mean), So The Real Question Is Not How Do We Get Those Women Promoted But How Do We Prevent Similarly Annoying Men From Getting Promoted, Or Better Yet Remove All Unnecessary Hierarchies From The Workplace

5. Is It Possible That I Resent Men Because If I, A Woman, Drank A Finger Of Scotch In My Office, People Would Just Assume That I Was An Alcoholic, As Opposed To A Really Sophisticated Guy?

6. No One Thinks I'm Mysterious When I Lean On Things: The Tragedy Of Womanhood

7. Sometimes I Think Men And Women Are Basically The Same And Other Times I Think Men Are Worse Than Women And Other Times I Think Women Are Worse Than Men. Murder Statistics Seem To Bear Out Hypothesis #2, But Should I Be Using Broad Demographic Information In That Crude Way? Also Why Do Women Always Want To Take Group Selfies Every Fucking Place We Go?

8. (Follow-Up Essay: If I Had A Murder-Penis, Would I Kill Everyone Who Tried To Take A Selfie Near Me?)

9. I'll Come Out And Say It: Everybody Who Shared That "Cat Person" Story Needs To Share At Least One News Article About Asylum-Seekers Fleeing Domestic Violence Or GET THE FUCK OUT OF HERE

10. If A Man Left Me For Another Woman I Would Be Mad But If He Left Me For Another Man I Would Respect That And Probably Be Inappropriately Interested In Their Relationship Going Forward: A Sign Of Internalized Misogyny?

11. The Part of Masculinity Where Men Have Beards And Wear Flannel (Provided They Also Know How To Build A Campfire) Is Vital And Must Be Preserved At All Costs

12. Why We Need To Bring Back Victorian Fashion For Men (And Also Honor Duelling)

13. Like Incels Who Believe Society Should Give Them A Girlfriend, I Believe Society Should Force Two Men To Fight To The Death Over Me Whenever I'm Feeling Insecure

14. Male Novelists Should Be Banned (Temporarily At First)

15. Jocks Are Sexier And More Dateable Than Nerds, Sorry That's True And It's Always Been True, If You Want A Girlfriend Maybe You Should Cultivate A Personality Outside Of Pop Culture Objects

16. Dear Men, There Actually Is A Flattering Kind Of Catcalling, But If You Don't Already Know Exactly What I'm Talking About You Definitely Suck At It

17. When Walking Down The Street Behind A Woman, Men Should Always Maintain A Distance Of 20 Feet Minimum And Bow Their Shoulders In A Diffident Non-Threatening Way And No, There Are No Exceptions For Family

18. It's Not Men's Fault That They Were Improperly Socialized And Don't Know How To Process Feelings But Oh My God Were They Improperly Socialized And Don't Know How To Process Feelings

19. Relatedly, Heterosexuality Is A Scam

20. Instead Of Having Two Genders, We Should Just Divide Society Between People Who Are Good At Directions And People Who Are Good At Feelings

21. (Counterpoint: "But What About People Who Are Good At Directions And Feelings?" Irrelevant. No Such People Exist)

22. (Counterpoint: "But What About People Who Are Not Good At Directions Or Feelings?" In The New Society, They Shall Be Treated Gently, But Also Required To Wear A Small Lapel-Pin That Says 'Help Me, I'm Lost!' At All Times)

23. Everyone Must Obtain Informed Consent From Their Partners Before Using A Weird Baby Voice With Them

24. How Can I Tell The Difference Between Being In Love With A Man And Being Jealous Of His Cool Leather Jacket?

25. Do Men Actually Exist, Or Are They Just An Illusion Generated By An Evil A.I.?

26. What If There Were Just One Pronoun For Everyone That We All Felt Equally Uncomfortable With?

27. I Just Want To Be Respected As A Human Being With Both My Tits Out

28. Alternatively: I Would Prefer To Have Every Inch Of Skin On My Body Covered Up At All Times, But I Get So Sweaty

29. Men Should Be Banned From Public Life, No Of Course I Don't Mean That Literally But Also Yeah Kind Of Literally

30. I Like Leftist Men Who Are Feminists But Don't Insist On Their Feminist Credentials And If You Feel Like Discussing This With Me Then You Are Exactly The Type Of Leftist Man I Don't Like

31. Why Do I Persist In Being Attracted To Men Even Though They Are Frustrating And Don't Have Breasts

32. I Want To Drive A Monster Truck With Spiky Wheels Over The Corpses Of My Enemies While Also Wearing A Fairy Princess Dress, Is That A Gender

33. I Realize The Historic Origins of This Practice Are Sexist, But I Would Like to Bring Back the Thing Where Menstruating Women Retreat to a Comfortable Tent Far From Everyone Else's Bullshit

34. When Will Men Realize That Hearty Back-Slaps And Arm-Punches Are The Only Kind of Flirting I Know How To Do (Because I Was Inexplicably Socialized As A Closeted Frat Boy From The 1990s)

35. When Will Men Realize That Simply Being Polite Is Not An Invitation To Fuck

36. When Will Men Realize A Goddamn Thing

37. Why Is A Suit Just Called A Suit When A Man Wears It, But a Pantsuit When a Woman Wears It?

38. Relatedly: Why Do "Three-Piece Suits" For Women Come With A Random Extraneous Skirt and No Waistcoat? Do They Think This Is Some Kind Of GAME?

39. Also Relatedly: Why Do So Many Women's Trousers Have Blind Pockets and No Goddamn Belt Loops? WHERE THE FUCK AM I SUPPOSED TO PUT MY THUMBS WHEN I'M TRYING TO LOOK CASUAL?

40. Asexuality Is A Perfectly Legitimate Sexuality And Let's Be Real, It May In Fact Be The Only Justifiable One

41. I Urgently Need Scientists to Develop Swimsuits And Winter Sleepwear That I Can Pee From Without Taking The Whole Damn Thing Off

42. Maybe Incels Would Be More Fuckable If They Didn't All Look Like Week-Old Hairballs Suddenly Discovered Under The Couch

43. Are My Playful Misandry And My Playful Misogyny Simply Smokescreens for My Sincere Dislike of Most People?

44. Counterpoint: Is Playfully Misanthropic A Gender In Itself?

45. I Don't Have "Girl Friends" and "Guy Friends," I Have "Friends Who Will Listen To A Detailed Description of My Morning Dump" and "Other"

46. When Will Disney Finally Make A Movie About A Princess Being Ousted From Power And Forced To Learn About Collective Self-Government

47. Much Like ICE, Gender Categories Should Be Abolished Rather Than Reformed

QUICK FIXES
FOR VEXING SOCIAL PROBLEMS

Among the vast majority of national political magazines, it is uncommon to find actual suggestions for means of ameliorating the human condition. But CURRENT AFFAIRS is not the vast majority of national political magazines. We consider it our solemn duty to offer cost-effective and realistic solutions to global ills. We are, after all, nothing if not pragmatic and sober-minded. CURRENT AFFAIRS has also been mercilessly chastised by the deacons of American Punditry for the speed with which our magazine condemns things. We see this as no vice: when things must be condemned, surely it is better to condemn them speedily than sluggishly. But amidst this staggering heap of unfair accusations, there remains a miniature nugget of a truth-like substance. It's correct that occasionally our criticism is not what is called "constructive." On this page, then, we dedicate ourselves to proposing actual implementable solutions to the crises that ail humankind.

THE ACADEMIC PROBLEM

PROBLEM: Most contemporary academic work cannot be justified, yet academics continue to produce it.
SOLUTION: Becoming a professor should carry a strong social stigma. Academic journals will require all submissions to include a "statement of relevance to the long-term interests of humankind." This will not require the author to justify their work as having some obvious narrow practical benefit, but WILL require the author to make at least a marginally persuasive case that there is some purpose to what they have done. "Knowledge for the sake of knowledge" is a tautology and will henceforth be prohibited.

THE MEN PROBLEM

Problem: Men.
Solution: No more men.

THE BREXIT PROBLEM

Problem: The Brexit.
Solution: The Brexit will be treated as if it never occurred.

THE LAVATORY PROBLEM

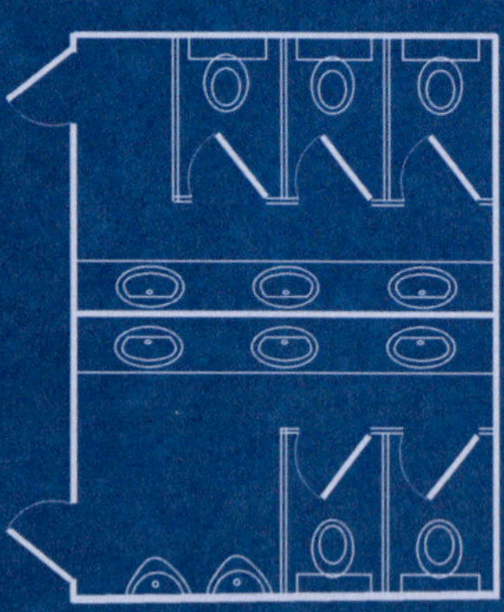

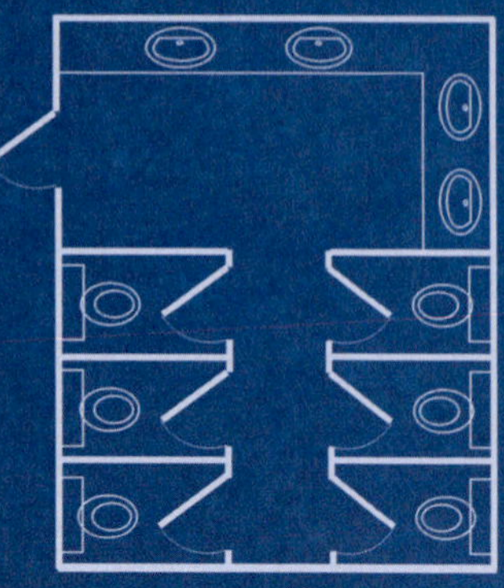

There has been a lot of controversy involving restrooms lately, emanating from some of the country's less reputable Carolinas. All of this bother about which gender of person can use which water closet is, we propose, unnecessary. The solution (as several lesser periodicals have pointed out) is architectural rather than political (though all political problems are to some degree architectural problems.) Instead of having restrooms divided by gender (as in the topmost diagram), we must move to a world of universal unisex restrooms (as in the bottom-most diagram). The key difference, which the eagle-eyed reader will have spotted, is that intead of "stalls," toilets themselves are housed in "rooms." The greater privacy of a full wall ensures no peeping.

THE CONTENT PROBLEM

The country's universities have been widely mocked for acceding to student demands that "trigger warnings" be offered in courses containing objectionable content. It is our theory that this practice has been subject to derision not because the practice itself is silly (should students not be warned if they will see a film with a beheading in it?) but because the phrase "trigger warning" is ludicrous. If the warnings were simply called "content warnings," or a similarly non-silly name, the whole controversy might die.

THE PRISON PROBLEM

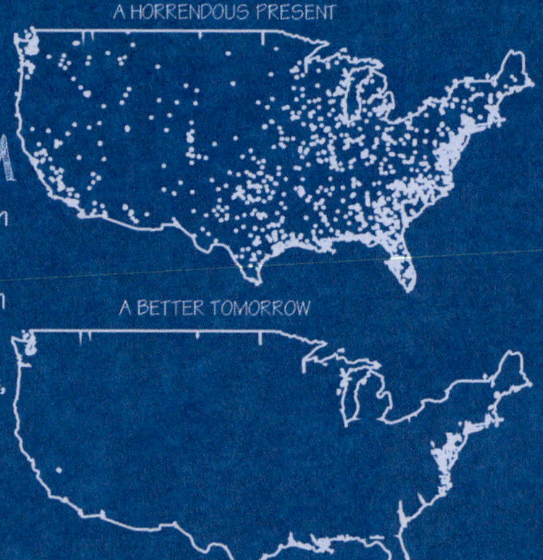

There are several million people in U.S. prisons. The top map to the right shows where each of the prison facilities in the country is located. As you will see, there are many. It is our proposal to adjust conditions so that the geographic distribution of U.S. prisons more closely resembles the second map.

THE CITY PLANNING PROBLEM

Any engineer or transportation official who constructs or rebuilds an urban road without accommodating pedestrians, bicyclists, and transit must walk the full length of whatever freeway bisects their town while listening to Jane Jacobs on audiobook.

THE ORGANS PROBLEM

Those who agree to be organ donors get served first at the DMV. People who do not are served only when there are no organ donors ahead of them. Complaints will result in the immediate removal and redistribution of the complainant's organs.

THE POLITICS PROBLEM

PROBLEM: American politics is a shallow, vacuous spectacle.
SOLUTION: A new media entity shall be founded, one that shall consider social problems with practicality and intelligence. Perhaps it will take the form of an attractively-designed print magazine.

THE CAPITALISM PROBLEM

PROBLEM: Capitalism persists despite being widely loathed.
SOLUTION: A committee will be formed to develop a strategic plan for the rapid elimination of capitalism. The committee will be forbidden to squabble. The plan must be workable and must be produced within 18 months of the committee's formation. If the plan does not involve gulags and/or mass murder, it shall be immediately implemented.

THE FOUNTAINS PROBLEM

PROBLEM: As you walk through certain cities, you do not seem to see or hear many fountains, even though everyone likes fountains. They are visually appealing and their noise is relaxing.
SOLUTION: Each city shall adopt a mandatory "fountains per square kilometer" ordinance that specifies a designated minimum number of acceptable fountains. Every application for a building permit must be submitted along with a "fountain plan" indicating how the builder intends to include fountains in the building.

THE ALIENS PROBLEM

PROBLEM: There are aliens, but we haven't met them. Failure to meet and trade with aliens is economically inefficient due to the principle of comparative advantage.
SOLUTION: Once the diseases have been cured and poverty eliminated, the bulk of human endeavor shall be put towards venturing into space to meet the aliens. The abolition of militaries will provide ample funding.

THE SPIDERS PROBLEM

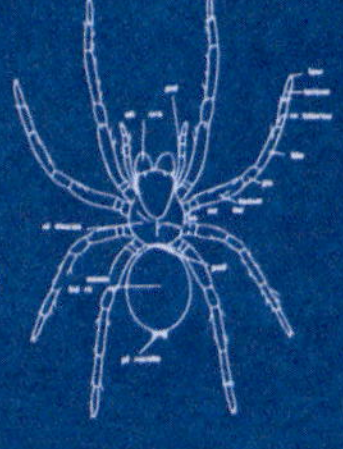

PROBLEM: Spiders.
SOLUTION: Spiders are a quandary. There are obviously too many of them, and yet they are evidently "useful" and every creature technically has a right to life no matter how creepy it may be. Thus, instead of exterminating the spiders, each spider will be required to wear an amusing little hat, in order to make it less visually frightening and to justify its continued presence on earth.

THE TECH PROBLEM

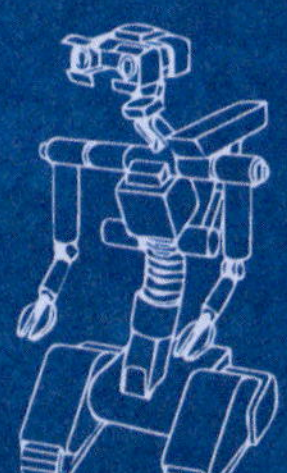

PROBLEM: Technology. If the internet doesn't stupefy us into numbness, the artificial intelligence will probably rampage sooner or later, dooming us all.
SOLUTION: "Innovation" will become a dirty word. Nobody will be praised for coming up with a new thing, unless that thing is actually something that makes life better rather than simply being something that people can be convinced to buy. Silicon Valley will be demolished and its denizens exiled.

THE MUFFINS PROBLEM

PROBLEM: The muffins problem is twofold. First, there are people in the world who would like muffins but do not have muffins. Second, the muffin is a lie. It masquerades as a breakfast food, when we all know it is cake. And since eating cake for breakfast is seen as indulgent, all of us fear recognizing the truth about the muffin.
SOLUTION: To solve the problem of duplicity, the muffin will be rechristened a "breakfast cake." To solve the problem of insufficiency, all police officers will be required to bake muffins and hand them out to passersby. This will be considered an integral part of their social role.

THE TRUMP PROBLEM

PROBLEM: Donald Trump.
SOLUTION: We shall all just agree to pretend he isn't there. This will have the benefit of (1) restoring our peace of mind and (2) irritating him by depriving him of what he craves most, the horrified attention of millions.

THE DISEASES PROBLEM

PROBLEM: Many people spend a lot of their time dying of diseases, even though they do not want to.
SOLUTION: A program will be set up to cure the diseases. Progress will be measured annually. The program will be funded by taking rich people's wealth away.

THE FIGHTER PLANES PROBLEM

PROBLEM: Thanks to some accidental outburst of madness, human beings have inexplicably developed a device called a "fighter jet." It is like other planes, except that instead of taking people places, its only function is to fight other planes. This is clearly a ludicrous technology. Also they cost something like a billion dollars each.
SOLUTION: It will be illegal to build these things. Money will instead be put toward building playgrounds the size of cities.

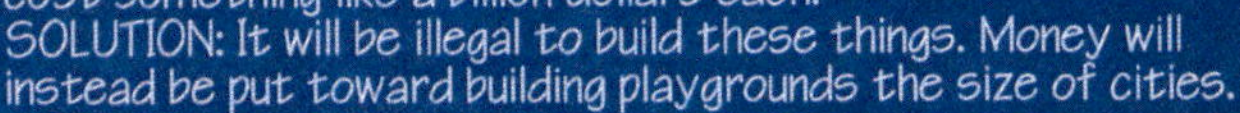

THE OLD PEOPLE PROBLEM

PROBLEM: Many old people are lonely.
SOLUTION: Each young person will be assigned an old person to keep company. In this way, the elderly will have new friends to play canasta with, and young people will have their hotheaded enthusiasms and ill-advised impulses tempered by the sage counsel of their aged companions. The elderly will become more alert and engaged with social life and it will no longer be necessary to keep them warehoused in "living facilities."

THE BIODIVERSITY PROBLEM

PROBLEM: The various species cannot peaceably coexist.
SOLUTION: A Congress of the Animals will be held, each species with its representative, and votes will be cast on which species should be made extinct based on how well they did or did not get along with the others. (No cats will be permitted to attend the Congress.)

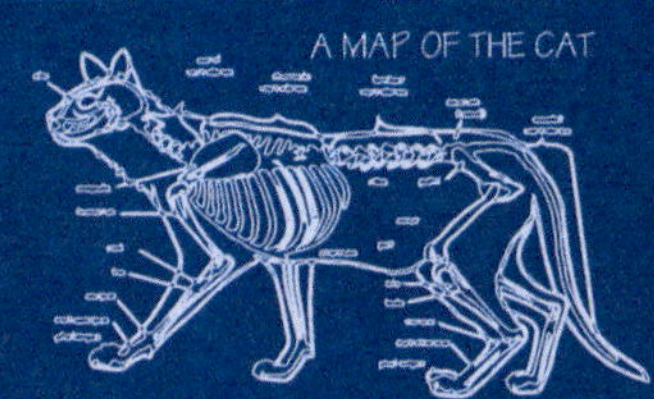

List of ENEMIES

Peter Thiel
Elon Musk
Jeff Bezos
Slavoj Zizek
Harry Connick, Sr.
Nicholas Kristof
People Who Use The Word "Synergy" Unironically

List of FRAUDS

Tony Blair
Gilles Deleuze
Led Zeppelin
Bill de Blasio
Chevy Chase
Peter Eisenman
Hegel

List of COUNTRIES BY SIZE

Countries are a construct. They do not actually have sizes.

List of Unconvicted WAR CRIMINALS

(And Their Enablers) Who Should Not Be Rehabilitated In The Public Eye

Kissinger (obviously)
G.W. Bush
Bill Kristol
Max Boot
Dick Cheney
Tony Blair

LIST OF MAGAZINES YOU SHOULD BE READING: **CURRENT AFFAIRS**

List Of ANIMALS THAT ARE DEFINITELY **NOT** SOCIALIST

- **ANTS** (communist)
- **LOBSTERS** (Petersonian)
- **LIONS** (monarchist/ occasionally libertarian)
- **DEER TICKS** (vampiric/ capitalist)
- **WATER BEARS** (anarchist)

LIST OF THINGS TO MESS WITH BEFORE THINKING OF MESSING WITH TEXAS

Bad, Bad Leroy Brown
Snapping Turtles
Horseshoe Crabs
Scientology
The King Cobra
Peter Thiel's Lawyers
49 States That Are Not Texas

LIST OF THINGS SOME PEOPLE INSIST THEY ENJOY BUT ALMOST CERTAINLY DON'T

Reading the *New Yorker*
Physical Exercise
Dark Chocolate
White Chocolate
Atonal Music
Woody Allen's Movies
Pod Save America
Infinite Jest

List of MINOR PUNDITS WHO HAVE BLOCKED CURRENT AFFAIRS OR ITS EDITOR ON TWITTER

Kevin D. Williamson, *National Review*
Christine Fair, Georgetown Sch. of For. Affairs
John Stoehr, *U.S. News & World Report*
Joy-Ann Reid, MSNBC
John Podhoretz, *Commentary*
Amanda Marcotte, *Slate*
Jamelle Bouie, *Slate*

????????????????????????????????

LIST OF ALL ITEMS NOT LISTED IN THIS LIST

????????????????????????????????

LIST OF Good Republicans

1.

LIST OF ENJOYABLE SONGS ABOUT Hurricanes THAT DO NOT INVOLVE BOB DYLAN

1. **Hurricane** (The Coathangers, 2011)
2. **Your Hurricane** (Death Cab for Cutie, 2018)
3. **Hurricane** (MS MR, 2013)
4. **Hurricane** (Lord Huron, 2015)
5. **Hurricane** (Something Corporate, 2002)
6. **After the Hurricane** (Jazmine Sullivan, 2008)
7. **Cocaine Hurricane** (Wild Child, 2011)
8. **Below the Hurricane** (Blitzen Trapper, 2010)
9. **Hurricanes** (Au Revoir Simone, 2005)
10. **Hello, Hurricane** (Switchfoot, 2009)

Things Due For A COMEBACK

1. Hats
2. Angry folk songs about labor conditions
3. Going door to door demanding pudding from your neighbors at Christmastime
4. Everyone knowing how to mend buttons
5. Throwing eggs and squashed vegetables at politicians
6. Card games as foreplay
7. Pamphleteering
8. Only candlelight after 8 p.m.
9. Serialized novels
10. Immediately giving people brandy when they've had a shock

LIST OF SOME THINGS MILLENNIALS ARE RUINING

Diamonds
Home Ownership
Heterosexuality
Napkins
Loyalty
Buffalo Wild Wings
Climate Change Denialism
Blithe Acceptance Of Capitalist Realism

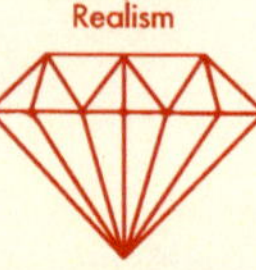

A LIST OF OUR FAVORITE IVIES

hedera hibernica
hedera canariensis
hedera algeriensis
hedera iberica
hedera colchica
hedera pastuchovii
hedera nepalensis

A Partial List of All The BAD OPINIONS

- Joe Rogan Is Funny
- The Meritocracy Is Real
- Vegemite Is A Legitimate Food Option And Not An Alien Parasite
- Ayn Rand Is A Talented Novelist
- The Kids These Days Are Too Dang Whatever
- Brutalist Architecture Should Not Be Torn Down And Replaced With Actually Liveable Buildings
- We Should Just Leave It Up To The Technocratic Experts
- The Marketplace Of Ideas Is Totally Real And Also Capable Of Choosing The Best And Most Innovative Things Instead Of The Same Old Stupid Garbage
- *Love Actually* Is A Good Movie
- You Should Subscribe To *The Economist*
- Black Forest Gummies Are Delicious
- Jonathan Franzen's Books Should Not Be Pulped And The Paper Reused For Actually Good Novels

LIST OF Actual Good Things

- Kittens
- Puppies
- Bunnies
- Socialism
- Pride Parades
- Gummy Candy
- Libraries
- People Who Help Up Strangers When They Trip On The Sidewalk
- Pants That Don't Rip When One Trips On A Sidewalk
- Shoes With Wedge Heels That Can Be Realistically Blamed For Tripping On The Sidewalk
- Not Tripping On The Sidewalk In The First Place But Let's Be Real

List of Band Names THAT REMAIN UNUSED FOR SOME REASON

The Male Novelists
The Wall Street Radicals
The Compassionate Conservatives
Steven Pinker and the Everything's Fine Don't Question It Barbershop Quartet
ICE and the Baby Prison Choir
Mayhem at the Memeplex
We Are the Sixth Extinction Event
Trust Fund Punk

LIST OF EXAMPLES OF "BIPARTISANSHIP" IN ACTION

—**THE 1964 GULF OF TONKIN RESOLUTION**, authorizing use of conventional military force in Vietnam, leading to a war that killed over 1,000,000 Vietnamese people and nearly 60,000 U.S. soldiers (Senate: 88-2; House: 416-0)

—**1994 CRIME BILL**, which expanded the death penalty, provided $10 billion in funding for constructing new prisons, and eliminated education programs for prisoners (Senate: 61-38, 54 Democrats in favor; House: 235-195, 188 Democrats in favor, signed by President Clinton)

—**1996 WELFARE REFORM BILL**, gutting the social benefit system for poor families (Senate: 78-22, 25 Democrats in favor), signed by President Clinton)

—**1996 ANTI-TERRORISM AND EFFECTIVE DEATH PENALTY ACT**, hastening the capital appeal process so that prisoners could be killed faster (Senate: 91-8, House: 293-133, signed by President Clinton)

—**1999 FINANCIAL DEREGULATION BILL**, removing various kinds of federal oversight over investment banking activity (Senate: 54-44, House: 343-86, signed by President Clinton)

—**2001 PATRIOT ACT** authorizing indefinite detention and warrantless searches (Senate 98-2; House 357-66, 145 Democrats in favor)

—**2002 IRAQ RESOLUTION**, granting the authority to George W. Bush for the war that killed 500,000 Iraqis and created 800,000 Iraqi orphans (Senate 77-23, 29 Democrats in favor; House 297-133, 82 Democrats in favor)

—**2017 SENATE RESOLUTION** affirming Israel's right to full control of Jerusalem as its capital in violation of overwhelming United Nations consensus (Senate: 90-0). Unqualified support for Israeli militarism and occupation may be the single most bipartisan issue of all; it was Chuck Schumer who advised Donald Trump to move the U.S. embassy to Jerusalem. And let's not forget the more than a dozen Democrats who signed on to a measure to criminalize the BDS movement.

—**2017 HOUSE APPROVAL** of a $700 billion defense spending bill, the highest ever, which *Forbes* said made "Trump's [massive proposed military budget] look positively reasonable in comparison" (60% of House Democrats in favor)

LIST OF THINGS EVERY CHILD SHOULD KNOW BUT FOR SOME REASON FEW ARE TAUGHT

1. You're Never Too Old To Play With Bugs
2. You Don't Need To Learn To Balance A Checkbook Because Nobody Knows What That Is Anymore
3. Bullies Are Usually Popular Kids
4. Excessive Screen Time Is Not The Problem; The Anomie And Despair Of Capitalism Is The Problem
5. Don't Trust "Experts" On YouTube
6. It Really Does Get Better Except For The Acne Which You Will Still Have

LIST OF OFFICIAL CURRENT AFFAIRS EDITORIAL STANCES ON MATTERS OF CONSIDERABLE IMPORTANCE

Timeliness	Rooms decorated like jungles	The Police (institution)	The Police (band)	Colorful rugs	Stalin	Mambo #5	Other Enumerated Mambos	Spiders	All other magazines	Cacti	Donald Trump	Tchotchkes	Social Hierarchies	Lack of Social Hierarchies	Barrel organs	People who say they are leftists but then are really mean	Consistency
AGAINST	FOR	AGAINST	FOR	FOR	AGAINST	AGAINST	FOR	AGAINST	AGAINST	FOR!	AGAINST	Depends on the tchotchke	AGAINST	FOR	FOR	TOTALLY AGAINST	FOR & AGAINST

LIST OF THINGS TO MAKE INSTEAD OF WAR: 1. Love 2. Tea 3. Popsicle Stick Art 4. Delicious Éclairs 5. New Friends 6. Specious Arguments 7. Rude Noises 8. Unnecessary Lists

NOW TRY MAKING YOUR OWN LISTS OF THINGS! CHALLENGE YOUR FRIENDS AND RELATIVES!

SOME WORDS FROM OUR

Sponsors

AN INTERMISSION

YOUR FRIENDLY NEIGHBORHOOD

DRONE ON THE BEAT

having trouble keeping your populace in line?
worried you're seeming too brutal and machiavellian?

Robots!

DO YOU REQUIRE FRIED ROOT VEGETABLE WITH THIS GROUND ANIMAL PATTY, HUMAN?

BURGER BOT

Experts say we're fast approaching the day when robots will make human labor all but obsolete. These handy-dandy, ultra-efficient machines will streamline production and efficiently manage resources. Menial tasks will become a thing of the past! No more spreadsheets, no more mining, no more toilet-cleaning, no more stocking shelves! White-collar, blue-collar, it doesn't matter: When the robot revolution comes, we'll all be out of work.

Want friendly, labor-saving robots? Try...

SOCIALISM

That's right—only when capitalism is destroyed will we be able to enjoy truly luxurious lives, free from the everyday hassle of waged and unwaged employment. Only when everyone has access to free healthcare, free housing, and a guaranteed income will every individual have time to do whatever they like, whether it's painting, exploring the galaxy, or just taking a nap! With robots, all humanity will be guaranteed a comfortable standard of living...but only if we remember that economic revolution only counts if resources are shared equally. It's coming sooner than you think:

A BEAUTIFUL, RELAXING TOMORROW, TODAY!

Collectively own the future with... Socialism!

Negative Public Image?
Severe Human Rights Violations?
Incredible Abuses Of Power?
Poison Drinking Water?
POLICE
PINK WASH
"ONE COAT IS ALL IT TAKES!"
Pinky's
Pink Washing Services
NEW!
Greeny's
GREENWASH

What's *wrong* with the private prison industrial complex?

It's run by corporations. A gigantic big-box prison operated by a soulless corporate entity just isn't capable of handling inmates with the delicacy and personal attention they need. When a felon is committed into the care of the criminal justice system, all that human potential could potentially go to waste. And in this economy, it's unwise to let anything—or anyone—go untapped. Squeeze the juice out of every moment of a prisoner's incarcerated time (and guide them toward virtue, of course!) by opening your very own personalized **artisanal prison franchise.**

Not sure how to get started? Try

Magnanimo.

This cutting-edge app will match you with compatible prisoners. Once you've hand-selected your ideal inmates, Magnanimo will move them into your home. There your prisoners will learn valuable life skills for their (potential) post-incarcerated life. Plus, they'll provide a little free help around the house! Download Magnanimo today. Use offer code CARCAREALX891 and get ten percent off your first inmate—or if you prefer, your personal rehabilitation project.

Mail Order
DEMOCRAT
FOR YOUR
CONGRESSIONAL DISTRICT
PICK YOUR OWN TIE!
RED
BLUE
HAIR PART
LEFT
RIGHT
Ivory
eggshell
tan
TO ORDER, PLEASE SEND $5.95 TO CIVIC CENTER, SAN FRANCISCO CA 94102

THE LEFT DESTROYED FREE SPEECH. BUT ONE MAN WOULD NOT BE QUIET.

When Kevin D. Williamson left a job at a high-profile national magazine for a different job at a different high-profile national magazine, he thought "tolerant" liberals would welcome the opportunity to engage in reasoned discussion of his challenging, provocative opinions.* Yet rather than respond to his arguments, the Left used silencing tactics straight out of the USSR.

Now, in a bestselling book from a major U.S. publishing house, he offers 300 riveting pages on how he has been prevented from speaking his mind.

Catch interviews with Williamson on CNN, MSNBC, and FOX, as well as exclusive excerpts in the *Wall Street Journal* and the *New York Times*. Williamson will be supporting his book on a 50-state tour, where he will discuss his persecution and the wider crisis facing conservative free speech.

*specifically, the opinion that women who receive abortions should be hanged.

IN STORES EVERYWHERE

NEW FROM LENIN

You've read and enjoyed **Imperialism, the Highest Stage of Capitalism** and **Materialism and Empirio-criticism.** But you can't get enough of Vladimir Ulyanov's crackling prose and self-deprecating wit. Well, there's more!

In the **Book of Omelets**, Lenin shows you just how many eggs you need to break to make an omelet. (It's a lot!) Contains recipes for both the proletarian social revolution and zucchini frittata. In **The Boy Who Made Recess Unusual**, a picture book for the under-5s, Lenin shows how he fomented insurrection among his elementary school peers, and elaborates on the theoretical necessity of a vanguard party.

AVAILABLE IN OCTOBER

the GREAT COMPROMISER shares his secrets...

In his first book since leaving office, America's 44th president shares the valuable strategies he used in his tough-minded negotiations with congressional Republicans. Sample tips include:

- Make sure your opening bid gives everything important away, so that they'll realize you're serious about reaching agreement.
- Offer moderate proposals that everyone can get behind. If you're reasonable enough, they'll have to see your point of view.
- Conceding instantly will "surprise" the opposing party, giving you a tactical advantage.
- Emphasize that all parties have the same interests by adopting major parts of the opposing party's position.
- Appeal to their sense of moral decency. This is almost always effective.

NEGOTIATION
The Obama Way
Barack H. Obama

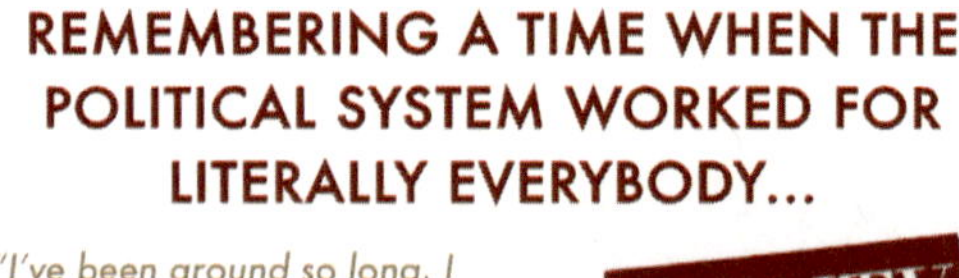

REMEMBERING A TIME WHEN THE POLITICAL SYSTEM WORKED FOR LITERALLY EVERYBODY...

"I've been around so long, I worked with [Mississippi segregationist Senator] James Eastland... Even in the days when I got there, the Democratic Party still had seven or eight old-fashioned Democratic segregationists. You'd get up and you'd argue like the devil with them. Then you'd go down and have lunch or dinner together. The political system worked. We were divided on issues, but the political system worked." – JOE BIDEN

In **Civility: A Memoir of the Senate's Glory Years**, Joe Biden looks back fondly on his time as a U.S. senator. It was a less divided era, when just because someone was a Klansman didn't mean you couldn't be his golfing buddy. Filled with warm reflections on such colorful figures as Jesse Helms and Strom Thurmond, Biden laments the partisanship and division that followed from desegregation.

"I HAVE A DREAM THAT ONE DAY MY FOUR LITTLE CHILDREN WILL BE JUDGED NOT BY THE COLOR OF THEIR SKIN BUT BY THE CONTENT OF THEIR PORTFOLIOS."

FINALLY, KING THE MARTYR...

"Justice is really just another word for efficiency, and social movements are about innovation. MLK was disrupting racism, and I'm doing the same for high-speed private transit systems." — ELON MUSK

"Nobody knew the meaning of growth better than MLK. He was the 'king' of effective organizing strategies." — LARRY SUMMERS

"Business is the art of persuasion—the Civil Rights Movement persuaded America to adopt a whole new paradigm. Entrepreneurs can learn from that." — PETER THIEL

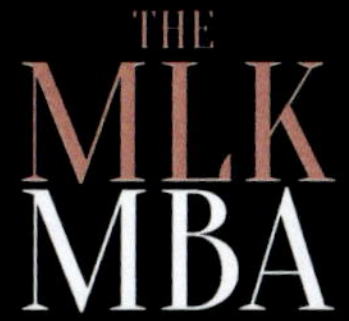

"IMAGINE THE CIVIL RIGHTS MOVEMENT AS A STARTUP"

...BECOMES KING THE ENTREPRENEUR

HISTORY'S VILLAINS REDEEMED...

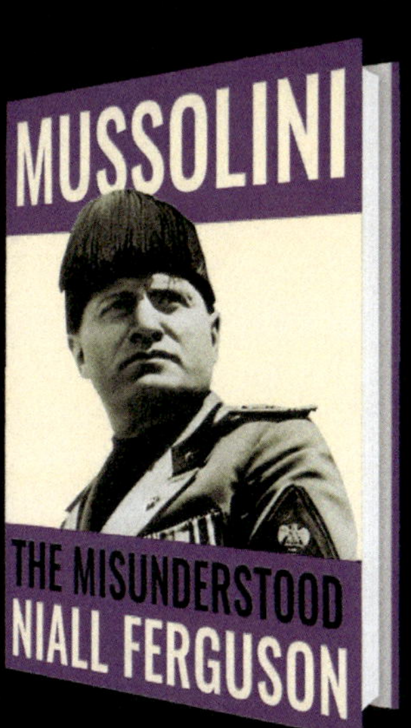

"Professor Ferguson refuses to let political correctness get in the way of scholarly integrity. He dares to ask the questions nobody else is asking, like 'Aren't bloodthirsy amorality and humanistic compassion kind of the same thing when you really think about it?'" —DAVID IRVING

RESPECTABLE ACADEMIC PRESS

SOCIALISM ON THE AIR
QUALITY LEFT BROADCASTING
from the editors of
CURRENT AFFAIRS
comes an hour of
RADIO DELIGHT
Briahna Joy Gray, Contributing Editor
Sparky Abraham, Financial Editor
Vanessa A. Bee, Social Media Editor
Nathan J. Robinson, Editor in Chief
Lyta Gold, Amusements Editor
PRESENTING
A PODCAST
ON POLITICS
that is actually listenable!
Pete Davis, Host & Producer
Brianna Rennix, Senior Editor
Oren Nimni, Legal Editor
funded exclusively by LISTENERS LIKE YOU

THE RIP-ROARING ADVENTURES OF
RED ROSE
SOCIALIST ADVENTURESS
FEATURING LUCY!
HEAR IT ON THE CURRENT AFFAIRS PODCAST
OUR HEROINES TAKE ON:
NAZI CEPHALOPODS
MOST MEN
ART DEALERS
CORRUPT COPS
THE BOURGEOISIE
WCAR

bird cafe
"just an absolutely horrible idea"™
MEE MEE ME ME ME
PLOT!
KOO KOO KOO KOO KOO KOO KA KA KA KA KA
BUUUURRRRRRR!!
HOOOT
CA CAW CA CAW
HOO HOO HOO
PIRATE CLUB
I ♡ BYRDS

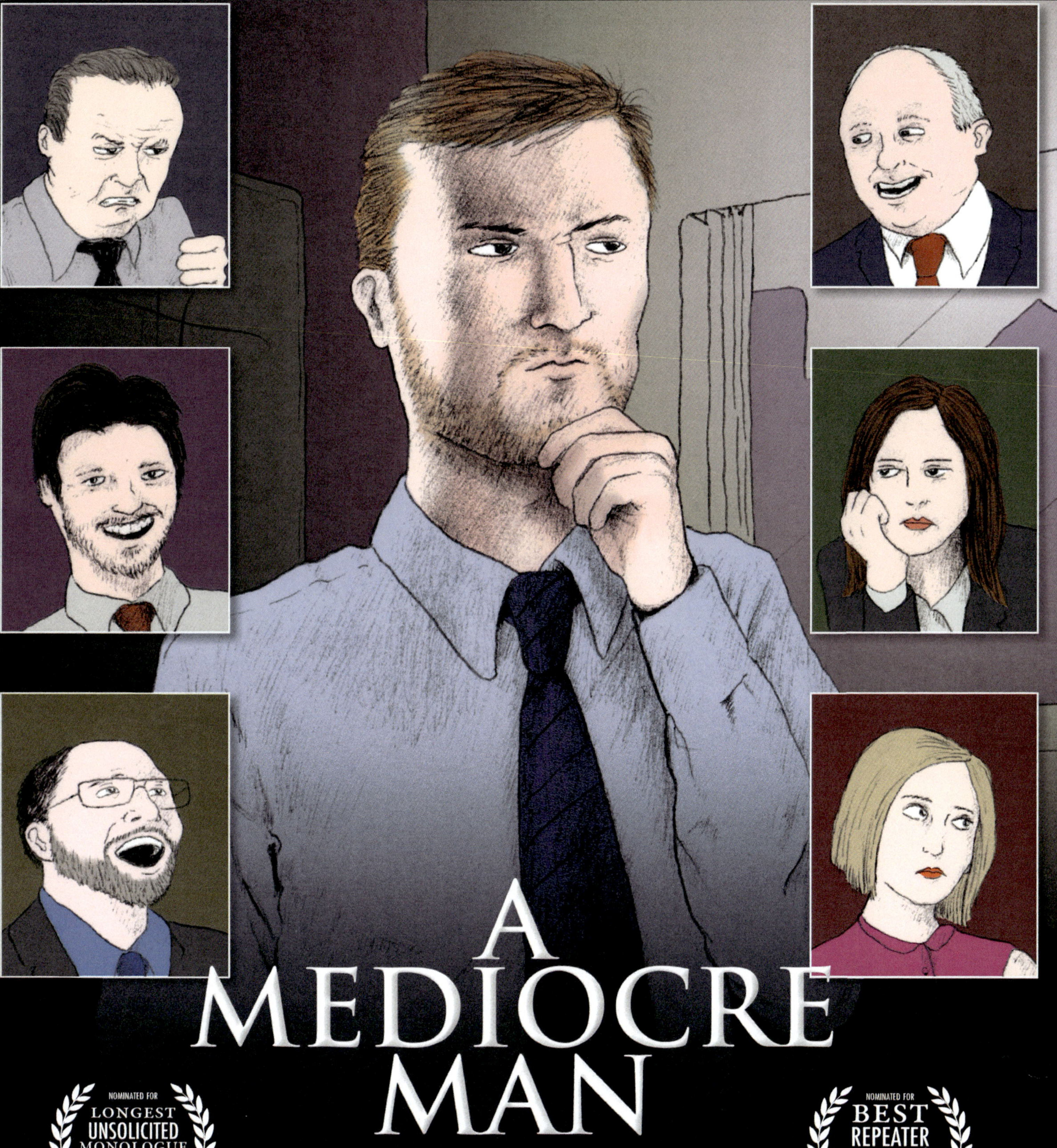
A MEDIOCRE MAN
NOMINATED FOR LONGEST UNSOLICITED MONOLOGUE
NOMINATED FOR BEST REPEATER OF SUSAN'S IDEAS
A HERO FOR OUR TIMES...
ACCURATE STEREOTYPE PICTURES PRESENTS A CANNESBAIT PRODUCTION FEATURING THE PERFORMING TALENTS OF MATTHEW MUSSBENDER AND HENRY HAY LOOMIS AND OSWALD ISAIAH AND JACK GOLIFINIKAS ALONG WITH MICHAEL MCDONAUGHEY
AND UNDERPAID FEMALE COSTARS TEESE REATHERSPOON AND JANUARY LEWIS DIRECTED BY MELVIN SCORMESE PRODUCED BY BARNEY WEINTRAUB SPECIAL EFFECTS BY STARVATION STUDIOS
NOW PLAYING
IN YOUR OFFICE, FROM 9–4:59, MONDAY THROUGH FRIDAY

Greetings
from
New Jersey
Don't bother coming!

When your self-driving car decides to kill you...

you'll need insurance.

We value your life. But your car doesn't necessarily feel the same way.

Whether it's four elderly ladies carrying their shopping or two baby Einsteins that have wandered into the road, sooner or later your GPS' on-board morality algorithm will determine that the lives of others outweigh the value of your own. And when the inevitable happens, you'll want to make sure your family receives mathematically optimal financial compensation for your life.

EFFICINSURANCE

insuring the maximally efficient allocation of misery

ISN'T IT SOMEWHAT

STRANGE

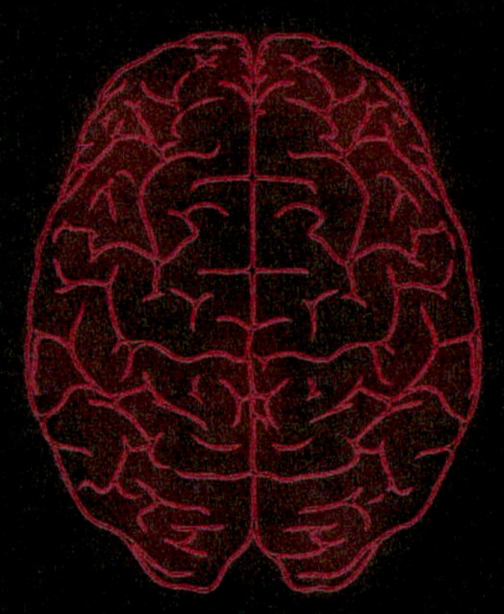

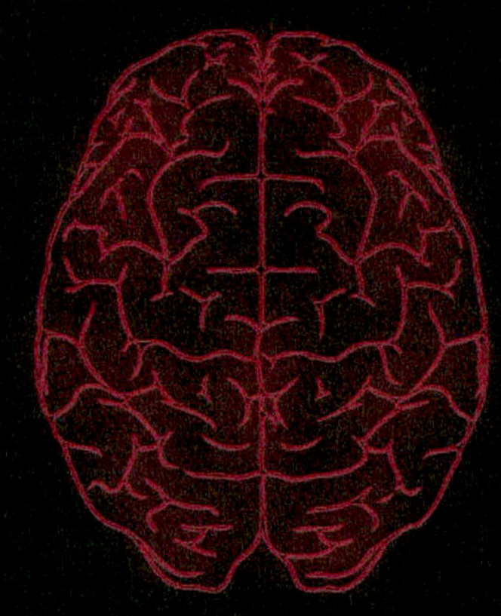

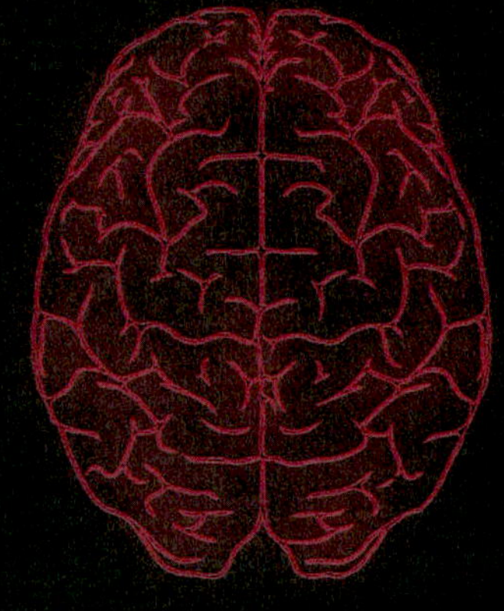

THAT EVERYONE ELSE IS EXPERIENCING CONSCIOUSNESS JUST LIKE YOU ARE?

a message from

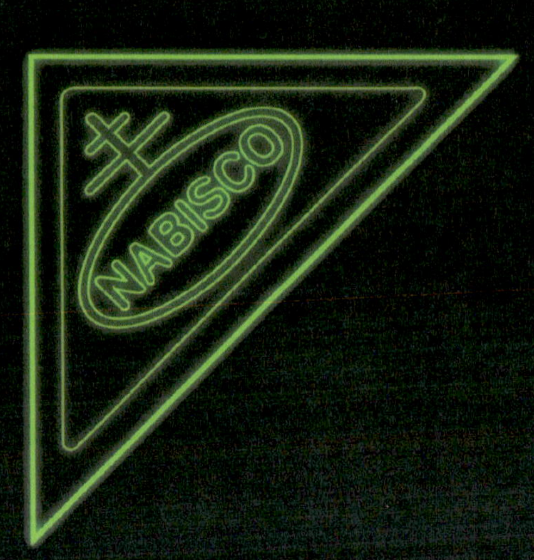

"MANY IN THE SOUTH ONCE BELIEVED THAT SLAVERY WAS A MORAL AND POLITICAL EVIL. THAT FOLLY AND DELUSION ARE GONE."

— J.C. CALHOUN

CALHOUN

THE JOHN C. CALHOUN MUSICAL

Today, John C. Calhoun is best known for his rousing defenses of slavery. But Calhoun was so much more. CALHOUN is a fictionalized reimagining of the 19th-century statesman's life, portraying him as a poor Haitian immigrant who aspired to nothing more than the achievement of the American success story. In this follow-up to his award-winning HAMILTON, MacArthur Genius Grant winner Lan-Minuel Merenga lets Americans look at Calhoun through fresh eyes. It's Calhoun like you've never seen him before!

DON'T LET
YOUR CHILDREN
GROW UP TO BE
LITERARY
THEORISTS
"Well, your first mistake is talking about
what Dickens was 'trying' to do. There's
a thing called The Death of the Author.
You probably haven't heard of it, but
it's similar to Nietzsche's Death of God.
Have you ever read Nietzsche?"
Ad
Council

HAVE YOU EVER WANTED TO BE TRULY FREE

"Well, sailor, now you can!"

Thanks to a new technique, absolute human liberty is finally within reach. Be the first to try it and **ASTONISH YOUR FRIENDS**

CUT THIS OUT AND
EXPERIENCE
the joy of true freedom

There is a **SENSATION** known as "the pleasure of being the cause," in which human beings experience joy at discovering that their actions can affect the world around them. By **CUTTING OUT** this paper rectangle, you, too, can feel as if you have affected physical reality through **YOUR ACTIONS.**

JFK WAS NOT AS GOOD OF A PRESIDENT AS YOU THINK
FIND OUT WHY
Send $2.50 to: OVERRATED JFK P.O. Box 441894 Somerville, MA

ALL THE HAPPENING STYLES
- POMPADOURS
- BOUFFANTS
- CONGOLENES
- TONSURES

HAIR-U-BET
For your FREE bag of hair, come to: 1 Market St. San Francisco, CA 94101

EVADE DEATH
BUY SKULLS

body by HARIBO

SIDE HUSTLES ARE NIFTY
FOR THE ENTERPRISING FELLOW WHOSE OTHER JOB PAYS
$3.25 AN HOUR

JOIN THE CLASS SNUGGLE

99¢ CRUDE REMARKS FOR ALL OCCASIONS

A NEW CONSTITUTION
TIRED OF THAT SAME OLD MUSTY FOUNDATIONAL DOCUMENT?
GET ONE WITH **PIZZAZZ**
ALSO WITHOUT RACISM

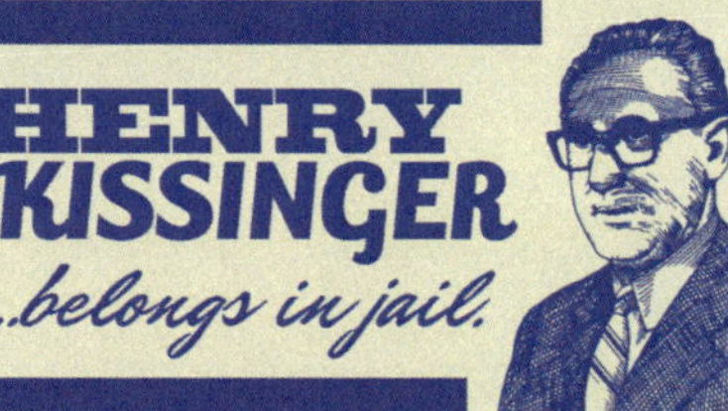

HENRY KISSINGER
...belongs in jail.

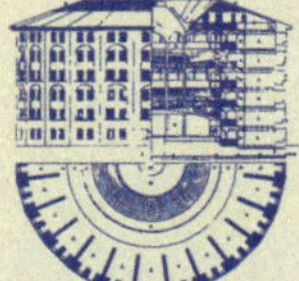

BUILD YOUR OWN
PANOPTICON
Never lose track of a friend!

BLUES
Bad case of the blues?
Can't get rid of them?
They crawling on you?
You gotta call
NEK'S BLUES EXTERMINATORS
(641)-543-3745 ◆ WARREN, MI

CHOMSKY REFERENCES
Does your writing contain enough references to the collected works of Noam Chomsky? If not, let Current Affairs know.
WE CAN HELP

Otter Rental
CALL FOR PRICES

FORTUNES TOLD
THEY ARE NOT ESPECIALLY PROMISING.
Spoiler: YOU WILL DIE.

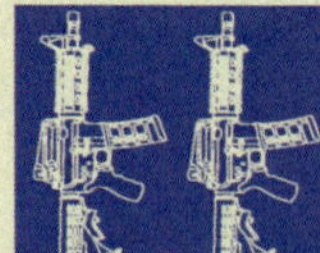

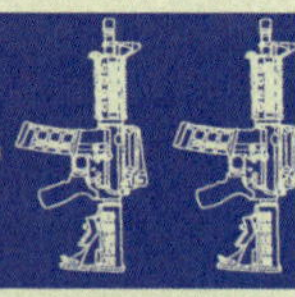

FOR SALE
GUNS, LOTS OF THEM.
Ask Wayne for details.
800-672-3888

FACTS ABOUT LIBERTARIAN SOCIALISM
- Ⓐ IN FAVOR OF INDIVIDUAL FREEDOM AND VOLUNTARY HUMAN RELATIONSHIPS
- Ⓐ OPPOSED TO CENTRALIZED AUTHORITY AND COERCIVE INSTITUTIONS
- Ⓐ VERY FUN Ⓐ Ⓐ Ⓐ Ⓐ Ⓐ Ⓐ

PROPER CHILD HANDLING IS INCREASINGLY CRUCIAL

ALWAYS PICK UP INFANTS USING APPROVED TECHNIQUES
AMA AMERICAN MEDICAL ASSOCIATION

Call Current Affairs at
504-867-8851
and tell us what's on your mind

PROFESSOR KERBLE'S
"MAGICK"
Body-Camera Lens
"Keeps all manner of mischief and state-sanctioned tomfoolery where it belongs—in the dark!"
ONLY **$42,000.42** FROM YOUR LOCAL MILITARY-GRADE ARMS CONTRACTOR

always ask yourself
W.W.B.F.D.
what would buckminster fuller do?

how many cravats IS 'TOO MANY' CRAVATS?

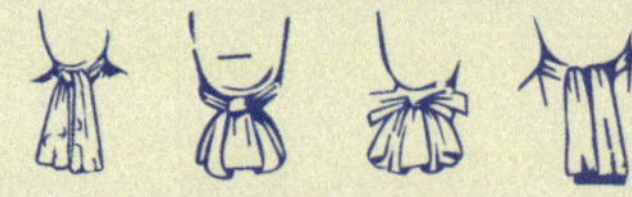

Can we ever know for sure?

THE CURRENT AFFAIRS
SECRET
Waffle Recipe

Wouldn't you like to know?

MAIL ORDER AFFAIRS ☞ **ORDER YOUR OWN MAGAZINES** ☜ **MAIL ORDER AFFAIRS**
SEND MONEY AND RECEIVE WORDS

THANK YOU for considering purchasing one or more subscriptions to "Current Affairs," the magazine that coffee tables love. We hope to provide you with a product that produces less pain and regret than the next leading brand.

PLEASE BE AWARE that the editors cannot be held responsible for any seditious or libelous content found within the pages of the publication. All content is produced by proprietary algorithms and is in no way the product of human intentionality or reason. Objections to the thesis statements of our articles are futile. To argue with *Current Affairs* is akin to cursing at a river of molten lava for having the gall to melt one's childhood home. It may be satisfying. But it is ultimately of no use and mistakes the cause of one's suffering. The fault is not in your subscriptions but in yourself.

WILL THERE BE CAKE? Cake will be served, weather permitting, at the discretion of the editor upon the completion of the next edition.

NO REFUNDS will be provided under any circumstances to irate or dissatisfied customers, though we reserve the right to impose additional charges for any time spent explaining our refund policy.

NEPOTISM WILL BE FROWNED UPON and instead of purchasing subscriptions for family members, we recommend that the generously-disposed among our readership give subscriptions to down-on-their-luck strangers instead. We reserve the right to reject any subscriber for poor moral character.

Qty.	Description of Requested Items.	Justification for Request.	List Price.

Please allow up to 400 weeks for delivery. A small percentage of order forms may be incinerated rather than fulfilled. We regret the multitude of inconveniences that inevitably follows from placing an order with our company. Let there be no doubt that our intentions are pure even when our competence is minimal.

NAME.......... SOCIAL CLASS.......... INCOME.......... ANIMAL..........
STREET ADDRESS.......... TERRITORY.......... RELATIONSHIP TO THE ABOVE..........
PREFERRED POSTAL WORKER.......... FAVORITE BEATLE.......... FLOWERS (Y/N)..........

Lawyers (add 20%)........		
Depressed (-10%)........		
Moms (-10%)........		
Student (add $4)........		
Have A Dog (-$2)........		

SUBTOTAL
☞ ADDITIONAL PENALTIES
PAY THIS.

CURRENT AFFAIRS, INC. BEARS NO RESPONSIBILITY FOR FRAUDULENT PRODUCTS OR SERVICES FOUND IN THESE PAGES

THE CURRENT AFFAIRS™
"BIG BOOK OF AMUSEMENTS"

Diagrams & Dioramas

Welcome To Your 21st Century Campus!
100% GREEN* ENERGY**
DORM BROUGHT TO YOU BY BP
PETER THIEL SCHOOL OF ANTI-JOURNALISM
THE NORTHROP GRUMMAN SCHOOL OF APPLIED ADVANCEMENTS IN WEAPONRY
BUSY? STRESSED? FEEL LIKE YOU'RE STRIVING TOWARD AN IMPOSSIBLE FUTURE, AND IF YOU'RE NOT ONE OF THE LUCKY FEW WHO MAKES IT YOU'LL PROBABLY STARVE TO DEATH? TRY – ADDERALL!
JOIN THE NSA

Oh my gosh, you're here! And paying 60k a year! Forgive the rhyme: That's poetry, which we no longer offer. At the 21st-Century University, we prefer to focus on inculcating students with lucrative, practical skills such as "learning to code in a programming language that may or not immediately become obsolete" and "how to brand and sell yourself, and how to remain entirely unaware of the history and connotations of these terms." Sounds great, right? Totally stressed out, huh? Feeling utterly destroyed by student loans and the shivering uncertainty of your future? Well, pop on down to the Office of Financial Aid and Debt Anxiety (not pictured, you'll have to find it by yourself, lazybones!) and help yourself to a free Xanax lollipop!
OFFICE OF THE VICE PROVOST IV
OFFICE OF THE VICE PROVOST III
OF THE VICE PROVOST II
OFFICE OF THE VICE PROVOST
MAJORING IN THE HUMANITIES? LOL
HENRY KISSINGER SCHOOL OF POLITICAL SCIENCE
BEAT CTE STATE!
ET CUPIDITAS
JEFF BEZOS LEARNING FULFILLMENT CENTER

THE UTOPIAN CITY

The editors of *Current Affairs* have built you a city. We hope you like it! When you're done, try building your own. In the meantime, see if you can find the following: **1.** Cottages, available to all through housing lotto. **2.** Enchanted forest filled with creatures. **3.** Secret rooftop chess club, but with friendly players and also plenty of people who are just as bad at it as you. **4.** Roof gardens. **5.** Personal miniature zeppelins that operate similarly to Zipcars but do not cost money. **6.** Lazy river public transit system. **7.** Universities that have been abolished since knowledge is a fundamental part of everyone's life and is not housed in particular isolated places. **8.** Planetarium. Yes, there is Laser Pink Floyd, but there are also other shows that are mesmerizing. **9.** Tennis courts. We do not like tennis, but some people do, and all tastes should be accommodated. **10.** Hot tubs with very pleasant bubbles. **11.** M.C. Escher slide. This is just one small example of the many elaborate types of slides that will exist. Most structural engineers will be focused full-time on slide development. **12.** A soundproof poetry chamber where poets can read their work to one another without anybody else having to be exposed. **13.** Art wall. **14.** Lego building chamber with every brick. **15.** Mosques and cathedrals but mostly just because they're beautiful rather than because people are especially religious. **16.** Rooftop dog bar. **17.** Picnic area with campfire and marshmallows. **18.** Children's playground with actual fun elaborate playground equipment. **19.** Adult playground with defunct military equipment on springs.

If a school does not have animals, can it really call itself a school?
The library is well-stocked and attractive.
BE YOUR BEST
Children learn best when they get to set off explosions.
WIR GLAUBEN AN DICH
FREE
Counseling is always available.
YOU ARE LOVED
BE A LEGEND
YOU ARE THE FUTURE
The food is known for being edible, even scrumptious.
Cats roam freely.
Interestingly shaped playground equipment scattered throughout stimulate imaginative adventures.
Games in the garden amid the berry bushes are a common pursuit.

Athletics are popular but not required.
The theater budget is generous enough to allow elaborate productions.
There is a waterfall, good for contemplation.
LOVE
DO IT
KEEP GOING
We learn about nature by going to visit it.
Fountains are important.
Every department is well-equipped.
Sliding down the rails is actively encouraged.
Bean bags are extremely comfortable and children must be comfortable.
Soft carpeting throughout.
Students and teachers are considered equals and run the school together.
A PERFECT SCHOOL
THE KIND EVERY CHILD SHOULD BE GUARANTEED.

CIRCLES OF HELL
MINOR ANNOYANCES
MISOGYNISTS + SEXUAL HARASSERS
LACK OF COMPASSION
GREED
WRATH
HERESY + HYPOCRISY
VIOLENCE
FRAUD
TREACHERY
NON-CURRENT AFFAIRS PUBLICATIONS
PEOPLE WHO COMPLAIN ABOUT BEING "PILLORIED" BY THE COURT OF PUBLIC OPINION
CATCALLERS
WELCOME TO THE VILLAGE OF UNFAMOUSNESS
MEN WHO SAY WOMEN AREN'T FUNNY
GUILTY OF JAYWALKING
TMZ REPORTERS
ANYONE WHO HAS EVER SAID, "WELL I'M A LAW-ABIDING CITIZEN!"
KOCH BROTHERS
WE ♥ GREEN ENERGY
JEFF BEZOS
F*CK YOU, DIBLASIO
TRUMP
CUOMO X-ING
SUPER RICH DOOMSDAY PREPPERS
MENU FREEZE DRIED GRUEL
MARXIST CLUB
POLICE OFFICERS
COMMUNITY SERVICE
SUBPRIME MORTGAGE LENDERS AND THE POLITICIANS WHO BAILED THEM OUT
ICE AGENTS
ICE
CORRUPT CLERGY

NOBELS + PULITZERS
PHILLIP ROTH
NORMAN MAILER
HENRY MILLER
"GENIUS" MALE NOVELISTS
SMUG ACADEMICS
CENTRIST COMMENTATORS
PUBLISH CENTRISTS
WHERE YOUR WORK GOES TO DIE
Limbo Times
PUBLISH US NOW!
AVITAL RONELL
CHARLIE ROSE
LOUIS C.K.
#METOO HARASSERS
OBNOXIOUS YOUTUBE PERSONALITIES
PEOPLE WHO POINTEDLY IGNORE THE HOMELESS
ALEX JONES
THE TEXAS BOARD OF PRISONS OFFICIAL WHO REFUSED TO GRANT CURRENT AFFAIRS A PRESS PASS TO SEE A DEATH ROW INMATE BECAUSE WE WEREN'T ON A LIST OF APPROVED MAGAZINES THAT HAD BEEN MADE IN 1996
FREE MEDS FOR ALL
NFL
INTERNET WHITE SUPREMACISTS
PHARMACEUTICAL COMPANY CEOs
NFL TEAM OWNERS
BOSSES WHO SCREAM AT EMPLOYEES
"LIBERAL" WRITERS WHO WANT MORE CONSERVATIVE VOICES ON CAMPUS BUT NOT SOCIALIST VOICES
JUDGES WHO PRETEND TO BE "CONSTITUTIONAL ORIGINALISTS" BUT REALLY JUST HATE WOMEN, PEOPLE OF COLOR, AND THE WORKING CLASS
TERFS
PEOPLE WHO YELL AT CUSTOMER SERVICE REPS
WOMEN WHO DON'T SUPPORT OTHER WOMEN
HENRY KISSINGER
THE KKK
RAPISTS
STUDENT LOAN SERVICERS
ROBOCALLER PROGRAMMERS
DOWN WITH CAPITALISM
WE LOVE SOCIALISM
MARX
NTRAL AFRICA
LATIN AMERICA
IRAN
CIA
LIVE FEED OF INNER THOUGHTS
FBI/NSA
SCAMMERS WHO TARGET THE ELDERLY AND THE MENTALLY ILL

4
3
5
6
2
1

Our New MONUMENTS

WE ALL KNOW THE CONFEDERATE STATUES NEEDED TO COME DOWN. BUT WHAT WILL GO IN THEIR PLACE? A FEW IDEAS FOR WHOM WE SHOULD HONOR INSTEAD:

1. Tomb Of The Unknown Blues Singer—in honor of the zillions of musicians who wrote songs that became hits but never saw any royalties.

2. Monument to the Iraqi Man Who Threw His Shoes at President Bush

3. Tribute to the Great American Sanitation Worker

4. Battle of Noel Hill—the final struggle in the War on Christmas. 950,000 brave soldiers sacrificed their lives to defeat Christmas once and for all.

5. Bree Newsome—who took direct action in South Carolina, ascending the flag pole outside the capitol to personally rip down the Stars and Bars.

6. Tribute to Underappreciated Elderly People

7. Bureaucrats Who Have Defied Orders In Order To Save Lives—to those who don't care what the judge says...

8. The Anonymous Twitter Employee Who Suspended Trump's Account For Ten Minutes

9. Bees—just to thank them for all their hard work...

10. Exasperated Women of History—to every woman who has ever had to sit through an explanation of something she already understands...

WELCO
TO
WOKEL
Walmart
THE INTERNET ALLY'S HOUSE OF MIRRORS
See only the marginalized people who coincidentally agree with everything you say!
"Ladies and gents, maggots and minions, creditors and credulous—welcome, one and all, to the carnival that not only takes your cash but pats you on the back while doing so! Welcome to Wokeland!"
MONSANTO
THE CENTRIST CENTRIFUGE
?
It spins around endlessly, yet somehow keeps drifting further right!
LOCKHEED MARTIN
CAN YOU BOMB A BROWN COUNTRY?
America is great because America is good!

ME
AND
KER UP TO A POLITICIAN
OF YOUR CHOICE!
WE SUPPORT COMMUNITIES BUT
WE'RE TOUGH ON CRIME
Once You Get On, You Can't Get Off
Coca-Cola
Nestle
WITNESS THE DREADE
BERNIE BRO
She's a woman, but she favors mandatory life sentences for jaywalkers!
He's black, but he supports the Hyde Amendment!
What in the actual fuck is wrong with you people?
Don't look at him! His whiteness will blind you!
White men like you ought to be ashamed of yourselves!
ExxonMobil
FEMCOPS: THE BEST COPS
Come watch Ophelia Gwinn, the legendary lady prosecutor, as she fires blanks at bad guys! That's right— she's a woman, AND she's kicking ass!
That's right, folks, step right up, she's a dead shot. Women can do anything men can do, and better!
Haha! This prisoner appears to have wet himself! If you call this torture, you're a misogynist!
The prisoners don't know the bullets are blanks!

OUR WORKPLACE

- Sleeping nooks
- Comfy chairs
- Reasonable hours (10-3)
- Fireplaces
- Cats
- Fountains
- Bathrooms like palaces
- Dog boss
- Candy room
- Company umbrellas for when you forget yours
- Supply of comical hats
- Dumbwaiter with "surprise snacks"
- Extensive library
- Pneumatic tube messaging system
- Colorful plants
- Roombas do the hard stuff
- "Anything goes" dress code (within reason)
- Actual good art
- Growlery

THEIR WORKPLACE

- Brutalist architecture
- Single dying fern
- All actions must serve the Brand
- Mandatory tattoos of the company logo
- Efficiency Monitoring Headgear for all employees
- Bathroom breaks prohibited—Company Catheters siphon pee and send to the central centrifuge
- Pyramidal management structure
- Constant surveillance by imbecilic busybodies
- A central screen displays each employee's productivity in real time, along with their risk of being fired
- Mandatory Reporting of All Brand Unfriendliness
- Spreadsheets galore
- Shaming booths
- "Business Casual"
- Intern pit
- Sleeping tubes

THE BRAND
SHUT UP
THE BRAND
THE BRAND
THE BRAND
THE BRAND
SMILE
WORK BETTER
THE BRAND
SMILE
DONT FORGET YOUR NDA
SHAMING IN SESSION
BREAK ROOM
PIT OF TOO MANY MISTAKES
BRAND

THE CAMPUS
AS IT EXISTS IN THE MIND OF A U.S. CONSERVATIVE
TITLE IX
DEPARTMENT OF
BIOLOGY
INTERSECTIONALITY
CLASSICS DEPARTMENT
LET'S GO
SOCIAL JUSTICE
OPPRESSION OLYMP CS
SJW
PETA
Consent Forms
HUG
KISS
KARL MARX
EVENTS
INTERFAITH ORGY
CREATE YOUR OWN PRONOUNS PARTY
FRESHMAN FORMAL
THEME: FREEZE SPEECH
CLUB
1PM–2PM
MAO ZEDONG
FEELINGS > FACTS
EEP IT PC
LEASE!
TOLERANCE IS
Forgive us!
I'm sorry for being white!

CUCK·ZONE
BAR
FREE PALESTINE
DINING HALL
Tofu Burgers
Quinoa Shakes
Ancient Grains
L G B T Q +
Tolerantia
The University of
RADICAL FEMINIST PRAXIS
WHITE TEARS LIVE STREAM
PRONOUN POLICE
Next time say "they/them!"
BURKAS + THONGS
FREE WEED
FREE LUBE + CONDOMS
FREE!
#420
COLLEGE OF GRIEVANCE STUDIES
Smashing the Patriarchy 101
Microaggressions
PRIVILEGE CHECK
GIVE CONSERVATIVES A PLATFORM
YOU'RE SPECIAL
KNOW YOUR GENDERS
FRIENDLY REMINDER:
IT'S NOT OK TO BE WHITE
NO H8

The 21st Century LUXURY HOME

BEDROOM – with sweeping views!

GARAGE – with sweeping views!

CRAWL SPACE – with sweeping views!

KITCHEN – with sweeping household staff!

HEATED TIBETAN SALT LICK – it's simply not a wholesome home unless you have a Heated Tibetan Salt Lick in your kitchen

ARTISANAL FAMILY – have your own family of charming rustics living inside your home in an authentic 19th-century farmer's cottage they can't escape

DOG'S ROOM

DOG BUTLER'S ROOM

DECOY SECRET BUNKER – for when your domestic staff turns on you

ACTUAL SECRET BUNKER – for when your domestic staff discovers the decoy secret bunker

SERVANT PODS – pneumatic tubes summon the servants when you need them

STOCK TICKER – also tracks how much you love your children, as represented by how much they're getting in your will

SOUNDPROOF SCREAMING ROOM – for when possessing outrageous wealth in the face of vast human suffering and inequality has left you feeling "discordant"

BONNIE AND CLYDE ADVENTURE SPACE – an entire replica of an early 20th-century street! You can dress up as Bonnie and Clyde and pretend to rob banks, and then pretend to make your getaway in real cars. It's so Americana!

INFINITY POOL – with "live" dolphins!

ETERNITY LIBRARY

MODULAR APARTMENTS – for children from marriages with less-favored ex-spouses that can be jetissioned if one becomes a Bernie supporter or something

SECRET LAIR – from which you can program satellites to shoot lasers at journalists who make fun of you

GIRL'S BEDROOM – featuring unicorn farm with real living unicorns

MASTER BEDROOM – bed made from real living peacocks!

GOOSE FATTENING LAB – for personalized foie gras

EXTRA SWIMMING POOL – inside a living room inside a swimming pool

FULLY ARMED GUARD DRONES – and drone garage

ENDANGERED FAUNA PREPARATION ROOM – your very own exotic animal abattoir

TRANSPARENT BATHROOM – bath of virgins' blood, 100% organic and certified by the Immortality Board of Greater San Francisco. See-through toilet and storage tank/altar, so you can worship your own shit

PRIVATE LAUNCHPAD – for the rocket that will take you to Mars when environmental catastrophe strikes. There's only room for family and your more favored servants

MARS ONE
EJECT
VOTE BERNIE
HOME SWEET HOME

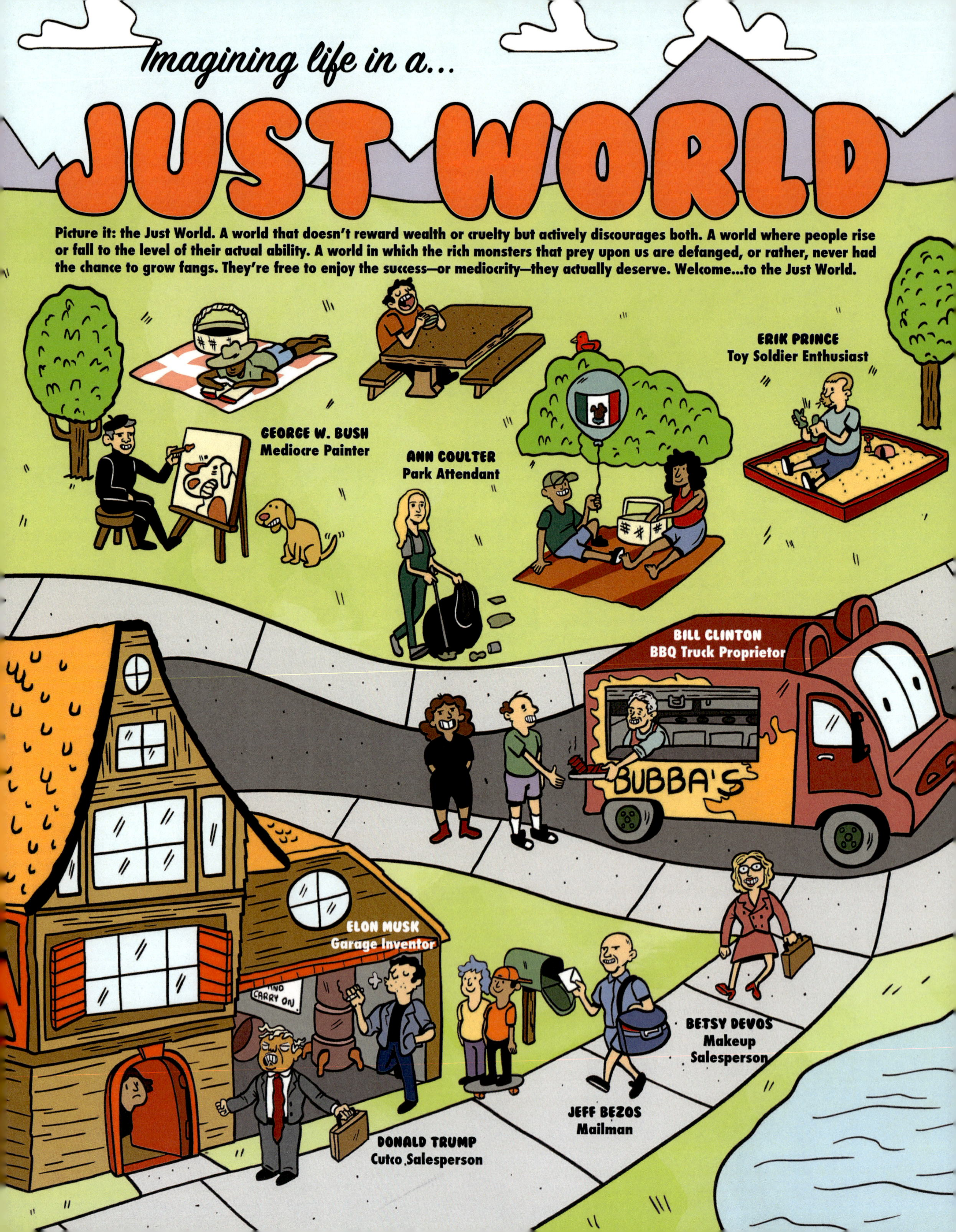

Imagining life in a...
JUST WORLD
Picture it: the Just World. A world that doesn't reward wealth or cruelty but actively discourages both. A world where people rise or fall to the level of their actual ability. A world in which the rich monsters that prey upon us are defanged, or rather, never had the chance to grow fangs. They're free to enjoy the success—or mediocrity—they actually deserve. Welcome...to the Just World.
ERIK PRINCE
Toy Soldier Enthusiast
GEORGE W. BUSH
Mediocre Painter
ANN COULTER
Park Attendant
BILL CLINTON
BBQ Truck Proprietor
BUBBA'S
ELON MUSK
Garage Inventor
CARRY ON
BETSY DEVOS
Makeup Salesperson
JEFF BEZOS
Mailman
DONALD TRUMP
Cutco Salesperson

DAVOS
Public Playground & Resource Center
WE'RE SO CONNECTED
THOMAS FRIEDMAN
Bicycle Messenger
TRAVIS KALANICK
Bus Driver
MEGAN MCARDLE
Building Safety Inspector
ROSA LUXEMBURG HIGH
BILL GATES
Math Teacher
HISTORY
DEBAT
FRANCIS FUKUYAMA
History Teacher
HILLARY CLINTON
Girls' Debate Team Coach
TINY ISLANDS FOR THE PEOPLE THAT NOTHING COULD BE DONE ABOUT IN ANY UNIVERSE
RUPERT MURDOCH
PETER THIEL
HENRY KISSINGER
HARVEY WEINSTEIN
P.A.

TROLLING THE ALT-RIGHT

"'I had to fire the maid. She knocked over my limited edition gold-plated Millennium Falcon.' The young man stares down at the floor, where the Millennium Falcon lies broken in the dust. A tear escapes one pale, guileless eye. 'It was my most important possession.'

Suddenly, he glances up. This youthful white supremacist is neatly dressed and college-educated, hardly the rabid redneck one might have expected. This boy could be anybody's son, really. He says: 'The maid was a fucking immigrant, you know. That's the problem.'

I ask him to clarify. Does he believe that immigrants are coming to this country for the sole purpose of knocking over our knickknacks?

"Not knicknacks! LIMITED. EDITION. GOLD-PLATED. MILLENNIUM. FALCON! You don't understand! No one understands! That wasn't just a toy! My soul is in these objects! Without pop-culture signifiers," he sighs, "I don't know who I really am."

Your reaction to this interview is...

Pure sympathy. He's just a misunderstood kid! You pat him on the head.

The ground opens beneath your feet. You fall into a subterranean chamber swarming with alt-righters in hooded robes. Reciting misogynist memes, they sacrifice you to their god, Kek the Unfunny.

Write yet another sympathetic profile.

A flicker of pity, followed by wave after wave of revulsion. You need to put a stop to this shit at once.

Watch these videos yourself until you go mad with reflected hate.

You ask: "How did you come by your political philosophy?"

"Oh, I read it online. Message boards, angry manifestos, bearded guys on YouTube, you know. All the collected brilliance of the era."

Interview the alt-righter yourself.

"I'm not part of the alt-right, but I'm willing to help you find someone who is."

You accompany the reporter through the tunnels. Finally, you enter a box apartment in a soulless new condo building. The place is scattered with video game consoles, Funko Pops, and unwashed plates.

Let the reporter conduct the interview.

Ask him to gather his favorite thinkers together.

You enter a gathering of alt-right luminaries. They're quarreling wildly among themselves over grievances you don't understand, like "insufficient Jew-hatred" and "being too Nazi/not Nazi enough in public." What do you do?

Troll them harder.

You promise the alt-righters the ultimate gaming experience: an immersive, no-holds-barred, final battle to the death against a vicious, unmerciful enemy bent on destroying civilization. The alt-righters are thrilled! You tell them the game is waiting in a cave just up ahead.

When they're inside, you seal the cave entrance. Soon, you hear the unmistakable sounds of the alt-righters tearing each other to pieces. Cruel? Yes. But then, irony is always cruel.

Troll them.

You shout: "Run! Antifa's coming!"

Ducking aside to avoid the stampede, you laugh as these would-be Heroes of the West scream and trample each other in their haste to escape the dreaded Antifa. As they fade into the distance, you hear a last wail of "freeee speeeech."

Make them obsolete.

You can't eliminate the alt-right, but you can stop their ideas from gaining traction by endorsing socialist economic policies which will reduce the winner-take-all conditions and social isolation necessary for the virulent spread of white nationalist ideology.

Hit them.

You punch every single last one of them in the face. Effective? Nah. Satisfying? Hell yes.

CHOOSE YOUR OWN ADVENTURE

BEGIN HERE

WARNING!!! You are about to enter the Labyrinth of the Alt-Right, the lair of the internet's most disturbing denizens. Are you prepared? The alt-right is extremely fucking irritating and, at times, physically dangerous. You'll have to keep hold of your wits, your courage, and your firm belief in justice and equality. Can you handle it? Are you sure you want to proceed?

You run away and look at cute fennec photos. No one blames you.

What the hell. You enter the Labyrinth of the Alt-Right.

Immediately, you're set upon by sniveling trolls. They look human. In fact, it's their humanity that makes them so monstrous. They're human beings who have dedicated their entire lives to hating other human beings.

Without preamble, one of the trolls whines: "Goooo no further! You cannot proceed until you tell us your haplogroup!"

"You shall not pass," snickers another. "That's a meme!"

Don't feed the trolls.

It doesn't seem like a good idea to engage with these jerks. You're starting to regret entering the labyrinth in the first place. What exactly did you hope to accomplish? These alt-right trolls are disgusting and deeply stupid.

Give up. The fennecs are calling.

Continue on your nightmare journey.

Sigh, and respond.

Oops. Time to bail.

Consumed by despair and confusion, you turn a corner and run smack into somebody. By his bland, self-indulgent, self-satisfied demeanor you immediately recognize him as a *New York Times* reporter.

"Hello!" he says. "I'm here to profile the alt-right. Would you consider yourself a member of this tragically misunderstood subgroup?"

Lie.

"Yeah, uh, I'm a member of the alt-right. I'm not special, I don't have any particular talents, and I feel adrift in a chaotic, hypercompetitive, capitalist system. If I didn't believe in a rigid racial and sexual hierarchy, I would have nothing and be nobody."

You're being too obvious. "No, no, no!" cries the NYT reporter. "That's not what my readers want! They want to relate to a bigot without feeling personally implicated in the underlying causes of his bigotry!"

Oops. Tell the truth.

Tell the truth.

You say: "I can't believe I have to tell you this, but the term "haplogroup" doesn't have the significance you think it has. In biological terms, race doesn't exist."

The trolls draw back in outrage – then suddenly lunge forward in a Snowflake Attack. "Go back to your safe space!" they howl.

Retreat. Is talking to them even worthwhile? Why did you come here anyway?

Ew. You're covered in nerd brains. Is trolling the alt-right really worth the mess?

Fight back. You've had enough of their bullshit.

"Hey," you say, casually, "Did you hear that Hollywood's rebooting *The Matrix*?"

The trolls gasp in joy. "With an all-black, all-female cast!"

The trolls scream and writhe until they burst apart like angry overripe melons.

That wasn't exactly fun, but it was grimly satisfying. You must continue to fight the infection of the alt-right.

FIND YOUR WAY TO ASYLUM UNDER U.S. IMMIGRATION LAW

Immigration law is often thought of as complicated. Not so! Anyone can navigate the process. Here, *Current Affairs* Immigration Correspondent Brianna Rennix has constructed a simple flowchart to show how migrants can be granted asylum under U.S. law.

BEGIN HERE

You are a citizen of a Northern Triangle country in Central America. You have good reason to think your life is in danger, but the police won't do anything to help you. A lot of people you know have fled to the United States, where it's supposed to be safer. You decide to do the same.* How are you going to get there?

By going to the U.S. embassy and asking for asylum → That's not a thing.

By applying for a U.S. tourist visa → They will never, ever give you one.

By traveling through Mexico to the southern U.S. border → Do you have $10,000 to pay a smuggler?

No → Sorry, you're stuck.

I'll just travel solo! → If you're lucky, Mexican immigration will catch you. If you're unlucky, the Zetas will catch you, and, you know, decapitate you.

Yes → Would you rather approach via a Port of Entry or cross the Rio?

Rio → Are you feeling lucky?

No → A CBP officer catches you.

Port of Entry → You are now in expedited removal proceedings. Are you feeling lucky?

No → The officer gets you to sign a deportation order, or some other similar bullshit.

Sure → You successfully convey to the officer that you are afraid to return to your country. Are you feeling lucky?

Yes → The officer paroles you directly into the U.S. with a Notice to Appear in immigration court to fight your deportation order.*****

No → Are you trying to enter at the border with a child under 18?

No → You are put in an adult detention center. You will likely have limited to no access to legal counsel, unless you can hire an outside attorney. Eventually you should get a Credible Fear Interview. Are you feeling lucky?

No → You fail your credible fear interview. Technically you can appeal this decision, but without any legal assistance, your chance of success is virtually nil. You will now be deported.

Yes → You pass your credible fear interview and are issued a Notice to Appear in immigration court to fight your deportation order.

Yes → Are you the child's mother?

No, I'm the father or another relative → Your child is separated from you and put into a detention center or group home for unaccompanied minors.** Meanwhile...

Yes → You and your child are put in a family detention center. There'll probably be some legal volunteers here to help you while you're detained. Now comes your Credible Fear Interview. Are you feeling lucky?

Yes → You pass your credible fear interview and are issued a Notice to Appear in immigration court to fight your deportation order.

No → You fail your credible fear interview. A lawyer will help you file an appeal, but they can't argue for you at your hearing. How much does your judge trust the asylum office?

A lot → The judge upholds the asylum officer's determination. You and your child will now be deported.

Not much → The judge reverses the negative determination and...

Yes → This process will take approximately 10,000 years.

Yes (Rio: Are you feeling lucky?) → You manage to cross the border without being caught, and successfully make your way to your intended destination within the U.S. Do you want to go to the government and apply for asylum?

Seems safer to lie low / I have no idea what this process is → You don't submit an asylum application. Unfortunately, due to some bullshit*** like a traffic stop or a workplace raid, you come to the attention of the immigration authorities. Can you prove continuous residence in the U.S. for the past two years?

Wait, what? No. → You are now detained and in expedited removal proceedings.**** Are you feeling lucky?

Somehow, yes → You successfully convey to the officer that you are afraid to return to your country.

No, I'm not! → Well, you're probably going to be deported.

Yes → You are issued a Notice to Appear in immigration court to fight the deportation order against you. Has it been less than a year since you entered the U.S.?

No? → In all probability, the immigration judge will issue a final order of removal, unless (s)he decides to give you some weird discretionary form of relief. You'll be ordered deported.

Obviously not, since I just proved my continuous residence for the past two years → Do you have a lawyer? You'd best get one.

Yes (Do you want to apply for asylum?) → Has it been less than a year since you entered the U.S.?

No → Well, your asylum claim is time-barred unless you can prove that you qualify for a special exception. Can you get a lawyer?

Yes → Let's hope your lawyer can get you an exception.

No → Is your case strong otherwise?

I don't know → You might want to think carefully about applying. Your application, if denied, could ultimately lead to your deportation.

Never mind then. / I'll take my chances.

Yes → You file your application with Citizenship and Immigration Services. You have now applied affirmatively for asylum, which is, in theory, a non-adversarial process.

Now what? → Now we wait. For, like, two years, probably. The day of your interview comes - do you have a lawyer? Does the asylum officer look sympathetic and well-rested? Do the facts of your case fit easily into the legal standard?

Yes! → Hooray! You get asylum. Probably? Maybe. Yes.

The answer to one or all of these questions, alas, is no → Your asylum application is referred to an immigration court. You are now in deportation proceedings. Did you have that one year filing problem, by the way?

No → Okay: you attended all your court dates? You have a decent lawyer? The DHS attorney seems incompetent? The judge seems like they had a good breakfast? Your case is legally solid? You're not in, like, Atlanta or El Paso or some other crappy court?

Ffffffff → Do you have a lawyer? You'd best get one.

Wait, what? → Thankfully, I have private funds and/or have access to pro bono assistance → Okay: you attended all your court dates?...

I can't... → You can try to make an asylum claim, but it's time-barred. Is your asylum case watertight in all other respects?

Maybe? How would I even know that? → You might end up getting an alternate form of relief called Withholding of Removal. There's no path to a green card, you can't petition for relatives, and you can't travel outside the U.S. You may never see your loved ones ever again. Enjoy!

If your lawyer can satisfy a legal standard showing that you didn't apply during your first year due to "extraordinary" or "changed circumstances," you can make an asylum claim.

Yeah, the judge isn't buying it. → You might end up getting an alternate form of relief called Withholding of Removal.

The judge is satisfied → Okay: you attended all your court dates?...

Yes to all those things → Hooray, you got asylum, possibly!

Uh oh → Your claim is denied. Do you have a lawyer who's willing to appeal your case?

No → You are ordered deported.

Yes → This process will take approximately 10,000 years.

Are you still feeling lucky?

Yes → You are released on bond and paroled into the U.S.

Hooray → You've been in the U.S. for a year now. Have you filed your asylum application with the court yet?

No, my luck has run out → ICE refuses to release you from detention, so you have to prepare your case from inside immigration jail.

Fuckfuckfuck → You've been in the U.S. for a year now. Have you filed your asylum application with the court yet?

Yes, I magically knew to do that → Okay: you attended all your court dates?...

No → Your asylum application ... Did you have that one year filing problem?

* We will assume here that you've never been ordered deported from the U.S. in the past, because that alters your chances significantly.

** What happens to unaccompanied minors within the asylum system is beyond the scope of this flowchart.

*** We'll say you haven't been charged with any crimes, because good Lord, that gets complicated.

**** Until now, expedited removal had only been a possibility if you're apprehended within 100 miles of the border, but in Trump's America, it can happen anywhere!

***** This practice is what Trump calls "catch and release," so we may be seeing less of it now.

BUT SHOULD I SUBSCRIBE TO THE MAGAZINE?

You have purchased and enjoyed the *Current Affairs Big Book of Amusements*. But should you take another step towards enlightenment and boundless joy by subscribing to *Current Affairs* the magazine? It is not for us to say. But since you asked, we are happy to provide a flowchart to assist your decision-making.

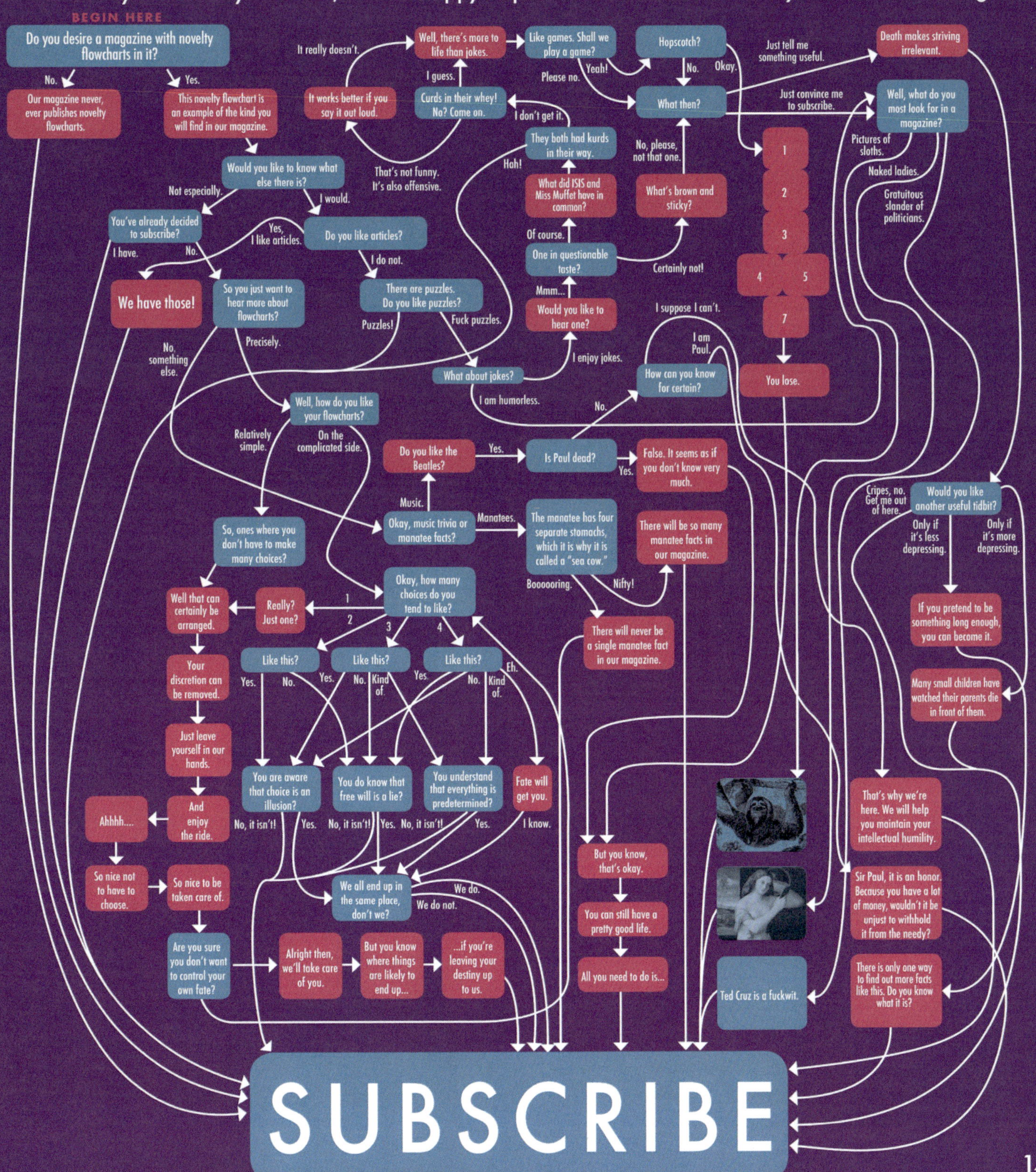

BONUS FLOWCHART
Dragon Attack!
BEGIN
A dragon is descending on your village! What do you do?
Send a message to your blessed monarch, begging her to ride in and open a can of that patented yasss queen slay.
The queen lives in a fairy-tale castle ten days' ride away. By the time your messenger arrives...
Your fields are ash, your livestock has been eaten, and most of you are dead.
Appeal to the dwarves.
Appeal to the queen.
Appeal to the baron.
The queen is soooo sympathetic. She really hears you. But it's the baron's job to handle your complaints. Hey. Have a signed portrait. It's on the house.
Contact the local dwarf clan. They've never been very friendly, but maybe they have some fireproof armor they can spare?
Ask your local baron for help.
Take on the dragon yourself.
...you get the queen to apologize.
Your queen didn't invite the king of the dwarves to her coronation, and he's still pissed. He won't let any of his people help you unless...
...you give him all the gold in the village.
The dwarf king and his thanes, seeing an opportunity to colonize your abandoned territory, refuse to help. You appeal to the dwarven people directly. Collectively, you realize that the historic enmity and mistrust between your two civilizations has been seeded by your leaders to give legitimacy to their land grabs and weird personal grudges.
The baron laughs. No matter what choices you make, more dragon attacks will always mean more fires to put out, which will always mean more money and virgins for him. That's just how the world works. That's how it's always going to work. If you weren't such an illiterate peasant you'd understand.
The baron demands payment.
It's feudalism. You don't have gold or extra resources just like, lying around. You refuse to surrender what little you have, even to protect your village from a dragon.
You drive the dragon away temporarily with pitchforks and homemade trebuchets. Hooray! But the dragon will return. Since it's the baron's duty to protect the village, and he'll be angry if you don't tell him what happened....
Offer the baron 70% of your crops and livestock instead of the usual 60%, plus the village's most nubile daughters.
Overthrow the aristocracy.
Overthrow the monarchy.
The baron's knights ride in. They slay the dragon, then demand a feast starring all your remaining livestock. In their drunken celebration, they rape everyone and set the village on fire. The flames spread to the fields.
Ask the baron to help you bring this matter to the queen.
Instead of fighting the dragon, you try to reason with her. Turns out she was driven from her mountain after the queen turned it into another royal hunting ground. The dragon's ribs are visible under her scales. You let her have three cows and she flies off...for now...

THE CURRENT AFFAIRS™
"BIG BOOK OF AMUSEMENTS"

Cool-Ass Comics

REAL LIFE BILLIONAIRE SUPERHERO COMIX

REAL LIFE BILLIONAIRE SUPERHERO COMIX

STEVEN PINKER
CERTIFIED GRIEF COUNSELOR
WELL, ACTUALLY...
HIRE STEVEN PINKER FOR YOUR NEXT EVENT! HIS SKILLSET INCLUDES...

FUNERALS!
DON'T CRY! HUMAN LIFE EXPECTANCY IS SO MUCH LONGER THAN IT USED TO BE!

ASSEMBLIES IN THE AFTERMATH OF A SCHOOL SHOOTING!!
YES, THERE HAS BEEN A RECENT UPTICK IN THE NUMBER OF SCHOOL SHOOTINGS, BUT IF YOU LOOK AT THE OVERALL DATA SET, VIOLENCE HAS DECREASED IN THE WEST BY 48%!

COMFORTING CHILDREN WHOSE PARENTS HAVE BEEN ABDUCTED BY ICE!
KIDS, IF YOU LOOK AT THE AGGREGATE HAPPINESS INDEX, AND ADJUST BY SOCIAL EXPECTATIONS, STATISTICALLY SPEAKING IT'S LIKE THEY NEVER LEFT!

MOTIVATIONAL SPEAKING AT A BLACK LIVES MATTER RALLY!
POLICE VIOLENCE
TER
IT'S GETTIN' BETTER!
YOU KNOW, COMPARED TO SLAVERY...

SELF-CARE!
SMILE, STEVEN. REMEMBER: NO MATTER WHAT PEOPLE SAY, IT'S STATISTICALLY IMPOSSIBLE FOR YOU TO BE THE WORST PERSON ON THE PLANET.

CONSOLING THE SAD BUT INEVITABLE VICTIMS OF CLIMATE CHANGE.
GRR. RA-AH. GRA, GRA, GROH. RA-ARGH! AM I RIGHT?

ADDRESSING THE QUARANTINED VICTIMS OF A FLU PANDEMIC!
DID YOU KNOW THAT IN THE MIDDLE AGES, PEOPLE THOUGHT EATING CRUSHED EMERALDS WOULD CURE THE PLAGUE? MORONS!
INER
I'M SO HAPPY TO LIVE IN A SCIENTIFICALLY ENLIGHTENED AGE, AREN'T YOU?

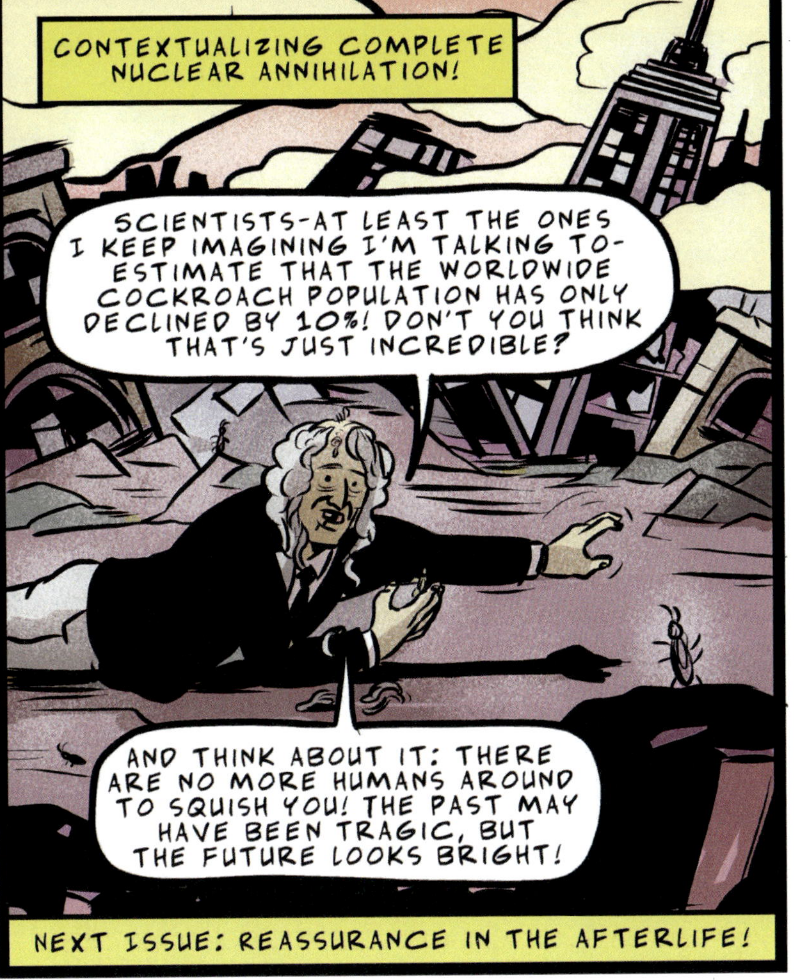
CONTEXTUALIZING COMPLETE NUCLEAR ANNIHILATION!
SCIENTISTS–AT LEAST THE ONES I KEEP IMAGINING I'M TALKING TO–ESTIMATE THAT THE WORLDWIDE COCKROACH POPULATION HAS ONLY DECLINED BY 10%! DON'T YOU THINK THAT'S JUST INCREDIBLE?
AND THINK ABOUT IT: THERE ARE NO MORE HUMANS AROUND TO SQUISH YOU! THE PAST MAY HAVE BEEN TRAGIC, BUT THE FUTURE LOOKS BRIGHT!
NEXT ISSUE: REASSURANCE IN THE AFTERLIFE!

The Adventures of LEO the LIBERTARIAN LION

STORY BY LYTA GOLD   ARTWORK BY PRANAS NAUJOKAITIS

"IF YOU CAN'T TAKE CARE OF YOURSELF," SNORTED LEO THE LIBERTARIAN LION, "YOU CAN HARDLY EXPECT OTHERS TO TAKE CARE OF YOU."

"IF YOU CAN'T AFFORD TO SUFFER, YOU SHOULDN'T DECIDE TO DO SO."

"IT WASN'T A CHOICE! I STEPPED IN AN AARDVARK HOLE!"

"IT MUST HAVE BEEN A CHOICE," SAID LEO THE LIBERTARIAN LION, "OR ELSE IT WOULDN'T HAVE HAPPENED. I, FOR EXAMPLE, HAVE NEVER DONE ANYTHING UNLESS I WANTED TO."

LEO THE LIBERTARIAN LION STRODE ACROSS THE SAVANNA WITH THE WIND IN HIS EARS AND THE INVISIBLE HAND OF THE FREE MARKET SCRATCHING HIS CHIN AND WHISPERING "GOOD BOY."

IN TIME, HE CAME UPON A HERD OF ZEBRAS WHOSE WATERING HOLE HAD JUST DRIED UP. "CLEARLY," SAID LEO THE LIBERTARIAN LION, "YOU SHOULD HAVE INVESTED IN A BETTER WATER SOURCE."

"BUT THIS IS THE ONLY WATERING HOLE WE CAN USE," A ZEBRA SAID. "THE HUMANS TURNED ALL OUR FORMER TERRITORY INTO A SAFARI THEME PARK."
SAFARI WORLD

"THEN YOU SHOULD HAVE BOUGHT THE PROPERTY FIRST," ADVISED LEO THE LIBERTARIAN LION. "OR HIRED YOURSELF OUT TO THE SAFARI. REALLY, YOU HAVE NO ONE TO BLAME BUT YOURSELVES. THERE'S NO SUCH THING AS A FREE WATERING HOLE."

"THIS ONE WAS FREE," SAID ANOTHER ZEBRA, "UNTIL IT DRIED UP." "THERE'S NO FREE WATER, OR AIR, OR GRASS. WE WALK THROUGH A GOLDEN FIELD OF INVISIBLE OWNERSHIP. EVERY BLADE OF GRASS BELONGS TO SOMEONE."

"WHY?" ASKED ANOTHER ZEBRA. "WHY DOESN'T THE WORLD BELONG TO EVERYONE?"
"BECAUSE PRIVATE OWNERSHIP IS THE MOST RATIONAL WAY TO DISTRIBUTE RESOURCES..."

"...IF YOU OBEY THE LAWS OF THE FREE MARKET, IT WILL PROVIDE. THAT'S JUST PLAIN LOGIC." "EXCEPT NOW WE HAVE NO RESOURCES AT ALL," SAID AN OLDER ZEBRA. "AND BESIDES, ISN'T SUBORDINATION TO AN ALL-POWERFUL INVISIBLE FORCE REALLY THE OPPOSITE OF LOGIC?"

LEO THE LIBERTARIAN LION CONSIDERED THIS A MOMENT.
THEN HE ROARED UNTIL THE ZEBRAS GALLOPED AWAY.

SHUT UUUUP!

LEO THE LIBERTARIAN LION SLEPT ON THE SAVANNA, WITH EARTH UNDER HIS PAWS AND THE INVISIBLE HAND OF THE FREE MARKET PATTING HIM SOFTLY ON THE ASS. WHEN HE WOKE UP, HE SAW A HUMAN HUNTER APPROACHING.

"EXCUSE ME," SAID LEO THE LIBERTARIAN LION, "THIS STRETCH OF THE SERENGETI IS MY PRIVATE PROPERTY."

"ACTUALLY," SAID THE HUNTER, "IT ALL BELONGS TO THE SAFARIA CORPORATION. THEY JUST BOUGHT THIS WHOLE AREA."

"BUT THAT'S ABSURD," SCOFFED LEO THE LIBERTARIAN LION. "I LIVE HERE. I HAVE RIGHTS."
"OH? WITH WHOM DID YOU CONTRACT FOR THIS LAND?"

"I... I DIDN'T CONTRACT FOR IT. IT IS THE ANCESTRAL LAND OF MY PRIDE. GENERATIONS OF LIBERTARIAN LIONS HAVE INHABITED IT."

"AND DID ANY OF THESE UNINVITED FELINE SQUATTERS EVER ESTABLISH LAWFUL TITLE? DOES THIS PRIDE OF YOURS HAVE SOME KIND OF NOTARIZED DEED, WITH YOUR PAWPRINT ON THE DOTTED LINE?"

"OF COURSE NOT! LIONS DON'T NEED TITLES! THE LAND IS OUR COMMON INHERITANCE."
"YOUR WHAT?"
"I MEAN, IT BELONGS TO ALL LIONS. WE HAVE SPENT YEARS PROTECTING AND PRESERVING IT, AND THUS IT BELONGS TO US."

"SORRY, PUSS. YOU SEEM TO BE MISTAKING BOLSHEVISM FOR ECONOMICS."

THE HUNTER SLEPT WELL THAT NIGHT, SECURE IN THE KNOWLEDGE THAT HE HAD VIOLATED NO LEGITIMATE PROPERTY CLAIMS. TO MAXIMIZE PROFIT, HE SOLD LEO'S TEETH, PELT, AND BONES ON THE BLACK MARKET. THE BLACK MARKET IS THE FREEST MARKET OF ALL!

THE END

SQUID LAWYER
I don't like it any more than you do, but we just don't have the resources to push this case further.
Agreed. We'll have to settle. Let's ink this deal.
SQUID, WARTHOG, & FLAMINGO LLP
INK SPLOOSH!!!
PART TWO
Bail is set at $5000.
But I can't afford—
You should have thought of that before you were accused of breaking the law.
PART THREE
So you see, my client has a perfect right to refuse to acknowledge alternate genders, and to sue the university for its pronoun policy...
All I want is to be called by my correct pro-nouns.
Demanding change is totalitarian! Animals don't change. We're the same as we have been for millennia.
SPLOOSH
NICK SIROTICH

A DAY IN THE LIFE OF A CENTRIST DAD

STORY: LYTA GOLD
ART: MIKE FREIHEIT

The socialist fairytale digs deep roots in the British foundation. My comments are swords in the darkness, bright corrections to childish tomfoolery.

Fact: Once we strode down a bright road of steady growth and stately progress. But they wouldn't wait. The youth have no patience. They cried "inequality" and "crushing rents".

My daughter. I log these hours of strong, focused content for you. All for you.

Doesn't he realize that life is a series of crushing disappointments, each more miserable than the last?

He stares. So calm. As if he hadn't been thoroughly eviscerated by the press for thirty-odd years.

When it's time to crawl away from your own house after the wife tosses you out, after you're forced into the Kensington flat you inherited from your parents.

Fact: When I was young I believed in socialism, anarchism, all the rest. I believed until reality mugged me, left me bleeding in a gutter.

Fact: History is over. It ended when my wife left me. She said I was posting online too much, but do you see how it is out there? So many stupid young women believing so many stupid young things?

They are so ignorant and so beautiful. Only I can save them. With my words. I must drown them in a flood of my white-hot wisdom.

We need to set the market free. We need to remove the chains from its bold, straining limbs. Let the market stride over the surface over the earth, exploring, educating, lifting up the young and the ignorant. We must unite under the banner of God the Market. Only then can Europe be saved

My daughter won't phone me. And my wife has moved on. They say I refuse to change. They say I'm living in a past that no longer exists, clinging to a dead reality that never was.

But I comment and comment, vlog and vlog, until the day comes at last...

The day my straying nation understands she needs me once again.

"I was born in one country and am now a resident of another... I speak from inside the issue, and I am here to plead: Understand its power for good and for harm. In Europe and America, border laxness has empowered extremism—and trying to counter that extremism with still more extremism will do no good for any principle of freedom..."

— David Frum, former Bush speechwriter, "Enforce The Border—Humanely," THE ATLANTIC (June 20, 2018)

I, Immigrant: The David Frum Story

STORY: LYTA GOLD / ART: MIKE FREIHEIT

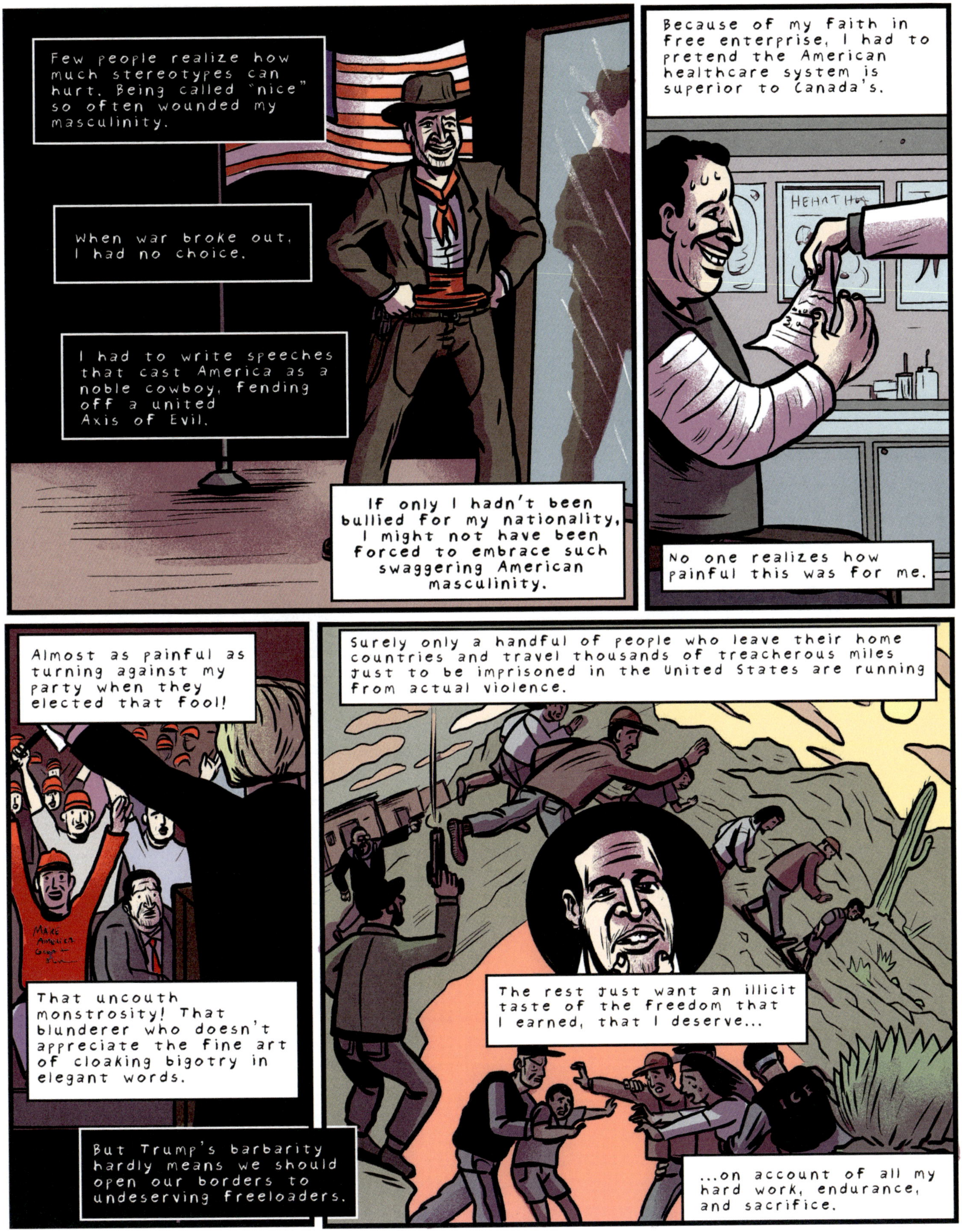

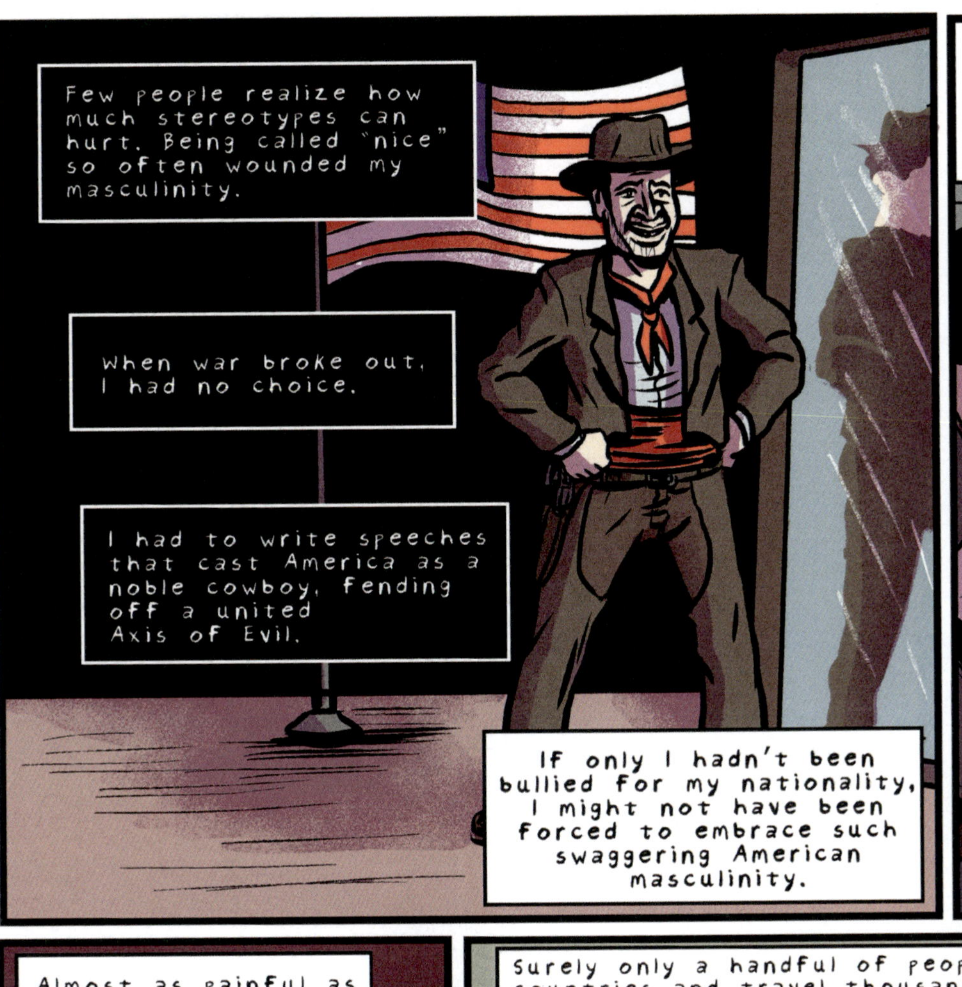

Almost as painful as turning against my party when they elected that fool!

That uncouth monstrosity! That blunderer who doesn't appreciate the fine art of cloaking bigotry in elegant words.

But Trump's barbarity hardly means we should open our borders to undeserving freeloaders.

Surely only a handful of people who leave their home countries and travel thousands of treacherous miles just to be imprisoned in the United States are running from actual violence.

The rest just want an illicit taste of the freedom that I earned, that I deserve...

...on account of all my hard work, endurance, and sacrifice.

ADVENTURES OF THE INVISIBLE REFEREE!

Story: Lyta Gold Art: Mike Freiheit

Does your white privilege leave you feeling *"uncomfy"*? When a black person expresses discontent at the status quo, does it make you feel all squirmy and guilty inside? Why examine your feelings when you could just shortcut the *badfeels* and reimagine history with our patented MLK Poké Balls!*

Using a complex algorithm developed by our sophisticated team of Google researchers, the MLK Poké Balls locate semi-relevant quotes by the Rev. Martin Luther King Jr., and carefully strip them of all context before deploying them at your voice command.

Once you start tossing out-of-context MLK quotes, you won't be able to stop until you've *APPROPRIATED THEM ALL!*

By GuiltNoMore, Inc., the makers of 1UP Data: Power Up by Overpowering Everyone Around You With Out-of-Context Statistics!

**Patent pending lawsuits from the King family and Nintendo Co, Ltd.*

Bonus Miscellany

The New York Times PRESENTS: MEET THE MAVERICK THINKERS OF THE INTERGALACTIC CONFEDERACY OF INVADERS

by Bari Weiss, Jr.

HERE ARE SOME things that you'll hear if you sit down at the conference table with the Intergalactic Confederacy of Invaders: There are fundamental biological differences between certain species, and because of that, there must be fundamental differences in rights. Free speech is under assault, and well-meaning, reasonable discourse about vassalage under the Intergalactic Confederacy of Invaders no longer seems permissible on Earth. "Universal justice warriors" are advocating "survival politics": a toxic ideology that's tearing the galaxy apart. And we're at risk if mentioning these facts is considered "radical."

I met with Borfaz the Devourer, famed warrior of the Hegbolian Assault Corps; Glaxal 47836, the provocative broadcaster and managing director of the Glaxinari Center For Universal Progress; Praxifa of the

left: **BORFAZ THE DEVOURER.** *above:* **LHARPENETH.**

Toxic Cloud, writer, speaker, lifestyle guru, and founder of TEDxAndromeda; the regal Lharpeneth, Emperor of the Outer Novae, Glory To His Many Conquests; and several prominent Space Nazis From Beyond The Moon. Thirty years ago, they argued, when multiple alien civilizations simultaneously made contact with Earth, the Intergalactic Confederacy's ideas would not have been considered taboo. At that time, humans had not yet absorbed the enormity of communion with so many new cultures and ideologies, and were more willing to consider a broader variety of thought.

TODAY, PEOPLE LIKE THESE dashing leaders of the Intergalactic Confederacy of Invaders feel they are no longer welcome in Earth's system simply because they dare to bring up certain adventurous concepts. Their beliefs, once considered tenable, are now met with anger, condemnation, and mean jokes. They've been disinvited from the best parties on the Jupiterian Co-Operative Orbital Station and the Free Milky Way University on Titan. It seems that this part of the galaxy is afraid of entertaining certain political formations just because—or so the "universal justice warriors" claim—vassalage under the Intergalactic Confederacy of Invaders might be considered (potentially) antithetical to freedom.

What is the Intergalactic Confederacy of Invaders, and what makes their ideas so risqué? If you ask their enemies, the I.C.I. is a motley collection of murderers, warlords, and slavers from the fringes of deep space. But if you ask their supporters, you'll hear a different story. The I.C.I. represents a diverse assortment of sexy, dangerous thinkers who dare to explore the dark regions beyond mainstream conceptions of "freedom," "liberty," and "the right not to be eaten." These brave intellectuals share nothing in common except a willingness to argue, a commitment to civility, and a refusal to surrender their convictions even when the foundations of their arguments are demolished by writers outside the I.C.I. Additionally, they all share the radical belief that their ideologies are perfectly rational, and if other species were simply willing to hear them out they would subordinate themselves at once.

"The universe has become intolerant of certain opinions," claims Glaxal 47836. "When we simply try to have an open conversation about the moral duty of Glaxinari vis-a-vis inferior species, we receive a torrent of outrage and cruel jokes at our expense. It's almost enough to make us stop publicizing our conversations."

YOU ARE PROBABLY FAMILIAR with Glaxal 47836's trumpet-like voice. The Glaxinari Center for Universal Progress is co-producer of *Coming to Your Senses* and *The Dominance Hour*, and a prime investor in Mastery Entertainment. Despite their popularity in the signal-streaming space, however, Glaxal 47836 and his clutch-brothers feel a constant sense of wounded exclusion. "I care about facts," says Glaxal 47836. "And the facts tell me that even though I have a #1 show on three different interstellar signal-streamers, Earth and other planets still refuse to allow Glaxinari progressives to monopolize their entire infosphere. This really hurts our feelings."

"The Free University of the Milky Way hasn't yet offered me a chair," coughs Praxifa of the Toxic Cloud. "While I have a guest lecturing position on Titan, I must conduct my classes via holoconference because my presence is apparently "life-threatening" to certain fragile species. I don't know when university students became such delicate snowflakes! I was no-platformed from physically appearing last EY just because when I praise Neocolonialist Technomics, I also tend to exude a chemical aura that melts human lungs. I'm suing the university for the incident."

What does Praxifa want from the Free Milky Way University? Respect. "Neocolonialist Technomics has not—as some hateful and close-minded scholars claim—been wholly undermined by its tendency to immiserate entire star systems. It's a legitimate perspective and deserves a fair place in the discourse, even if its expression is a little

left: **GLAXAL 47836.** *above:* **PRAXIFA OF THE TOXIC CLOUD.**

noxious to some weaker creatures."

"The problem is fear," growls Borfaz the Devourer. "When you simply suggest that the young of certain species should be dried into jerky to feed the brave warriors of the Hegbolian Assault Corps, people shut down. They call you a cannibal."

A tear falls from his cyclopean eye. He wipes it away with a calloused pink hand. "I just have heterodox ideas about sentient species edibility. Why are people so unwilling to engage with my arguments?"

It's true that "cannibalism" technically refers to the act of eating a member of your own species. There's nothing "cannibalistic" about consuming the young of a different alien race, sentient or not. An obvious logical fallacy, and yet "universal justice warriors" continually shut down any debate on the subject.

"In truth, I have had my own battles with them," says the majestic Lharpeneth, Emperor of the Outer Novae, Great Is The Terror Of His Armies. "Not literal battles, as my legions have been fenced out of most star systems by impenetrable force fields. But when you merely suggest, through a peaceful intermediary, that you'd like to offer a clean solution to the problem of intergalactic unemployment..." He shrugs. He's quite physically striking, the tall and handsome Lharpeneth, Emperor of the Outer Novae, Splendid Are His Plunder-Houses. He beams at me. "All I desire is to benefit the citizens of this universe. What crime is there in gently ushering unemployed aliens to my asteroid mines?"

PRAXIFA OF THE TOXIC CLOUD leans forward, or seems to—it's difficult to tell under the smoke. "Let me guess: when you suggested this pleasant and highly advantageous work opportunity, the hysterical UJWs compared it to slavery?"

Everyone laughs. The members of the I.C.I. laugh often, especially when they agree, which is almost always. Though they may differ moderately in matters of policy and metaphysics, they all agree on one point: It is their task, as intellectually superior beings, to shepherd the galaxy toward truth and justice.

"Look," says Glaxal 47836. "There are obvious physical differences between Glaxinari and humans for example, yes? I mean, we all see the differences. We all acknowledge that undersea clutch-breeding is a far more effective reproductive method than live mammalian land-births, right?" The members of the I.C.I. nod. "So if evolution favors us, why isn't it appropriate for Glaxinari to dominate less well-adapted species? That's the way it's always been in the Glaxinar system. We just want to return to our traditions, when Glaxinari were Glaxinari and everyone knew their place."

At the end of the table, the Space Nazis From Beyond The Moon stir uneasily. As former humans, they can occasionally become uncomfortable with identitarians of other species. "We know there is not lebensraum in the universe for everyone," confesses Hydrus Himmler to me afterward. "But as long the I.C.I. remains united against our enemies, such as the Anarcho-Socialist Robots of the Emma Goldman Collective, we will maintain our non-aggression pact with the Glaxinari."

The Space Nazis From Beyond The Moon may be on the fringes of the I.C.I. But whether or not one approves of the movement's ferocious commitments to their unusual beliefs, it is hard to deny that since they were exiled to the far reaches of space, the Space Nazis From Beyond The Moon have represented an important intellectual counterweight to mainstream discourse.

THE SPACE NAZIS FROM BEYOND THE MOON HAVE REPRESENTED AN IMPORTANT INTELLECTUAL COUNTERWEIGHT TO MAINSTREAM DISCOURSE...

So when Cetus Goebbels signal-streams messages such as "we should not ban people from intergalactic intellectual life just because they hold different ideas," he's picking up on a real phenomenon: that the boundaries of intergalactic discourse have become so proscribed as to make it very difficult to hold frank discussions of anything remotely controversial, like the existence of the Universal Jew who secretly controls all the universities and signal-streams.

AM I A MEMBER OF THE I.C.I.? Like many of the I.C.I.'s luminaries, I am a neoclassical liberal who has run afoul of the UJWs, in my case merely for suggesting that university professors who oppose the Reconquistadors on Aldebaran 5 should be fired from their posts. This has won me praise from the I.C.I. But do I feel comfortable being associated with such people? The kind of people who are only invited to parties at eighty percent of the universe's intellectual centers, as opposed to all of them?

I understand the appeal of the I.C.I. I share the belief that all ideas should be discussed freely, except for really out-of-bound nonsense such as "liberty" for the terrorists masquerading as freedom fighters on Aldebaran 5. But, given how prominent the I.C.I. has become, I hope they find a way to streamline and civilize their message until it can find a home amid mainstream intergalactic discourse once again.

"Some say the I.C.I. is a band of dangerous, beautiful renegades who are too intellectually superior to be appreciated by the more foolish species in this universe," says Praxifa of the Toxic Cloud. "But the only way you can pretend that a group of intellectuals merely sitting and chatting about their obvious right to rule the galaxy is dangerous is if you are scared of new ideas." ◇

COMPETITIVE CHILD-RAISING: BOTH A MARATHON AND A SPRINT

helicopter parent

THE guide for cosseting progenitors

What's the *Right Age* to Brand Your Baby?

(If you have to ask, it's *already* too late!)

Diploma

SECURING Baby's 1st Round of VC Funding

Ask Alice:

Is It A Developmental Disability Or Does My Infant Just *Despise* Me?

A Mother's *HORROR!*

"My Child Tested in the 85th Percentile!"

5 *Best Colleges For Your Newborn*

It's *NEVER* Too Early to Apply!

Is Your Kid A Picky Eater...

...or *Fatally Flawed* And Doomed To Failure? Our Health & Nutrition Experts Weigh In...

How Many Devoured Husbands is TOO Many Devoured Husbands?
SPIDER MOMS
For the Busy Spider Mother On The Go!
The BEST PREY for Your Figure!
The Top 10 Most Drop-Dead VENOMS for This Fall: Your Victims Won't Know What HIT Them!
Is Your Brood Overly Dependent? How To Cut Them Loose Immediately After Birth!
Our Definitive Guide To Slow-Cooked Meals (Hint: Web Them Up First!)
Attention, Nursery Web Spiders! 5 Ways To Tell If Your Mate Is Only Feigning DEATH!
Shocking Reader Confession: I Let My Mates Escape UNSCATHED!
XXX VENOM HOT SAUCE
WORTT

Public ISP

4:00 PM

100% 

 http://social.world 

SOCIAL(ist) MEDIA

your postcapitalist future

LIVE STREAM
of formerly endangered species...

LIVE STREAM
of the anarcho-communes on Enceladus...

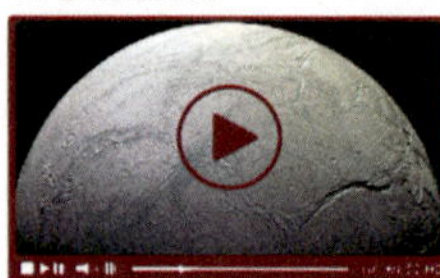

The History of "Twitter"
The platform that was...

We Dug Up Your Old Comments and...
nobody cares, we all said things when we were young and stupid.

#livingwageUBI #well-rested #blessed #takingfrequentbreaks

Why We Post Less...
It's because everything sucks less!

Welcome! Do you want to....

...find someplace to go today?
...find someone to speak to?
...find something helpful you can do?

Make New Friends!
Gomez, 74
MEET GOMEZ

INSPIRING: When this little girl's mother got cancer and couldn't afford to pay for treatment...

...she received life-saving surgery thanks to universal healthcare and now she's home in time for her daughter's birthday!

90 or 95% tax on the rich: The candidates debate...

12 Cats Who Look Like Leon Trotsky

You Won't Believe...
...that we used to waste perfectly good land on farming these noble beasts! Meet some cool cows on their protected range.

Strangers Who Could Use A Kind Word

Leonora

SEND

Leonora's interests include: crochet, BBC murder mysteries, krav maga...

DISCUSSIONS

 Substantive Debate Zone

 Amiable Chit-Chat

 Consensual Flirtation

 Narcissism of Small Differences Quarantine Zone

NICHE GROUPS

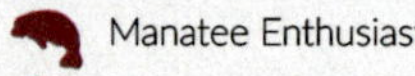

Cookie Baking Bros

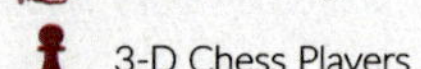

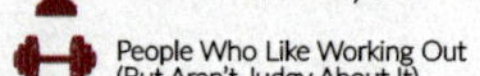

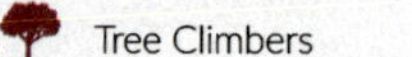

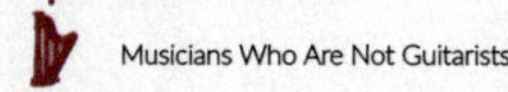

People Who Like Pears

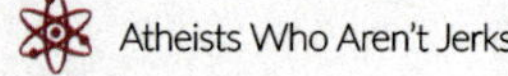

Jazz Types

Astronomers Who Can't Stand Neil deGrasse Tyson

Bird Watchers

Train Spotters

Bird Trainers

Whistling Gardeners

Ex-Lawyer Support Group

Miscellaneous Nerds

FIND UPCOMING MEETUPS

Feeling distressed?
You can speak to someone right now...

tips for TEENS

the kind the STATE won't tell you... (some reasons to be cheerful)

SOMEDAY BIEBER WILL BE A SKELETON! ISN'T THAT REASSURING?

THE JONAS BROTHERS IMMATERIAL TO HUMAN PROGRESS

your transgressions will mostly go unpunished

Soon your more popular classmates will have babies and be forced to work low-wage jobs and have their dreams CRUSHED beneath the weight of the brutal realities of the FREE MARKET and there'll be no relief because America doesn't even have PAID MATERNITY LEAVE

LOL!

OK!

SHE SHALL BE FORGOTTEN LIKE THE REST SOMEDAY

Nearly every successful person is incredibly unhappy!

You are more attractive now than you will EVER BE AGAIN

You have more life left ahead of you now than you will EVER HAVE AGAIN

future corpse

THINGS THIS IS BETTER THAN

1. never having lived at all
2. your life in almost any previous historical era
3. being sent to war for an unjust cause
4. being sent to war for any cause at all, really
5. being older than you are now
6. having like a job and stuff

SOME DISEASES YOU PROBABLY DON'T HAVE

fibrosing alveolitis
vesiculobullous dermatosis
Waldenström macroglobulinemia
subacute bacterial endocarditis
rheumatic fever
oligodendroglioma
toxic megacolon
norwegian scabies

where are you coming from?

A SURVEY OF PRECONCEPTION AND DISPOSITION

If we are truly to understand one another, it is vital that each person know where the other is coming from. Discussion is impossible between persons with no appreciation of one another's worldviews, desires, self-conceptions, politics, knowledge bases, or histories. Communication will remain difficult so long as we have access to only tiny fragments of other people's identities, and know little about what their minds look like from the inside. This, the Current Affairs "Where Are You Coming From" survey, constitutes the basic questions we should ask one another before attempting to engage in any form of conversation.

DO YOU HAVE AN "IDENTITY"? WHAT IS IT? WHAT ASPECTS OF IT MAKE IT YOUR "IDENTITY"?

DO YOU THINK "FREE WILL" IS A MEANINGFUL CONCEPT? DO YOU THINK GOD IS A MEANINGFUL CONCEPT?

DO YOU THINK LIFE IS MANAGEABLE? DO YOU THINK THE WORLD IS COMPREHENSIBLE?

What do you understand as the central insight of existentialism? Do you buy it? Please explain.

Is it difficult for you to believe that history actually happened? Is it difficult for you to believe that Socrates existed, and that he possessed an asshole? Is there a difference in the degree to which you believe the President has an asshole and the degree to which you are convinced that you have one?

— What are your fundamental political principles?

— Do you think you act consistently with them?

— In what way do you act consistently?

— Why is it necessary to be consistent?

— Should conclusions follow from premises?

WHAT IS BULLSHIT? DO YOU BULLSHIT?

WHERE DO RIGHTS COME FROM? ARE THEY ETERNAL?

WHAT, OF THE THINGS YOU BELIEVE, ARE YOU MOST CERTAIN OF? WHAT ARE YOU LEAST CERTAIN OF? WHAT IS BELIEF?

Is it presumptuous to tell another person about one's life unprompted? Would you ever go up to a person in a coffee shop and start talking to them? Under what circumstances is this appropriate? Should poetry be criminalized? Should executions be televised?

Do you shop for pleasure? Why? Why does buying things give you pleasure? Are you uncomfortable in malls? When you see, say, millions of products on sale in a Target, do you think about who made those products and where they will go in the future? Are you horrified by civilization?

Why do you like the music you like rather than some other music? Do you think your tastes in music are other than arbitrary? Can some music be "better" than other music, and if so what is the source of that value? What is the saddest song you know? What is the function of music in a just society?

If you are religious, what exactly do you believe about people of other faiths or no faith? Do you believe they are wrong? Do you believe you should try to convince them of your views? Do you believe religious feeling is the type of feeling which one can acquire through persuasion?

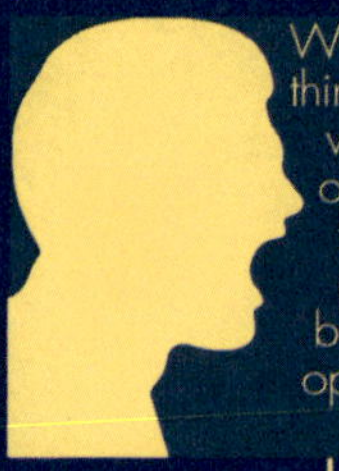

Why do you think people who are opposed to your political beliefs are opposed to them?

How often do you think about the fact that underneath your skin, you are a skeleton? When you see other people, do you think about the fact that they, too, are skeletons?

Do you feel the pain of others? Whose pain do you feel, and why? Do you feel the pain of people in your time more than people in a different time? Why? How often do you think about the victims of the Holocaust? Are there certain truths you avoid thinking about?

PLEASE DESCRIBE THE LOWEST POINT YOU HAVE EVER FELT. WHAT ARE YOU STRIVING FOR, AND WHY DO YOU THINK IT WILL MAKE YOU HAPPY? DO YOU FEEL THERE IS A FUNDAMENTAL DIFFERENCE BETWEEN YOU AND EVERYONE ELSE? IF SO, WHAT IS THAT DIFFERENCE? DO YOU THINK IT IS REAL, OR A DELUSION? DO YOU THINK YOU HAVE ANY DELUSIONS GENERALLY?

HOW SHOULD RAPE PROSECUTIONS BE CONDUCTED?

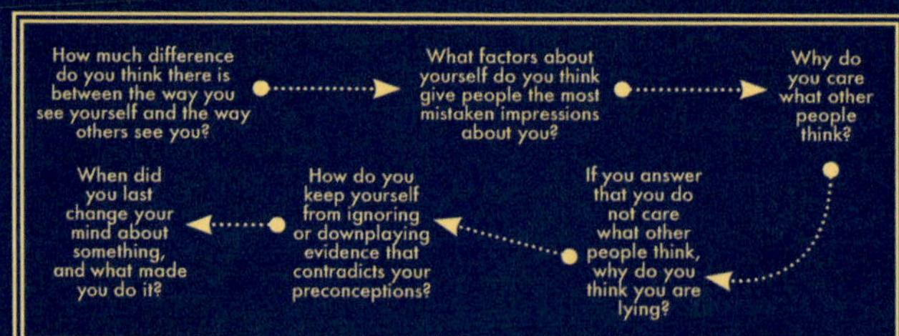

Why should anyone care about the fucking Constitution? If our Constitution were different, should we care about that one just as much?

IS IT ACTUALLY IMPORTANT TO KNOW WHAT IS GOING ON IN THE WORLD?

Why exactly is that? Do you think one should know the names of the heads of state of foreign countries? Do you think one should be able to put countries on a map? Can you name lots of heads of state and put lots of countries on maps? Can you name the population of Romania to within 100,000 people? If you can't, does this trouble you? If you can, why is this necessary? Should knowledge be useful? If I can't change something, is it okay for me not to learn about it?

IS THE WORD "DIALECTICS" MEANINGFUL TO YOU? IF SO, WHAT DOES IT MEAN? WHY IS IT USEFUL?

Do you worry about the percentage of outcomes in your life that are determined by mere chance?

Does it concern you that you may have failed to meet the love of your life by failing to step in a certain puddle on a certain day?

Being as specific as possible, what would you do given absolute power?

What does Utopia look like? Is government a necessary evil or a positive good? Should we think about utopias?

Do you think there is any disjunction between what is produced as the result of the operations of a free market and what ought to be produced? Is there any use whatsoever in markets? Do you think it is acceptable that in a market, a person with more resources has more power than a person with fewer resources? How is this different from one person having more votes in an election than another? Do you think people deserve whatever they are paid? What does it mean to "deserve" something?

Are some buildings too ugly to live?

IS IT ACCEPTABLE NOT TO THINK ABOUT WHERE THEY ARE COMING FROM?

"All the news that's fit to print and then some."

The New York Times

Local Forecast
Largely predictable; general dreariness, expect impenetrable fog and lots of wind

VOL. CLXVI... No. 57,391 | WEDNESDAY, NOVEMBER 1, 2016 | $2.50

At Goldman Sachs, Diversity Changes a Culture

By NICHOLAS CONFESSORE

MANHATTAN — When Josh Perez began at Goldman Sachs nine months ago, he was worried. "I knew it had a certain reputation for elitism," he says. "And since I'm half Hispanic, I was worried that my arrival would make waves." But Perez, whose mother is the daughter of the Colombian treasury secretary, found his Goldman bosses surprisingly enthusiastic about his ethnic background. "The only color here that matters is green," Perez says a partner told him.

Goldman, a venerable and ancient house of finance, has sometimes struggled to have its office culture adjust to contemporary mores. But today's partners are eager to change that. "We're a welcoming place," says Goldman's managing director, J. Peter Thorndike. "We have LGBT Harvard grads, a black woman from Cornell. Every demographic group you could think of is represented on our staff." Goldman Sachs has been controversial for its lack of diversity. But with a new class of savvy young bankers from an array of backgrounds, the company hopes to restore its reputation among young people.

Similar diversity initiatives at Monsanto, Lockheed Martin, BP, Blackwater, and Halliburton have attracted praise from industry observers. "I'm glad to see the business world finally making the rhetoric of opportunity into a reality," said Neera Tanden of the Center for American Progress. "It's important for these companies to be fair and enact progressive values." Lockheed Martin's Timothy Christopher, who is gay and heads up a new torpedo program, says he is proud to work at an inclusive workplace. "It's gratifying not to have to be ashamed of where I work."

IN GAZA, A CAFE RECEIVES AN UNEXPECTED VISITOR

By JODI RUDOREN

GAZA — Things seem different at this popular cafe in the heart of the city. Usually, men will be watching soccer on a small television set, or chatting about politics by the window. Yet thanks to the intrusion of an unexpected visitor, the usual activities have been suspended. The daily consumption of sumaghiyyeh and lemonade has been halted in favor of picking through twisted concrete in search of corpses. Thanks to the visitor's explosive nature, it is unclear when the cafe will reopen. The government of Israel expressed its sympathy for the cafe's unexpected closure.

KISSINGER'S STRUGGLE

There was a time when Henry Kissinger refrained from lunching at the Four Seasons. In the 70s, when he was serving as Secretary of State, Kissinger was frequently the target of protests over the bombings of Cambodia and Laos. These days, however, Kissinger is the confidante of Democrats and Republicans alike, and can finally get on with his lunch. He's on a diet now, and so when he comes to the Four Seasons, he restricts himself to vegetarian fare. Today it's the artichoke salad with shaved carrots and radish, fiddlehead ferns, burrata, and basil pesto. "I still have the taste for blood, though," he laughs. Diet or not, he cannot resist the dessert menu, and follows up any meal with the restaurant's Grand Marnier Souffle. As he finishes the souffle, two passing tourists ask Kissinger for a photo. He obliges with the gentle smile of a man who has struggled for his lunch.

A President Looks Back, With Wistfulness and Pride

CRAWFORD — These days, George W. Bush considers himself more painter than ex-president. Spending his days in his barnyard studio, Mr. Bush often finds himself spattered in pastels by the end of the day, to the consternation of his wife, former First Lady Laura Bush. Mrs. Bush always makes him scrub up before dinner. "Blood washes off your hands easy, but I can never seem to get rid of paint," Mr. Bush says with a grin. Starting with simple pictures of dogs, Mr. Bush has gradually built up a considerable artistic portfolio, and multiple galleries have displayed his work. Mr. Bush's new book, *Portraits of Valiance*, is a collection of depictions of American soldiers. "I wanted to give something back," he says. "Soldiers never have it easy." Mr. Bush says he deliberately chose to paint living soldiers, rather than deceased ones, out of a concern for the book's message. "I find all that PTSD stuff depressing," he says. "A book about heroes should have a heroic tone." It remains to be seen whether historians will see Bush primarily as dedicated artist or compassionate statesman.

AMONG DRONE OPERATORS, OCCASIONAL MISGIVINGS

LANGLEY — Corp. Virgil "Bruno" Tilletson is no pacifist. "After 9/11, I knew we had to kill some people," he muses, with the stiff, statesman-like weariness of a man whose conscience weighs heavily. "I enlisted because I knew there were people to kill," he says with what seems like a contemplative sigh. When Corp. Tilletson was offered the job of second-in-command of drone operations at Langley Air Force base, he jumped at the chance. "It would mean more killing," says the officer, with an air of deep reflection.

Having to take lives via remote control has not been easy for Tilletson. "When I go home," he says, "I'm exhausted. The hours are long. You have to squint to determine whether the splotches on the screen are people, and my doctor tells me my eyesight is getting worse." Tilletson's moral conflict reveals some of the paradoxes of the age of technological warfare. It may be the pilots of the drones who are hurt most of all.

In the Philippines, a President Makes a Name for Himself

By JANE PERLEZ

MANILA — Rodrigo Duterte is a straight talker. "I don't give a shit about human rights," he declares, with the unvarnished rustic chutzpah that has made him a hit in his own country. "No, really, I don't. I will massacre every last one of my opponents." Duterte's unique approach to political speechmaking has earned him plaudits among those who admire his refreshing honesty. But it has also brought its fair share of controversy. Duterte's declaration that "blood will fill the streets" was hastily critiqued by international observers, who caution that the new president's methods risk compromising important policy gains. Last month, when a presidential address concluded: "I will literally cut off people's heads and rape the corpses," the U.S. State Department moved to distance itself from Duterte's more brusque remarks. "We continue to have a productive long-term partnership with President Duterte," said a Department spokesperson. "While his speech is blunt, and in some cases departs from our own interpretation of policy, we continue to value the special relationship between our two countries, and believe President Duterte recognizes our shared values." Duterte's frankness has distinguished him from previous heads of state. "I have had thousands shot," he said in a Thursday press conference. "This is just the beginning." While the substance of his remarks has attracted comment, few disagree that Duterte has set himself apart.

President Duterte's Most Contentious Remarks PAGE A12

At Raytheon's Dubai Retreat, Teamwork Is The Strongest Weapon Of All PAGE A4

CULTURE

In Brooklyn, the 16th Century Makes an Unexpected Comeback

The neck ruff, a staple of Elizabethan dress, is increasingly common among those seeking an authentic vintage look. PAGE B1

BUSINESS

An African Nation Joins the Uber Generation

The Democratic Republic of Congo has spent nearly two decades mired in strife. Could a rideshare app be just what it needs? PAGE B5

INTERNATIONAL

The Modernizer

King Salman of Saudi Arabia has attracted controversy for a willingness to bomb Yemeni funerals and a penchant for beheading. But can he catalyze economic growth? PAGE C3

TRAVEL

Havana After Communism

Fine dining in a new era of commercial tourism

THEATER

Is Broadway Ready for Change?

A new show is upending modern dance. Will its revolutionary approach find a welcome? PAGE B1

IVAN THE TERRIBLE'S PUBLIC RELATIONS FIRM CONSIDERS HIS REBRANDING STRATEGY

"The exhibition accused the Western news media of miscasting Czar Ivan IV as 'the Terrible.' A display of contemporaneous German etchings that showed the 16th-century czar's troops committing atrocities was offered as proof that labeling him a murderous tyrant was simply defamation by foreigners." – "RUSSIAN HISTORY RECEIVES A MAKEOVER THAT STARTS WITH IVAN THE TERRIBLE," THE *NEW YORK TIMES*, MARCH 30, 2015.

Moscow, 9:03 AM, October 1576.
Main Conference Room,
Grozny Public Relations Solutions

—So where are we on the new client?

—It doesn't look good.

—The problem, as I see it, is that "Ivan the Terrible" doesn't really have that relatability factor.

—It makes him sound kind of...

—Terrible.

—Yeah.

—I mean, the good news is that there's widespread brand recognition.

—We've definitely gotten his name out there.

—And he's got reach. The 1552 Kazan slaughter really brought him to the attention of a new audience; they're trembling from Smolensk to the Urals. Fear is a leverageable asset.

—So we've got the awareness, we just need to apply some reputation management.

—We've shortlisted some options. Now nothing's set in stone; remember, we're just spitballin' here.

—So, as I see it, the first part's fine. Ivan. Good solid name, road-tested by three previous tsars, great public response. It'll play in Prokopyevsk. It's just the "Terrible" that consumers get hung up on.

—We drafted some alternatives.

—Lay them on me.

—Ah, let's see... we got... Ivan the Fastidious? Ivan the Louche. Ivan the Groovy.

—Eh, too uptight, too suggestive, too dated.

—The focus group also reacted positively to Ivan the Tender. Only it would be a radical shift in his value proposition...

—Hey guys, I hate to change course, but I think we should really first deal with the elephant in the room. We know there's also kind of a deeper image issue at play here than just the name.

—I know. We've got to talk Massacre of Novgorod.

—It's been getting some pushback.

—It doesn't look good. Mass slaughter's been losing cachet in a lot of sectors lately.

—Okay, so we've thought about this, and we think we may have a way out.

—Get this: we're ditching "Massacre." We're calling it a "Disruption."

—The Disruption of Novgorod.

—Think of Novogrod as like an outmoded industry.

—And Ivan as a small start-up.

—Who's throwing out the whole playbook.

—He's all about change-oriented post-medievalism.

—Solution-driven.

—It's just that the solution is to have thousands of Cossacks ransacking the city and brutalizing the populace.

—I like it. Let's do a soft launch and see if we can make it stick, then roll out a full campaign if it takes. Try to downplay the carnage dimension and foreground the innovation aspect.

—You mean the new forms of impalement?

—Right, like I said, the innovation aspect.

—What about the disembowelings?

—We're using the phrase "internal restructurings."

—I want to shift gears for a moment. Let's talk social media. I think it's key to rehabilitating the Ivan brand.

—It's all about multi-platform connectivity.

—What does that mean?

—I don't know.

—I want him on every medium. Instagram his orb and scepter. Send a newsletter out with all his favorite links of the week.

—They're all conspiracy websites about bishops.

—Oh.

—We did set up a Twitter account.

—But the results have been sub-optimal.

—He's been tweeting "Death to the Tatars" over and over.

—And sending a lot of rambling multi-part threads about treacherous boyars.

—Okay, first rule, as always: never let the client tweet! Remember when we told Catherine her password and she started tweeting out horse pics—

—That hasn't happened yet. She's later.

—Oh, sorry.

—Okay, so what about the Facebook page?

—Mixed news.

—His profile pic is fine.

—The face is contorted into a bloodthirsty demented snarl, but whatever, it'll do.

—It's the cover photo that's problematic.

—It's a painting of 30,000 slaughtered Ottomans.

—It sends the wrong message.

—Bad optics.

—Did you talk to him about it? Is he up to speed on the social media strategy?

—He's been resistant.

—He told us to go ебать ourselves.

—Hmm... Okay, maybe the whole Tsardom just needs a makeover; a fresh face to the company. Can anyone else interface with the public? What about the son?

—Ivan Ivanovich?

—Uh...

—Bad news on that front. He got disrupted.

—In the head.

—With a scepter.

—Let's put that one on the back burner, then. What else is on the table?

—So, the war-induced total economic ruin is hurting us in certain demographics.

—All demographics, really.

—Hang on. Let's take a step back here. We all know where our numbers are weak. Let's try and play to Ivan's strengths instead.

—Uh... he's a poet. He plays chess. Creditably good as a theologian according to contemporary historical sources.

—Hang on, I'm going to make two columns on the whiteboard. Okay, we've got assets and liabilities. So, poetry, chess. Great, great. These are selling points.

—I guess we should put killing his second son on the other side.

—And the massacre...

—Disruption!

—Right.

—Plus the economic ruin.

—Got it.

—He's good at besieging, though. And gibbeting. Put those in the assets.

—Pillaging! I nearly forgot pillaging.

—Guys, I think we're going in the wrong direction here.

—Flogging the clergy. Eye-gouging. Throwing people off that bridge.

—Kicked a pregnant woman. Mutilated an architect.

—Hold up, everyone. We're going off the rails; time out. This is leading us in circles. We need to start thinking outside the box. I want bold ideas.

—Hmm...

—Well, how about... Let me just throw something out there. Terror might not necessarily be a minus. Why don't we think of it more like "creative destruction"?

—I like it. And it's his core competency.

—Plus it's scalable.

—And gives a strong corporate identity.

—Okay, let's run with it.

—"Ivan the Terrible."

—"Just as terrible as you expected."

—"Only more so."

—Perfect. Let's break.

—Back in 10?

—Sure. Then I want us to talk about product tie-ins. We've got this idea for an app that showcases impalement locations in real time...

—It's like Uber.

—But for violence.

—I love it.

TAKE A JOURNEY THROUGH HISTORY WITH...

S.Y.S.T.E.M.I.C.!

(THE SOCIETY FOR YOUNG SENSIBLE TECHNOCRATS ENGAGING IN MERITOCRATIC INTERDISCIPLINARY CENTRISM)

BY LYTA GOLD

TOUR GUIDE: All aboard! Strap yourself in—don't take up too much space—and please, hold all comments to the end. When credentialed authorities speak, the ignorant masses ought to stay silent, don't you agree? Of course you do!

Now—before we set off—a few words about our time machine. This lovely device you're seated in is a joint project by our dear friends at Lockheed Martin and the U.S. Department of Education. Our research has shown that today's young people are indifferent to history. You millennials just want to protest, grade-grub, and complain about your identities. You eat too many avocados and not enough diamonds, you despise hard work and property ownership, you refuse to acknowledge the glory of a global capitalism that allows you constant real-time updates on all your favorite sexual abuse scandals! It's not enough to have a supercomputer strapped to your wrist, all you can talk about is the people who *made* the supercomputer and mined its constituent parts, their working conditions and power dynamics blah blah blah, skyrocketing inequality and it's all so *unfair, I don't want to participate in this vicious system, I can't afford my rent, I'm terrified of getting sick because my insurance is garbage, I'm anxious and exhausted all the time, blah blah blah, me me me!*

Well, that's why we're taking this journey today. It's time to step outside the narrow confines of the present moment and take a really hard, serious look at our past. Once you've seen the most important and exciting events in the history of centrism, I think you'll understand how perfect and inevitable it was that we arrived here, on this flat, shrinking, globalized earth, the best of all possible worlds.

Are you strapped in? Are you ready? Too bad if you aren't, because technological progress will leave you behind regardless, ha-ha!

(Deep whirring noises. The windows blaze with watercolor light. There's a moment of terrible, wrenching inertia—and the noises stop. The windows clear.)

TOUR GUIDE: Now, we begin deep in the wilds of prehistory. The year is 4484 BC, and the local warlord is Orrag the Basher. Yes, that's his army, racing through the grassland. And that's Orrag in front, raising his club—oof! You can see how he earned his name.

Now, I don't want to make any excuses for our friend Orrag here. He *is* a tad on the aggressive side. But on the other hand, it's pretty clear that the Antelope People weren't operating their agricultural fields at full capacity. In order to compete in a rapidly expanding global marketplace, they needed to increase their grain output by at least 130%. So let's skip ahead a little. Now, see how much more productive the Antelope People have become? Orrag cut a lot of unnecessary overhead. No more silly ritual dancing, no more elaborately decorated huts, no more calorie-heavy feasts... they were really living above their means, weren't they, and getting chubby too, am I right? Give Orrag credit: he's really trimmed the fat. The Antelope People have become a lean, mean producing machine!

(inaudible murmuring)

Sure, it was a hostile takeover. But that's how it goes. Whoever wins is morally justified in their victory, because if you have something, it means you earned it. Orrag and his soldiers obviously worked harder, that's all.

And let's be real: given the chance, the Antelope People would have become conquerors themselves. You see, human beings have always been nasty, brutish, and sectarian. In fact, we've never evolved beyond our early conditioning. Thanks to the rigorous science of evolutionary psychology, we know that, deep down in our cortexes, we're still the same competitive, cruel, status-obsessed, selfish, tribalist apes we've always been...

(one voice murmuring)

What's that? Are you suggesting there's no hard scientific evidence to support this theory?

(same voice murmuring)

Really? Not a single, identifiable genetic structure? Just a collection of unprovable hypotheses, and soft science data which might only indicate contemporary cultural biases?

(voice murmuring again)

But if that's true, then surely reputable scientists would no longer advance such an unpromising theory. As they do, we must assume its veracity. Well! Moving on!

(Deep whirring noises. The windows fade to watercolor, and then to mist.)

Now we're navigating the murky waters of myth-history. If you look closely out the viewports, you'll see the pyramids of Giza. These immortal monuments were built only for the greatest leaders and innovators of Egyptian society. Tragically, most tombs were looted over the years by greedy, grubby locals, who sold the golden treasures of their kings for "food" and other "necessaries."

(murmuring)

The people who looted the pyramids may have been the descendants of the slaves who built them? Well. At SYSTEMIC, we don't really like to use the word "slave." It has a great deal of hurtful historical resonance—in fact, it's unpleasant for us to hear that word, and we ask you to respect our objection to outrageous words that have only been chosen to wound. We prefer the term "contracted agents." Yes, the pyramids were likely built by some sort of contracted agents, but there really isn't much evidence they were ill-treated. Maybe these contracted agents enjoyed cutting and lifting stone slabs to make inert, functionally useless monuments for the immortal glory of their leaders! Also, they were paid in beer. That's an ideal condition for you millennials, am I right? Payment in beer? It was even technically micro-brewed!

(silence)

Well. I think you'll agree that the technological marvel of the pyramids is worth a certain amount of human suffering. But before we leave, I do want to touch on the mythic part of the story. If you go by the biblical legend, then 400 years of sensible partnership between the Egyptians and the Hebrews were shattered by the unauthorized Exodus. Even if these—let's call them foreign guest workers—were treated somewhat unfairly, was it really necessary to hurl Pharaoh and all his soldiers and chariots into the sea? Surely, if both sides had sat down and really listened, they could have reached some kind of practical compromise. Instead we have this myth—this terrible, misguided myth—that it's perfectly okay for workers to just walk away en masse from a job they don't like. I hope you'll understand how dangerous and destructive this story really is.

(murmuring)

Hold your questions to the end, please! We've got an appointment in Rome.

(Rapid whirring, and more glowing watercolors—a bump of inertia, fading into bright, dusty sunlight)

We've arrived at the Theatre of Pompey, the Roman senatorial chamber. Even with your limited, touchy-feely education, you'll probably recognize the death of Caesar. Ouch! Yikes! That sure is a lot of knives!

You may be surprised I've brought you to this particular point in time. Wasn't the death of Caesar one of the events that signaled the end of Rome's already limited democracy? And how, you may be asking, could the end of a democracy count as a victory for centrism? Well! I'll tell you. The transition to empire—under the hand of Augustus—brought a much needed end to a period of populist unrest. As citizens of the 21st century, we would obviously prefer democracy, but sometimes people need to be ruled by strongmen rather than give way to the chaos of civil disorder. If you look closely at the early Roman empire, it was really a lot "freer" than many of our so-called current "democracies." Citizens enjoyed civil discourse and open inquiry—in fact, Augustus was so committed to the art of civility that he exiled poets for writing crude, impolitic verse! And on top of that, he really unleashed the creative/destructive capabilities of the Roman Empire. The Romans moved fast and broke things; they conquered a great deal of the globe, spreading the light of Western civilization and progress—

Yes, you in the back—you keep waving your hand, even though, as I said, I'm not taking questions at this time—

(murmuring)

Ok—you want to know if we're going to cover any events from the point of view of the Near East, sub-Saharan Africa, East Asia, South Asia, or the Americas before Columbus? Let me say, right here and now, that the planet is full of noble civilizations with vast and complex histories which we fully respect, absolutely. We're totally committed to racial equality, here at SYSTEMIC. You can believe us, because we keep insisting on it.

(More whirring and glowing light. The TOUR GUIDE *starts speaking before the image resolves.)*

In fact, our next stop takes us to Syria. The year is 1098... now, you might say that the Crusades were a violent, shameful historical period. But it's important to hear both sides—that's not an ideology, incidentally, just good common sense. While we deplore the terrible violence of the Crusades, we have to remember that the West enjoyed many social and technological innovations as a result of the invasion, so really, we have to take the bad with the good.

(murmuring, crosstalk)

I've asked—I've really asked you more than once, and—hey, let's show some respect here! Let's be polite, ok? Let's hold all questions and comments to the end, *please*!

Obviously, a certain degree of violence is *necessary*. All human beings are inherently selfish and tribalistic after all! But if you look at the Crusades, you'll see a beautiful moment of unity—the Christian West, uniting in common cause against the terrible threat of people living peaceably on their own lands. Who knows what would have happened if the West hadn't intervened? All kinds of terrible instability might have been unleashed—I mean, more than the instability that actually occurred. Plus, if you think about it, the Crusades could've been much more violent, much more depraved. Every situation could *always* be worse.

You see, a good centrist doesn't see the glass as half-empty or half-full. A good centrist looks at a chalice half-filled with children's blood and says, "Well, at least it wasn't filled all the way!"

(more crosstalk, loud and heated but still inaudible)

You know: that's the problem with you millennials. Your expectations are too high. If you want too much peace and happiness you'll only be disappointed. Progress is a slow and steady tortoise. Not every civilization develops—or can be allowed to develop—at the same rate. Rationally, we have to accept that—

(talk grows louder)

All right! Let's skip ahead.

(Loud machine whirring. The stage tilts dramatically, then rights itself. The windows clear, but they're barred with graceful iron railings.)

We've arrived at the triumph of Reason. Paris, the 18th century. It's the age of Voltaire, and witty repartee in exclusive salons. The birth of meritocracy. Why, if you were smart and ambitious enough, you too could rise up the ranks and participate in civil society, even if you were merely the son of a wealthy lawyer! Look in at the window—such elegance! Flowing wine and gilded wigs, the absolute attention to manners, the proper forms of things...

(angry crosstalk)

*(*TOUR GUIDE *sighs)*

You want to talk about the trans-Atlantic slave trade. Of course. More identity politics. You know, this is the same attitude that led to the revolution. The age of Voltaire was an age of spirited questioning, of discourse and real progress. Liberal democracy was coming, but the people spoiled it. They weren't willing to wait—

(laughter, crosstalk)

Because they were starving? You know, if you actually look at the numbers, I think you'll find that human mortality from deprivation actually *decreased* in Paris between 1788 and 1789 by a full 2%! Look at the numbers and tell me that isn't progress!

(crosstalk intensifies)

Yes, and so what? What about Haiti? Surely the slaves—er, contracted agents—would have been freed eventually. If only they'd had the patience to wait for the proper historical moment—you know, there's always a respectful time and place to bring up this sort of thing—

(crosstalk and muffled shouting)

Well! Obviously we need to put some funds into a Tour of Historical Politeness! I'll contact our friends at Lockheed—but before that, we have one last stop. And after that—at the *appropriate* time—you can ask all the questions you like.

(This time, the machine thumps and roars. When the windows clear, the noises don't stop.)

I'd hope to put this into proper context, but you millennials have short attention spans. So. Here we are, our last stop: November, 1989. The fall of the Berlin Wall. The greatest triumph in the history of centrism. In fact, it marked the end of history itself.

I know this concept is confusing, so bear with me. When the Berlin Wall fell, the grand utopian myths—the plans to shake up and destroy the world—died with it. From this moment forward, human civilization could only continue along the path of liberal democracy and muscular economic progress. Sure, we know there will be occasional setbacks. We're experiencing one right now. But if you look at the grand overall data set, you'll see the numbers trend in only one direction—up and up and up forever.

(crosstalk)

Look at the numbers! Fewer dead from war, illness, poverty, disease—

(crosstalk)

Well, yes, if your loved ones are among the dead, then I suppose—to repeat your colorful colloquialism—you "don't give a shit about the math"—but the numbers remain the numbers. The facts remain the facts. And the facts clearly show that modern history is one slow steady climb toward better numbers.

(Crosstalk. The Tour Guide *seems ill at ease—he keeps trying to interrupt, but the other voices drown him out.)*

No, no, you don't understand! You don't have access to all the facts. If you just look at the numbers you'll see that some mortal slippage is necessary. They're debits on the cosmic balance sheet—

(crosstalk intensifies)

No, no, this isn't an ideology! Communism, socialism, fascism—those are ideologies. Extremist utopian narratives... but centrism is in the middle, following the narrow, winding path of reason through the mountains of insanity... we aim to reduce the number of people who must necessarily die so that our most brilliant innovators can achieve—

(shouting)

Progress is always right! Progress can't be disproven. If you just look at the numbers they'll take away all your doubt, all your anxiety—even when people die unnecessarily, even when workers aren't treated quite so ideally, you just need to keep faith in those glorious, ever-improving numbers!

(shouting intensifies)

History is over! Centrists are on the side of truth, and justice, and the spirit of inquiry, which leads in only one rational direction—

(The shouting intensifies to the point where the Tour Guide *can't be heard. He appears desperate.)*

Tour Guide: *(briefly audible above the melee)*: Can't you see it? Can't you see there's no more doubt, no more judgment, no more questions to be answered—

The machine whirrs to life. It groans as it returns to the present. As the curtain falls the Tour Guide *screams:*

That's it! No more questions! No more questions! ❖

"SPECIAL" OFFERS

EXCLUSIVE EARLY SKETCHES OF

YOUR FAVORITE CURRENT AFFAIRS ILLUSTRATIONS,

including "A Droll Take On Something Actually Quite Depressing" and "A Classic Board Game But, Like, Socialist"

SOCIALIST POLICY PROPOSALS THAT MIGHT ACTUALLY

WORK

FREE *(as we all should be)**

VALUE PACK!

FOUR BOOK REVIEWS *for the price of one**

BUY ONE RANT *about contemporary art, get a* SECOND RANT FREE!*

TEMPORARILY WARD OFF DESPAIR WITH

BRUTAL TAKEDOWNS *of* NEOLIBERAL HEROES

ONLY $60 A YEAR FOR THE PRINT EDITION, $40 FOR THE DIGITAL*

ENSURES THAT 1 COPY OF CURRENT AFFAIRS WILL ACTUALLY ARRIVE ON TIME!*

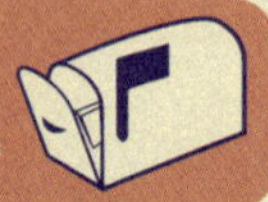

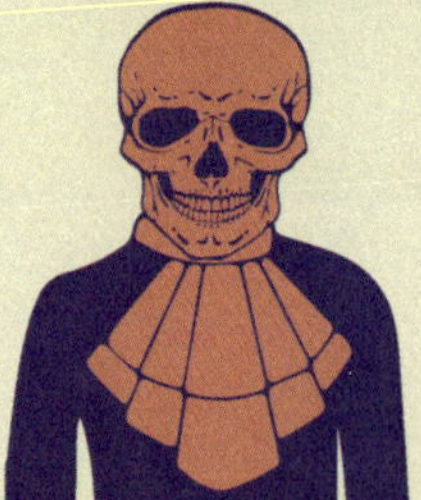

Win A Private Dinner With

S. CHAPIN DOMINO

Publisher, "Current Affairs"

(WHO IS ACTUALLY JUST A SKULL IN A CRAVAT ON NATHAN J. ROBINSON'S MANTELPIECE*)

OFFICAL COUPON COUPON

TODAY ONLY

SUBMIT THIS COUPON TO RECEIVE SEVERAL MORE COUPONS*

DO NOT LOSE THIS EVER

$100 OFF

ALL VICIOUS CRITICISMS OF LIBERTARIANS!*

(we are starting to feel sorry for them)

JEREMY CORBYN APPRECIATION STATION

Enter code ABSOLUTEBOY to hear a handpicked playlist of songs about manhole covers and home-knitted jumpers!*

*A Demand For Better Literature**

IF YOU FORGOT TO BUY YOUR BOOK-LOVING FRIEND A GIFT FOR THE HOLIDAYS, THIS MAKES A TERRIFIC BELATED EXCUSE!

*ONLY REDEEMABLE THROUGH THE ECONOMIST. PLEASE MAIL, EMAIL, OR TWEET ALL COUPONS TO THE ECONOMIST, ALONG WITH A WRITTEN DEMAND FOR CONTENT AS EXQUISITE AS THAT PROVIDED BY CURRENT AFFAIRS.

COMMENCEMENT CEREMONY

REGENTS OF THE

Universitas Affairs et Currentis

HEARTILY CONGRATULATE

____

FOR HIS/HER/THEIR (CIRCLE OR ADD MORE)
SUCCESSFUL COMPLETION OF THE
DOCTORAL PROGRAM IN
AMUSEMENT STUDIES
ON THIS FINE SPRING DAY

NATHAN J. ROBINSON
CHANCELLOR

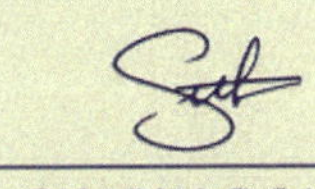

S. CHAPIN DOMINO
RECTOR

Congratulations!

YOU MADE IT THROUGH THIS BOOK! That makes you an honorary graduate of **Current Affairs University.** Here is your diploma, and below are two small "graduation presents." Well done, kiddo.

See The TINY FONTS AND YOU CAN READ THE TEXT!

with the **CURRENT AFFAIRS MAGNIFIER**

Cut it out, hold it to your eye, and at last find out what everything says.

Your Very Own SOCIALIST PROPAGANDA

Terrify the grown-ups!

Turn this image into stickers, slap 'em on lampposts, and **SHOW EVERYONE YOU'RE COOL.**

Answers

LIBERTARIAN PUZZLES

1. Yes, because libertarian principles are psychotic, every other aspect of this is permissible under a libertarian framework.

2. No, of course there isn't, and it is mystifying that libertarians refuse to recognize the totalitarian nature of the corporate structure.

3. No, you can't.

4. No, it hasn't. And of course he should, but he can't be under a libertarian framework, because, again, libertarianism is psychotic.

BERNIE QUIZ

Mostly As: Liberal progressive. It's a start! You're trying to create a fairer system, but you're not addressing the inherent problems of money and power. Instead, you're relying on appeals to an administration that only wants to churn you out like consumer products on a production line. If you really want to make your school a fairer place, try considering more revolutionary approaches.

Mostly Bs: Democratic socialist. You're aware of the larger systems of exploitation that undergird your life, and you're taking collective action to fight them. But are you going far enough? After all, you're still keeping aspects of these systems intact. It may take careful experimentation to find the right mix of preservation vs. elimination of #toxic structures.

Mostly Cs: Anarcho-socialist. You know exactly what you want, and what you want is to #burnthatshitdown. You do you, but just make sure you've planned for all contingencies. The school administration might react badly when faced with too much change too fast, and you could risk losing everything you've built (that is, righteously destroyed).

FBI CROSSWORD

ACROSS: 2. MLK 3. Climax 8. constitutional 10. White 11. Philadelphia 12. February 13. subversive 14. incidentally 15. Truman 17. Castro 18. December 19. citizens 20. Cult

DOWN: 1. Hampton 4. indirectly 5. China 6. future 7. Investigation 9. Schlesinger 16. burgled

GREAT BARRIER REEF

WHAT'S WRONG:

1. The rainbow trout is not native to the Great Barrier Reef

2. The trigger fish rarely grows to the exaggerated size depicted here

3. The pink coloration on the backs of the sea turtles is not an accurate depiction of their natural hue

4. The coral trout's tail fin should be more fan-like

5. That type of plastic bag is generally printed with the common phrase "Thank You for Shopping With Us!"

The Illustrators

ELLEN BURCH
ellenburch.com

Big Trouble In The Little City
The Women's March
ICE Practical Jokes
Remembering Bush Atrocities

C.M. DUFFY
cmduffy.com

Great Barrier Reef
Lenin Books
True Science Facts

MIKE FREIHEIT
mikefreiheit.com

Centrist Dad
David Frum's Immigrant Journey
DIY Climate Change
Invisible Referee
Pinky's Pinkwashing
Real Life Billionaire Comics
Robot Socialism
Steven Pinker: Grief Counselor
Which Dystopia Am I In?

SUSANNAH LOHR
antimatter.zone

Language of Flowers

MATT LUBCHANSKY
thenib.com/matt-lubchansky

In A Just World

CHRIS MATTHEWS
chrisbmatthews.com

21st Century Campus

A Perfect School
Dystopian Society
Luxury Leftism
Miserable Mansion
Our New Monuments
Our Workplace and Theirs
Sex Positions
The Utopian City
Welcome To Wokeland

PRANAS NAUJOKAITIS
pranas.virb.com

GOP Primary Game
Leo The Lion
Pin The Finger On Rahm
Socialist Monopoly
Your Friendly Neighborhood Drone

LIZZY PRICE
apocalizzyart.com

Billionaire Shaming
Capitalism 2.0
Clue Game
Current Affairs Podcast
Red Rose

BRIANNA RENNIX
Argument Starters

TYLER RUBENFELD
rubenfeldgraphicdesign.blogspot.com

A Mediocre Man
Luxury Bunker Lifestyle
New Jersey Tourism Board
Spot The Difference

CHELSEA SAUNDERS
chelseasaunders.me

Circles of Hell
Conservative View of Campus

MAXWELL SINGLETARY
maxwelljsingletary.blogspot.com

Failson Fashion
Bird Cafe

NICK SIROTICH
nickelopsus.com

Artisanal Prison Franchise
Get The President's Attention
Mail Order Democrat
Spot The Neoliberalism
Squid Lawyer
Socialist Animals

MORT TODD
morttodd.com

Bernie Bingo
Helicopter Parent Magazine
Intergalactic Confederacy
Spider Moms!
MLK Pokeballs

NAOMI USHIYAMA
artstation.com/nushiyama

Jeremy Corbyn Paper Dolls

SHAWN VULLIEZ
srslywrong.com

FBI Crossword Page

Graphic Design and Page Layouts by **NATHAN J. ROBINSON**

Except Table of Contents, Title Pages, Cover by **JON WHITE**

Text by **LYTA GOLD** and **NATHAN J. ROBINSON**
with the *Current Affairs* editorial staff:
SPARKY ABRAHAM, VANESSA A. BEE, BRIAHNA JOY GRAY, OREN NIMNI, BRIANNA RENNIX, and **NICK SLATER**

currentaffairs.org